Farming Inside Invisible Worlds

Contemporary Food Studies: Economy, Culture and Politics

Series Editors: David Goodman and Michael K. Goodman
ISSN: 2058–1807

This interdisciplinary series represents a significant step toward unifying the study, teaching, and research of food studies across the social sciences. The series features authoritative appraisals of core themes, debates and emerging research, written by leading scholars in the field. Each title offers a jargon-free introduction to upper-level undergraduate and postgraduate students in the social sciences and humanities.

Kate Cairns and Josée Johnston, *Food and Femininity*

Peter Jackson, *Anxious Appetites: Food and Consumer Culture*

Philip H. Howard, *Concentration and Power in the Food System: Who Controls What We Eat?*

Terry Marsden, *Agri-Food and Rural Development: Sustainable Place-Making*

Emma-Jayne Abbots, *The Agency of Eating: Mediation, Food, and the Body*

Henry Buller & Emma Roe, *Food and Animal Welfare*

Farming Inside Invisible Worlds

Modernist Agriculture and Its Consequences

Hugh Campbell

BLOOMSBURY ACADEMIC
LONDON • NEW YORK • OXFORD • NEW DELHI • SYDNEY

BLOOMSBURY ACADEMIC
Bloomsbury Publishing Plc
50 Bedford Square, London, WC1B 3DP, UK
1385 Broadway, New York, NY 10018, USA
29 Earlsfort Terrace, Dublin 2, Ireland

BLOOMSBURY, BLOOMSBURY ACADEMIC and the Diana logo are
trademarks of Bloomsbury Publishing Plc

First published in Great Britain 2021
This paperback edition published in 2022

Bloomsbury Publishing Plc does not have any control over, or responsibility
for, any third-party websites referred to or in this book. All internet addresses
given in this book were correct at the time of going to press. The author and
publisher regret any inconvenience caused if addresses have changed or sites
have ceased to exist, but can accept no responsibility for any such changes.

A catalogue record for this book is available from the British Library.

Library of Congress Control Number: 2020939738

ISBN: HB: 978-1-3501-2054-9
 PB: 978-1-3503-2774-0
 ePDF: 978-1-3501-2055-6
 eBook: 978-1-3501-2056-3

Series: Contemporary Food Studies, 2058–1807

Typeset by Integra Software Services Pvt. Ltd.

To find out more about our authors and books visit www.bloomsbury.com
and sign up for our newsletters

This book is dedicated to Tom Atchison and Leigh Campbell.
One farm, two generations, two ontologies.

Table of contents

List of illustrations

Figures

Maps

Table

Acknowledgements

Great powers are the subject of this book and they deserve acknowledgement. I acknowledge the power of our land Aotearoa New Zealand and all the things it makes possible. I acknowledge the successive waves of our ancestors who arrived here over the last thousand years and turned an unknown land into a home. I also acknowledge the many and various places where our land and our ancestors formed farming partnerships – for better or for worse.

This book was a work of collaboration, kinship and friendship. The intellectual ideas that informed most of the central ideas in this narrative were developed over many years with a diverse group of fellow travellers.

The emergence of new, critical approaches to agricultural change consolidated in Australasia around the activities of the Agrifood Research Network. I owe a large debt to the founding leaders of that network including Geoff Lawrence, David Burch and Roy Rickson, along with many of the members of that group who have become both academic collaborators and friends over the last two decades – particularly Carolyn Morris, Jane Dixon and Bill Pritchard.

The Biological Economies group has been foundational to my re-evaluation of the ontologies of my academic and farming worlds. I am grateful for the tireless energy of Richard Le Heron, the barn-burning theoretical experimentation of Nick Lewis, Chris Rosin, Katharine Legun and Matt Henry, and the affability and discipline of Eric Pawson, Mike Roche and Harvey Perkins.

Much of the work in this book is drawn from a series of research projects about the emergence of alternative agriculture in Aotearoa New Zealand. I would like to acknowledge my co-leaders and key interlocutors in the Greening Food, ARGOS and NZ Sustainability Dashboard projects, in particular John Fairweather, Jon Manhire, Caroline Saunders, Henrik Moller, John Reid, Lesley Hunt and Paul Dalziel. As well, the Empires of Grass team led by Tom Brooking and Eric Pawson has done much to open up new vistas in New Zealand history; without their work this book would have been impossible to conceptualize.

The Centre for Sustainability at the University of Otago has provided academic inspiration and collaboration. Its director Janet Stephenson and administrative staff Nicki Topliss and Gwenda Crawford have made the Centre a unique and supportive place to work. I also wish to thank the numerous postdoctoral fellows and postgraduate students who have passed through the Centre, especially my long-time collaborator Chris Rosin who drove many of the theoretical innovations that began to shape our collaborative work over the last fifteen years. As well, Ruth Fitzgerald, Carmen McLeod, Annie Stuart, Angga Dwiartama, Cinzia Piatti, Maddie Hall, Karly Burch, David Reynolds and Abbi Virens made their mark on elements of this book; Paul Stock and Jeremie Forney introduced me to food utopias, assemblages and the importance of generosity in all academic dealings; and Julia Haggerty brought new insights into land and environment in Aotearoa New Zealand, and has made Montana our second home.

Many of my academic friends have read chapter drafts and given superb feedback. I am indebted to Anne Murcott and Geoff Lawrence for being the first readers of every draft and for their support over many years leading up to the commencement of this project; Eric Pawson, for carefully reading every chapter and encouraging both a serious engagement with environmental history and an equal engagement with contemporary legacies of that history; Richard Le Heron, Chris Rosin and Nick Lewis for their insightful commentary on ontology and assemblages; Julia Haggerty for tuning up my ideas about frontiers; Tom Brooking for advice on key historical sections; and Chris Perley for his commentary on new ways to farm (and for putting me in touch with Don Miller who shared his personal collection of photographs of hillside erosion after Cyclone Bola).

I also thank my editors at Bloomsbury, Lucy Carroll and Lily McMahon and my series editors, Mike Goodman and David Goodman, for their unfailing support and encouragement. I also want to thank Imogen Coxhead and Les O'Neill for their expert editorial and map-making assistance.

I would like to thank the various organizations that contributed to allowing this book to be published under an open access agreement. The Division of Humanities and the Centre for Sustainability at the University of Otago, and Ruralis (Institute for Rural and Regional Research) in Norway, all made a contribution to this goal and I am very grateful for their support.

Many other friends and colleagues have provided insights that informed aspects of this book – at conferences, on field trips or fishing trips, over shared meals and various adventures. Thanks to David Craig, Jane Higgins, James Hale, Sean Connelly, John Stenhouse, Helen Leach, Ian Frazer, Alison Loveridge, Anne Pomeroy, David Rice, Stephen Horton, Scott Willis, Jenna Packer, Mike Hirst, John Dawson, Tony Ballantyne, Kate White, Sue Wards, Morgan Williams, Michael Bell, Michael Carolan, Julie Guthman, Hannah Gosnell, Harriet Friedmann, Philip McMichael, David Evans, Bruce Muirhead, Michael Burgess, and my Norwegian colleagues and friends at Ruralis – in particular Reidar Almas, Hilde Bjorkhaug and Rob Burton.

I have also relied extensively on a host of amateur historians and genealogists in my wider family. The Campbell story at Ashburn and Glenn Rd was meticulously researched by Dawn Isles. Research into the Bailey and Roberts families and farms was informed by Kristin Wickens. The remarkable adventures of Dennett Heather and his two families have been a long-time passion of Shirley Heather, Bruce Heather, Peter Wakeman and Alison and Jo Mewett. Unaiki Te Watarauhi came to life thanks to the work of Marri Pureu and William Kainana Cuthers, and the three of us benefitted greatly from Anaru Eketone's advice about the history of Ngāti Tamainupo. While my kinfolk have often debated long and hard about various aspects of these histories, I take sole responsibility for the particular way in which I have come to understand and characterize them.

Much of the work in this book draws on the insights and practices of farm families in Aotearoa New Zealand. During the last twenty-five years of researching hundreds of farms and orchards, I have learnt about the great variety of ways to pursue futures for farming. One of my most difficult tasks was choosing a tiny fraction of this group as case studies to illustrate this narrative. I appreciate the cooperation and assistance of all these families.

Close to home, my grandparents Tom and Dorothy Atchison loom large in this story mainly because they insisted their grandchildren should understand what it meant to be a good farmer. My recollections of growing up on Longridge and Windsor Lodge were aided and expanded upon by my parents Leigh and Graeme Campbell. Both of them passed away during the writing of this book but, true to family form, kept up a constant stream of narrative until the very end. My parents and grandparents stand at the front of a great muster of farming relatives who participated in my farm education and shared their farms with me at many different moments during my life. While I have deliberately not named any farms in this narrative that still are owned by my kinfolk, those experiences certainly inform the wider narrative. My brother Douglas gave excellent and timely advice – drawn from his own long experience as an author – as to the most effective styles of incentivization needed to commence, endure and complete a book. My sister Phillipa not only shared that early on-farm education with me, but also clarified a couple of my own recollections about our shared experience of Windsor Lodge. I am grateful to my two sons, Finn and Niall, who circled around this venture and made sure that it maintained fealty to the cause of enacting a better world for future generations. And I continue, as a scholar and a human being, to be hugely grateful for the friendship, good humour and unfailing support of my soulmate and wife, Marion. She both kept me pointed towards completion and made an immense contribution to this book by drawing beautiful illustrations of old family photos that had become too degraded to be publishable.

In the same way that farms enact landscapes, this book was enacted by a large family. I will always cherish this collective time of co-creation.

Glossary of Māori terms

hapū	(clan, sub-tribe; to be born)
hīkoi	(march, walk)
hui	(gathering, meeting)
iwi	(tribe)
kai	(food)
kaitiakitanga	(guardianship, protection, environmental management)
kaumātua	(Māori elder, holder of tribal knowledge)
kaupapa	(principles and ideas that act as a base or foundation for action)
kauri	(large native conifer)
Kīngitanga	(the King Movement)
mana	(prestige, reputation)
mānuka	(small bushy tree – 'tea tree' or 'ti-tree')
Māori	(indigenous inhabitants of New Zealand; the language of the indigenous inhabitants of New Zealand)
moa	(large flightless bird, now extinct)
pā	(traditional Māori hill fort)
Pākehā	(New Zealander of non-Māori descent, usually European)
pāmu	(farm/to farm)
rāhui	(restriction, prohibition, a ritual ban on resource use, a place captured by force)
taonga	(treasured possessions or cultural items, anything precious)
te reo Māori	(the Māori language)
tītī	(sooty shearwater or 'muttonbird')
waka	(canoe, vehicle)
whakapapa	(lineages, genealogy, to recite genealogy)
whānau	(family)
whenua	(land, homeland)

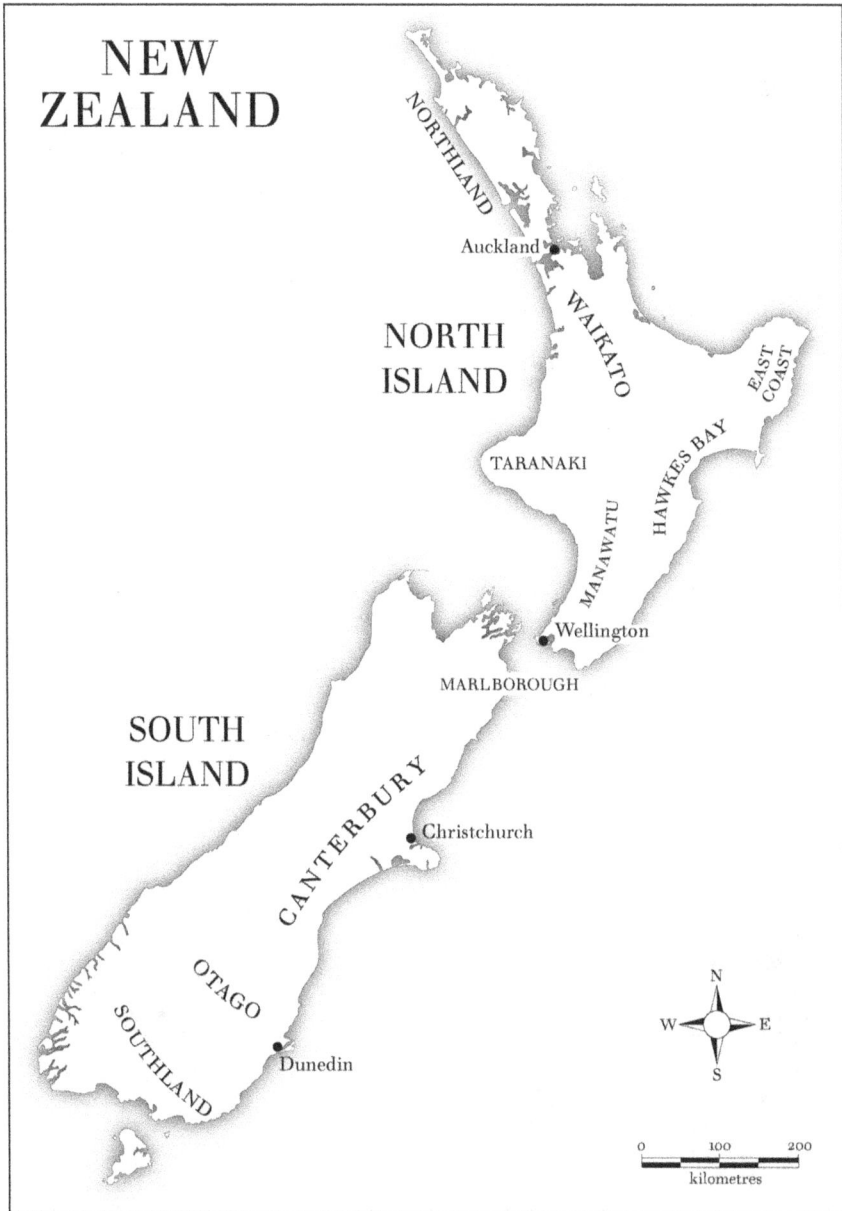

Map 1 New Zealand with major farming regions

NEW
ZEALAND

NORTH
ISLAND

CLOVERNOOK:
Joe & Jane Roberts, 1857–1973

THE FENCIBLES' GIFT:
Thomas & Mary Ann Bailey,
1847–1855

WINDSOR LODGE:
Tom & Dorothy Atchison, 1972–1999

HEATHER'S HOMESTEAD / MAROTAHEI:
Dennett Heather & Unaiki Te Watarauhi,
1850–1863

TE RAHUI:
Ned & Reine Roberts,
1890s–1925

GLENN RD, KAUPOKONUI:
James & Isabella Campbell,
1883–1910

LONGRIDGE:
Tom & Dorothy Atchison,
1946–1972

SOUTH
ISLAND

N
W ← → E
S

ASHBURN ESTATE:
John & Elizabeth Campbell,
1868–1882

0   100   200
kilometres

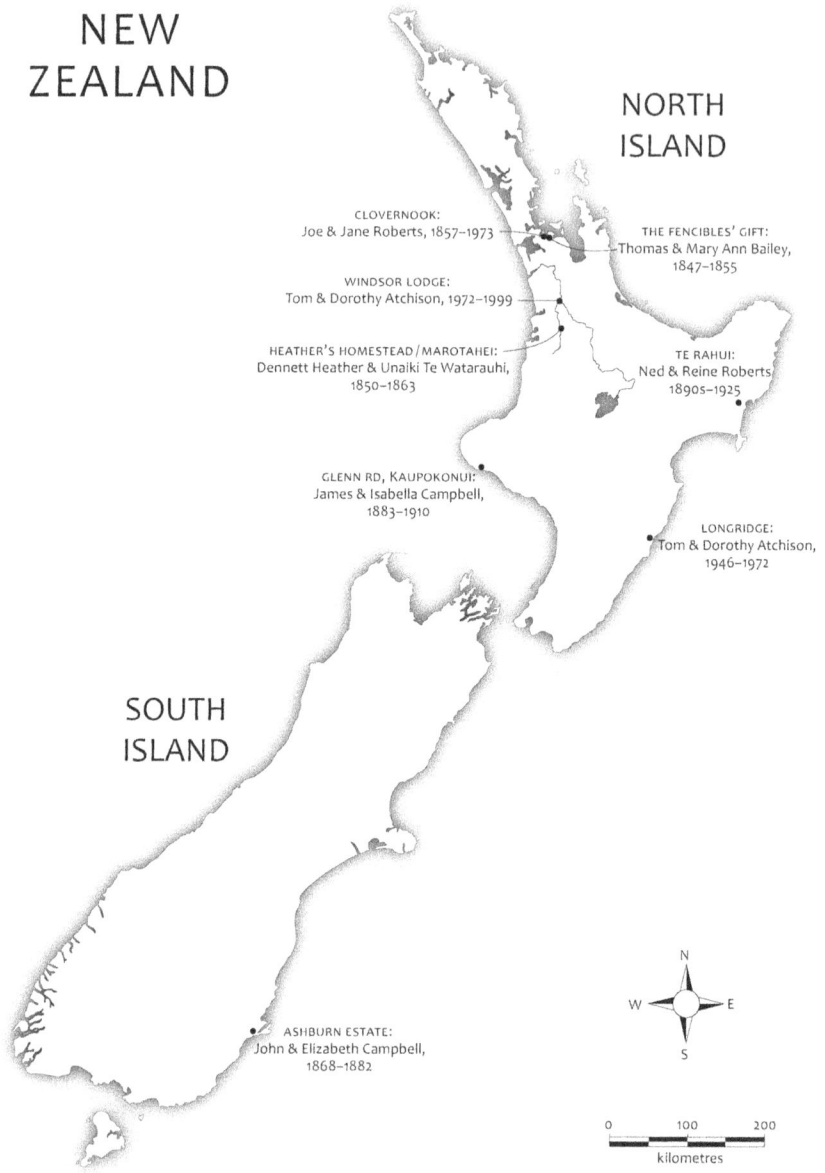

Map 2 Family farm locations

Prologue: Visible and invisible farming worlds

When we examine power in social worlds – even in a place as seemingly mundane as a farm – our eye is inevitably drawn towards visible expressions of power. For critical social theorists, activists and practitioners, a farm makes a particular kind of empowered world visible. We can see it in the way that farmers treat animals, cultivate fields, and in the relations and inequalities of gender, labour or ethnicity on farms. All such relations and practices visibly express different kinds of power. We can also see different forms of visible capital that demarcate status and worth. We can see the vital power of farms made manifest in production, yields and the flow of goods. And we can see settled landscapes of orderly activity and aesthetic worth. This visibility is not just a trick of the eye. A farm is a thing that makes a particular kind of empowered world exist – a world with consequences that social scientists can immediately engage with and visibly appraise. But what if power is also manifest in making things invisible? In enacting a particular kind of farming world, what has been *unmade* by a farm or rendered invisible by its actions? What hasn't happened, what choices weren't taken, what worlds that might have been are now no longer able to exist? In this book I argue that the power of farms can only be understood if we examine both their visible and invisible powers. Farms are anything but mundane, their histories are both triumphant and catastrophic, and the consequences of their invisible powers shape the crises of our contemporary worlds. These histories also point us towards alternative futures.

New Zealand is an interesting place to think about particular kinds of invisible powers in relation to farming. It speaks to the invisible consequences of the actions of farms in colonization as well as the special place that farming has as a site of elaboration of scientific expertise and modernity.

Intriguing contradictions and extremities abound. As a Developed World country, the role of agriculture in the New Zealand economy is atypically large (and historically the subject of strong political celebration) relative to the usual reliance of wealthy countries on manufacturing and services. While over 80 per cent of New Zealand's population resides in cities, the core of the national economy and much of the nation's identity are based upon the exporting of primary produce from rural New Zealand. In a wider world where indigenous and local foods are in the ascendancy New Zealand has the distinction of being one of the most export-oriented food producers in the world – exporting over 90 percent of the food that is produced! At the same time, it displays little elaboration of indigenous cuisine in mainstream food culture and commerce. The once abundant and variable forms of food and fibre production undertaken by indigenous Māori now inhabit a tiny fringe of land-use. The country's relentless pursuit of agricultural exports is built on profound discontinuity with past land-use.

New Zealand agriculture also displays vexing ecological contradictions – inhabiting an 'empire of grass' where less than two centuries ago stood dense native forests and wetlands. New Zealand is, at the heart of its colonial history, a country where farming was the agent of change that breached critical ecological frontiers. Multiple times in early colonization, and now again in the twenty-first century, farming has been an agent of ecological chaos and disruption. Despite this history, since the 1990s New Zealand has cheekily traded on a 'clean and green' image for food products, sold using imagery of pristine alpine landscapes, native bush and congenial rural society, while at the same time the country is situated poorly on international comparisons of biodiversity loss, is currently in the grips of a crisis in freshwater ecologies partly induced by agricultural intensification, and is also notable for the extremely high proportion of greenhouse gas emissions that are produced by agriculture. It seems that many of New Zealand's claims of agricultural greatness reside alongside strange contradictions and silences.

This kind of extremity and contradiction has been the pattern for New Zealand ever since its establishment as a British colony, which, after periods of conflict and crisis, transformed the indigenous space of Aotearoa into Britain's 'Farm in the South Pacific'. Because of all these imbalances and contradictions, New Zealand is a country that is particularly interesting for thinking about how such an extreme pattern of agricultural land-use, founded in the colonization of an indigenous landscape and culture, was rendered invisible, pacified and came to feel entirely normal and ordinary to most if its participants – which included me.

A family of 'good farmers'

Being normal as a farmer and farm in New Zealand is often a family affair. I was born in 1964 during the last years of the 'golden age' of twentieth-century prosperity in New Zealand farming. The wider family that I was born into was, on the whole, composed of farmers going back multiple generations. Four lines of my family disembarked into the new colony between 1840 and 1880 and immediately started farming. All my grandparents were farmers (as well as six of my eight great-grandparents) and around half my wider family was still farming as I was growing up. Even by New Zealand standards this is a lot, meaning that, from the outset, I was encultured with the importance of farming and the centrality of pastoral family farms in the great narrative of New Zealand life. Becoming a scholar in my adult life was always postdated by these initial truths. I became a researcher who was interested in agriculture with a pre-existing set of known cultural 'facts' about the agricultural world: farms are an important thing, they convey high social status (particularly, when I was growing up, sheep farms). Family farms are good, farm men are tough, farm women are educated and resolute, farm children are lucky, rural communities are 'close knit', agricultural scientists do good work, we are feeding the hungry of the world, all these things are important to New Zealand and help to explain why we are a good society.

Put together, what I grew up with was a strong sense of what it meant to be both a good farmer and what comprised a good farm. These kinds of evaluation did not seem to be founded in any kind of overt political contest; rather they were, as I'll go on to argue in this book, generated in the day-to-day experience of living on a farm. While my wider farming family was influential in forming these evaluations, the primary influence was my grandfather – Tom Atchison – who started farming with a soldier settlement loan after the Second World War and died when still residing on the family farm six months before the end of the twentieth century. He carried enormous moral weight in our collective lives. Another important dynamic was the tacit influence of the farm itself: a sheep and beef farm nestled among a sea of dairy farms outside the village of Ngaruawahia in the Waikato region (see Figure 1). The farm had an interestingly symbolic name – Windsor Lodge – that perfectly conveyed a sense of Englishness, horsy-ness (important for my family) and respectability. On closer inspection in later life, I did eventually ponder that the House of Windsor in Britain was actually the bearer of an invented name specifically intended to draw attention away from an inconvenient foreign past. This turns out to be an apt observation for both our own farm and the great venture of pastoral farming in New Zealand.

Figure 1 Windsor Lodge, *c.* 1980 Artist attribution: Marion Familton

By the time I was growing up under this tutelage in the early 1970s, Tom Atchison had clear views and evaluations on how to be a good farmer. He was, fundamentally, a sheep farmer. He valued his independence and his capacity to deploy particular embodied skills and capacities he had learnt through farming. His enthusiasm for science extension activities – particularly anything concerning New Zealand's famous rotational grazing system – often took him into farmers' field days and science demonstrations at the local research centre. Driving us around the district, he'd give voice to his approval of other farmers' pastures when they showed a uniform growth pattern of grass; no weeds; with pasture growing right down those tricky gully slopes where gorse, broom and blackberry liked to dominate; and nice tidy fences with tight wires and healthy-looking animals grazing within. He also liked large 'park-like' trees in shelterbelts or strategically placed in prominent vistas (as long as they didn't intrude on potential space for pasture). This aligned with his ideas of an English landscape. It is notable that the pretty combination of pasture and trees was positioned in view of the main road, while the barer production areas and embarrassing 'swamps' were mostly out of sight of other farmers driving by. This ensemble of elements comprised a 'good farm' and signalled to him that it was being orchestrated by a 'good farmer'.[1]

The heart of his evaluation of both himself and his neighbours as good farmers was productivity. He waited for the vital information that told him all was well in his world: the weight of his lambs on delivery to the abattoir, the amount of wool shorn off his hoggets and the number of lambs he bred from his flock of ewes each year. These yields and measures resonated across his farming landscape and told him that he was a good farmer because he was a productive farmer. Strangely, though, given all the attention to productivity and the technical aspects of everything that was happening on our farm, there was a rather contradictory lack of curiosity about where our beef cattle and sheep ended up being consumed. They went off to an abstract land somewhere else where someone, in some capacity, clearly needed to eat them (not many details beyond the farm gate were required apart from the cheque from the meatworks). Rounding off this mystery over 'smoko' in the farm kitchen, my grandfather explained that farming was a morally good way of life because the world was hungry and we were producing food for the hungry people of the world. The higher our levels of productivity as farmers, the lower the moral burden of world hunger on our souls.

Modernity's colonial farms

The world that I inhabited when walking across our farm as a child in the early 1970s was a knowable, stable and 'good' place to live. We inhabited a farm that, along with its thousands of close cousins, was numbered among the most virtuous and obedient offspring of the great scientific project of modernity. I took my first steps out onto our farm at a time when agricultural science, and its many and various endeavours, was central to the 'world-leading' status that we accorded to our pastoral farming practices. New Zealand had developed a reputation as a global leader in agricultural science in the twentieth century, a prowess built around managing the chaotic consequences of the breaching of major ecological frontiers in New Zealand: the massive expansion of grass-based production onto land that was once inhabited by indigenous grasses, forests or wetlands. Breaches in these frontiers, as I'll describe at length in this book, had consequences beyond imagining that persist as legacy issues in the contemporary ecological crises of farming in New Zealand. Growing up inside this world we had no such sense of the trade-offs and conquests that lay hidden inside our agricultural history. Agricultural scientists were the heroes of our farming narrative: they 'modernized' pastoral farming by identifying suitable grasses to stabilize slopes, developed their combination with artificial fertilizers, diagnosed the lack of certain critical elements in New Zealand soil and helped the control of the pests that thrived in these disrupted frontier spaces.

My extended family were enthusiastic consumers of this kind of scientific knowledge. My grandparents' first farm, Longridge, was cut out of mānuka 'scrub' on the hills of the province of Hawke's Bay and required constant management for erosion and non-stop application of fertilizer to promote pasture grasses that could stabilize those newly de-forested slopes. My other farming grandparents deployed some innovative engineering solutions to drain their share of the Ngaere wetlands in Eastern Taranaki to create a successful dairy farm. As avid de-foresters and wetland-drainers, my family over multiple generations had turned to science to manage the consequences of breaching these ecological frontiers. Our farming systems were settled, scientific and existed inside tight boundaries. They were, as I'll go on to argue, modern – and modern worlds are typically settled and pacified. They make it hard to contemplate alternatives.

The politics of the farm: Disruption and re-visibilization

My first memories of our farming world anchor themselves in the last few years leading up to 1973. The year is important. These were the last moments of the 'golden age' and the end point of a period of stability for New Zealand farming that had stretched from the 1920s through to the very last days before the UK was going to 'betray' New Zealand and enter the European Common Market. My lessons were commencing just as the world they related to was about to move into profound crisis.

Fifteen years later, New Zealand farming was in a very different place. First, our long-term trading relationship with our colonial 'home' collapsed when Britain entered the European Common Market in 1973 and ended New Zealand's privileged access to the British market. Then, as the ramifications of the loss of the UK market rolled through a series of crises for the next ten years, New Zealand embarked on a process of radical economic liberalization of both farming and the wider economy. The resulting crisis in the mid-1980s – caused by what we now refer to as neoliberalization – tore apart rural worlds along with the complacent assumptions they were founded upon.

The crisis of neoliberalization – which was the first subject I studied in my academic career – forced me to see a different world of farming to that in which I grew up. My childhood experience of family farming was anaesthetized in a passive and de-politicized world that was enacted anew day by day on the farm. It induced a state of what later writers would characterize as 'ecological amnesia', along with 'historical amnesia', 'social amnesia' and 'political amnesia'.

Observing from within the crisis of neoliberalization, it turned out that my farming world was not so much set in concrete as perched on top of a cultural glacier. There was a simultaneous sense of how we were inhabiting an immense and slow-moving cultural mass that was almost inert (and appeared highly secure when viewed from a paddock on a Waikato farm before 1973), which, when seen from a different scale and temporality, was actually an unstable pile of ice and rock crashing down a disintegrating mountainside. Crisis disrupted the seemingly solid habitus of farming; it destabilized the quotidian serenity and predictability of our farming lives, and revealed a disturbing level of grinding tension, deep below the icy surface.

The British betrayal of 1973 and the subsequent crisis of neoliberalization revealed to me what had been hiding in plain sight. Behind the crisis of the 1970s and '80s was a much longer, but much better concealed, history of crisis: farming in New Zealand, like every other settler colony in the world, was founded on the dispossession of indigenous people of their own land and the ecological colonization of New Zealand by non-indigenous plants and animals. Many of the strange contradictions that I identified at the start of this prologue had their origins in the peculiar and, at times, dramatic dynamics of why and how New Zealand came to be colonized by Europe. Our farms are, at heart, agents of colonization, and they retain that character, and are vexed by its consequences, to this day.

Farming inside invisible worlds

Our farm didn't feel like a site of colonization, yet it most certainly was. It had a hidden history, the invisibility of which seemed the necessary precondition to our existence as farmers at all. When I was wandering around a paddock in the 1970s, there were other worlds that were simply unthinkable and unseeable from inside our farming world. This omission clearly took some achieving. Windsor Lodge, just outside the important Māori village of Ngaruawahia, was situated six kilometres from Turangawaewae Marae. This is the historic home of the King Movement (Kīngitanga), which originally contested the colonial invasion of Māori farmland in our region in the 1860s, and is still the current place of residence of the Māori King. Our land surely features in family whakapapa (lineages) linking local Māori families to the land going back centuries, yet now we neither sought nor saw any trace of such claims.[2] We were not simply farmers, we were Pākehā[3] farmers – a distinction that would only start to penetrate our thinking after the empowerment of a tribunal in 1985 to investigate the flawed outcomes and injustices of the Treaty of Waitangi, which was signed in 1840 at the founding of the European colony. The Waitangi Tribunal would, alongside the betrayal of 1973 and crisis of neoliberalism, be the third looming crisis, causing alarm in the Pākehā farming community by bringing into view a history of land confiscation, invasion and duplicity that were the previously invisible dynamics at the heart of how we came to inhabit the landscape.

Alongside the erasing of past owners and users of our land, another site of erasure was our landscape ecology. The paddocks were grass, where previously they had been covered in groves of kahikatea pine (*Dacrycarpus dacrydioides*). The wetlands that once supported flax, fish and waterfowl had been drained and their remnant contained inside two small fenced-off areas ('the swamps') outside the fenced pastures at the back of the farm. Our farm's boundaries were protected by legal title that privileged us in planning regulations and allowed us freedom to do many things on our farm that, with hindsight, were ecologically troubling: cutting and burning native bush, altering waterways, draining wetlands, dumping and burning waste, allowing contaminated water to flow away along our drains to an invisible destination and shooting semi-protected native birds.

The political character of this history of erasure – which had magically rendered invisible prior owners, indigenous claims, indigenous ecologies – was reproduced in our daily lives and actions. We were standing together in 1973 in a secure Pākehā farming world, while the political rock and ice slowly moved underneath us. We were, effectively, farming inside invisible worlds. Or, looked at a little less charitably, we were able to farm peacefully and successfully precisely because other worlds had become invisible.

The political agency of farms

This is the kind of contradiction that lies at the heart of the enquiry in this book. The narrative that I will relate commences with three inter-related sets of questions:

1. How do we understand the power of farms as agents of colonization? How did farms act to silence some worlds and close down possible futures in colonial New Zealand?
2. How did farming undergo a significant transition from a chaotic world of colonization into a pacified and increasingly homogenized world of modernist farming? What kind of new reality was created by the modernist farm?
3. Finally, how did this world become disrupted in the latter part of the twentieth century, and how do we understand the power of farms themselves to reveal alternatives, create new opportunities and enact new futures?

New Zealand is an extreme version of farm-based colonization, but in its extremity it reveals important dynamics about wider transitions in farming under modernity. It is a lens into dynamics that are shared not only with other settler states like Australia, Canada and the United States, but also with all those regions and economies where modernist farming arrived into prior worlds of land-use with tumultuous consequences and vexed legacies. In this book, I explore the idea that social, ecological and economic power – particularly in colonized worlds – is enacted as much through invisibility and silence as it is through visible relations and vocalized contests in our farming and food worlds. It has, as I'll go on to elaborate in the next chapter, a particular kind of 'ontological politics'.

To tell this story, I focus on farms and orchards themselves as sites where these kinds of political effects are enacted.[4] The farm stories that I will tell come from diverse worlds, both personal and scholarly. These stories partly follow my own biography, and also a two-decade sequence of academic collaborations that brought me into contact with a range of farms exhibiting both familiar modernist characteristics, but also, increasingly, a range of ways of being 'alternative'. In a book that is partly about the way that scholars and researchers help 'make' the worlds they study, it is important to briefly acknowledge these academic influences. First, the great crisis of neoliberalization that was unfolding as I undertook my PhD brought me into contact with the vigorous critiques of 'farming under capitalism' that were taking shape in Australasia (and across the Developed World) during the 1980s and '90s.[5] From that point onwards, a series of projects and collaborations began to examine different kinds of alternative farming arrangements that were increasingly becoming visible in New Zealand, and were disrupting notions about what farms were as well as how they might act in the future.[6] Finally, a long-term collaboration with a group of scholars seeking to innovate around theories, methods and ontologies of agrifood scholarship – called the Biological Economies group – opened up new potentials for theorizing the kinds of major historical transitions, and their fateful consequences, that are the central concern of this book.[7]

The narrative is built around specific farms in different historical periods. At the centre of my account of the great colonial crisis of land-use are several clusters of colonial farms settled by my forebears. The story of these early farms is informed by a strong body of scholarship on the environmental and post-colonial history of New Zealand. This book isn't a work of historiography, but nevertheless relies greatly on the work of prior historians to inform much of the narrative.[8] The farms that inform the latter part of this book are partly drawn from my own research collaborations, or are well-known exemplars of new options for farming in New Zealand. To try and keep the text as accessible as possible, I've engaged with some of the more complex social theoretical discussion in extended footnotes. While some chapters are strongly oriented towards theoretical discussion relating to critical agrifood theory (particularly Chapters 1, 4 and the Epilogue), I've tried to write the rest in a way that will be accessible to a wide range of readers.

What this account shows is that farms reveal particular kinds of political agency that have consequences in social, ecological and economic worlds. As an object of study, the farm is not a passive bearer of other more significant powers – those of nation state, Promethean inventions and science, the great political projects of modernity or capitalism, natural vitalities, or of socially constructed worlds of inequality and cultural symbolism. All these things happen within and around farms, but our key mistake has been to miss the strange, mundane powers of the farm itself as the maker of such worlds. By rendering visible the invisible powers of farms, we find both dark histories and contradictory outcomes, as well as ways to grasp how farms are sites of vitality, renewal, experimentation and hope.

Notes

1   Good farms also, to his mind, seem to exhibit stable and well-defined social and
     gender hierarchies and well-defined boundaries. On a typical weekend I was, as
     a grandson, out in the paddock being instructed how to farm. My older brother
     was two steps ahead of me in the same paddock. My sister was riding a pony. My

grandmother and mother were preparing cheese on toast for Sunday brunch. Such instruction followed a schedule. We (the boys) could start learning to drive the tractor at age nine, shoot the rifle at fourteen and use the chainsaw at sixteen. We met and talked to neighbours over our fencelines. We were all white.

2   Such a search would be interesting – as the farm lies in a contested borderland between the powerful Waikato tribes and neighbouring Ngāti Hauā.

3   The signifier that we were not indigenous New Zealanders, but colonial imports, predominantly from Europe, especially Britain. Māori and Pākehā are important cultural designations in New Zealand and derive their meaning from the dynamics of European colonization. Neither Māori nor Pākehā existed as terms prior to the colonial moment.

4   To simplify what will be a complex narrative, I use often use the term 'farm' throughout this book to indicate a range of styles of land-use. That looseness is deliberate. The tightening of the definition of the farm under colonization and modernity in Aotearoa New Zealand, to be a single unit of legally bounded land commercially producing food and/or fibre and usually privately owned by a family, is one of the interesting hegemonies that will be revealed in this narrative. For simplicity's sake, the word 'farm' does useful work in this book. But it also simplifies a complex world of land-use-particularly the way that farms are actually complex assemblages of human and non-human relationships and agencies. It is not my intention to search out one new term to describe what, to paraphrase Annemarie Mol, might signify 'the farm multiple'. Alternatives in farming worlds have emerged around animals, domesticated plants, with trees, vines and through a breaking of barriers between land and sea. To avoid slipping too early into this complexity and alterity, I'm going to characterize land-use in the same way that the land-users themselves characterized their own land in different parts of this narrative – often using 'farm' to suggest pastoral farming, and 'orchard' to designate specialist fruit production – while also recognizing other indigenous ways of describing worlds of gardens, hunting, foraging, whenua (land) and pāmu (the Māori verb 'to farm').

5   Work that has its most obvious legacy in the work of the Australasian Agri-Food Research Network that still provides vibrant and creative critique of the current state of food and farming worlds (see www.afrn.co).

6   Particularly the 'Greening Food' project on organic and IPM innovations in horticulture and pastoral farming that ran from 1994 to 2002, and the ARGOS and NZ Sustainability Dashboard projects that ran from 2003 to 2018 (see www.argos.org.nz and www.nzdashboard.org.nz).

7   See Le Heron et al. (2016) and Pawson et al. (2018).

8   If I were seeking to write a comprehensive farming history, I wouldn't concentrate solely on my own family's farms as they miss one important ecological frontier – the indigenous grasslands of the South Island's 'High Country' – as well as not engaging with the great class transition from 'Great Estates' to family farms during the 1890s in many parts of New Zealand.

1

Farming and ontology

Trouble at modernity's farm

Farms have an interesting relationship with modernity.[1] For many in the 'Developed World' the farm has been the bearer of some of the strongest claims about the way in which science and technology have delivered 'progress' and provided benefits to humankind. Yet, after having spent most of the twentieth century as one of the previously unchallengeable 'goods' delivered by the modern world, the farm has come under attack in ways that would previously have been unthinkable for many farmers, scientists, economists and politicians. Weren't farms one of the quiet achievers of a better world, delivering a reduction in world hunger and advancing the betterment of humankind through the advantages of abundant and cheap food produced under ever more sophisticated and predictable, scientifically informed systems of production? How could such modernist certainties start to unravel?

Ever since Rachel Carson published *Silent Spring* in 1962, an environmental critique of intensive farming practices has been emerging in wealthy industrialized nations, rising to open concern in the last decades of the twentieth century. The global food crises of 2008–2011 punctured another certainty: that the only future for farming would be a continuation of the existing trajectory of increasing industrialization, productivity and efficiency delivering ever cheaper food. At the same time, new realizations about fossil fuel reserves and climate change raise concerning questions about the extent to which the modern farm is now in an intimate relationship with a fuel source that is strictly time limited and has dire climatic consequences. UN reports now openly discuss the need to double our production of food by 2050 to keep ahead of world hunger, but that we need to do so *sustainably*.[2] On a broader social and political stage, there are now multiple social movements that characterize the modern farm as expressing pathological ethical, social and ecological effects. This contentious turn in the political virtues of the modern farm in the Developed World arrived much later than earlier crises in the indigenous world, where colonization, high-minded development schemes and a related embrace of farming as the bearer of modernization and progress in ventures like the Green Revolution devastated prior social and ecological worlds.[3] This is the complex politics of modernist farming: on one side lauded as a bearer of enlightenment and progress, on the other as a destroyer of worlds with pathological social and ecological consequences. For scholars who research and elaborate on farming worlds, this divide runs through the middle of our professional lives. This book approaches this divided world via an unusual theoretical question: how did farms themselves enact both these outcomes? I'm going to argue that farms aren't just the bearers of modernity: they are powerful makers of modernity. They have their own particular kind of political agency that needs to be understood in order to grasp the importance and vexed consequences of the relationship between farming and modernity – particularly in many parts of the world where 'modern societies' emerged from the farm-led colonization of indigenous worlds.

This story has two distinct halves. While much contemporary academic and political focus is directed towards the increasing level of challenge and disruption currently being experienced by modernist farming, this leaves out the equally important, and much less frequently considered, question of how modernist farming became so powerful in the first place. The first half of this book will examine the making of this modernist farming world as parts of the British Empire were colonized, eventually stabilizing into the coherent and politically untouchable entity that became the normative pattern for farming in much of the Developed World through the twentieth century. The focus on colonized settings involving settler farmers is unusual. Most discussion of the emergence of modernist farming either situates it inside the industrialized Developed World in places like the UK or Europe – where a long transition from peasant to modern agriculture took shape – or is directed towards the Green Revolution where a dramatic clash between peasant and modernist farming occurred across much of the rest of the world. This book examines a specific kind of 'third space' in this great transition – the 'settler states' where modernist farming by European settlers acted as a powerful agent of colonization of indigenous worlds.[4] Modernist farming in colonial settings enacted powerful effects – breaching key ecological frontiers and unleashing chaos in landscapes that previously supported much more diverse and complex worlds of food, land and resource-use – before stabilizing into uncontested and normative worlds of modernist, scientific agriculture during the twentieth century. This is a pattern that took shape in the United States, Canada, Australia and my own home, New Zealand.

The second half of this book will examine the unmaking of this powerful farming world as it became increasingly contested in the last decades of the twentieth century. After a long period of stable and uncontested modernist farming, this seemingly monolithic world became increasingly disrupted and the politics of its existence became openly exposed by destabilizing new materialities, new ways of understanding the world through science, ecological crises and new social and political movements. Into this disrupted space, new alternatives and many possible futures have begun to emerge.

Both halves of this story can be told using one compelling national site of farming endeavour – New Zealand – which was colonized with the explicit intent of becoming Britain's 'farm in the South Pacific'. In this particular space, the colonial encounter was intimately related to the specific project of establishing settler farming in British colonies, with significant consequences for the culture, politics, economics and ecology of land-use of New Zealand. The speed, chaotic qualities and scope of New Zealand's transformation were remarkable. One of the first geographers to ponder this colonial transformation suggested that the extent of landscape change that had happened in New Zealand in only one century was so vast and all-encompassing that it could only be compared to the impacts of four centuries of colonization in the United States and twenty centuries of land-use change in Europe.[5] Put simply, no country can do a better job than New Zealand of describing the impacts and consequences of colonization undertaken in service of a sudden need for food during the Industrial Revolution. It tells a story, however, of more than just the impacts of colonization. It reveals how an important transition from colonial battle zone to uncontested modernist normality was partly enacted by the power of farms themselves. A particular kind of modernist farm – grasslands-based sheep, dairy and beef farms – breached a series of ecological frontiers and established a new landscape order inside the chaos and disruption of colonized worlds. These farms reveal the hidden politics of how, out of chaos and disruption, an increasing homogeneity of landscapes and uncontested cultural normality was enacted.

Such actions have long consequences. By considering contemporary farm politics in New Zealand, the great pivot around the making and unmaking of modernist farming can be revealed. New Zealand may remain the most export-oriented food producer in the world,[6] but it has now also become a site of important political motions and reactions to modernist farming over the last two decades.[7] This comes into stark focus around a new frontier conquest. Previously, farms were celebrated agents of colonial conquest, breaching ecological frontiers and then acting, in concert with the state, science and broad cultural consent, to stabilize the chaos that such breaches unleashed. In the twenty-first century, however, a final ecological breach – this time using irrigation to bring intensive dairy farming into previously dry pastoral landscapes – has unleashed chaos that its participants are now struggling to contain. The making and unmaking of modernist farming pivots around the (un)containability of ecological and social disruption, and around this pivot, new futures start to take shape.

By telling the story of both the rising and the falling of the modernist farm project in a colonized landscape like New Zealand, a narrative emerges that is applicable to all the regions of the world in these 'third spaces' where indigenous landscapes were colonized through the agency of modernist farms. Placing the modernist farm into its rightful central role in this rising and falling trajectory poses a considerable challenge for how to academically narrate dynamics that have happened across such a long period of time and which traverse diverse fields of academic interest. The story is part political, social, ecological and economic, and it involves questions about both how farming is practised and how researchers and scholars participate in stabilizing or critiquing farming worlds. In this book, I want to attempt this task by following the 'ontological turn' in social theorizing.

Farming and ontology

This book is an extended consideration of the ontology of farms, which places what follows into a narrow and unfamiliar place for many scholars.[8] Ontology is the study of *being*: more specifically, what exists and how we characterize and identify things as real. It characterizes objects, sets boundaries and limits, and decides what is and isn't part of an object or process. For philosophers, it is a highly specialized field which cultivates its own world of academic interest, and does so in ways that are not quite the same as what I mean, as a social theorist, when I use the term 'ontology'. Over the last two decades, a number of social theorists have started to take an interest in ontology as part of their wider focus on how the shape and form of social phenomena are enacted not just in intentional human actions, but also including materials and relations between human and non-human agents.[9] What are the social and material relationships that combine to create a thing (ranging from the State[10] to the human body[11]) that we then act on as socially 'real'; or what are the ways in which social and material processes set boundaries, limits, categorizations and hierarchies in and around social objects?[12] This has become a compelling area of sociological thinking around questions like: what is nature? Is nature separate to culture? Are humans distinctly different to other non-human actors in social worlds? And what kinds of limits, boundaries and hierarchies do we enact when we undertake research into issues concerning ontologies of nature, sustainability and ecological transformation?[13] For many scholars interested in the critical social scientific study of ontologies, this has coalesced around an explicit focus on the *political* implications of ontologies, which question the outcomes, inequities, silencing and privileging that emerge from struggles between ontological worlds – both large and small.[14]

In this book, such questions are directed at both the ontologies that have enacted modernity – giving a particular character, relationality and shape to modernist worlds – along with the specific ontology of the farm: what comprises a farm? How do we, as researchers and practitioners, understand and enact the limits, boundaries, key relationships and human/non-human actors on a farm? Or, even more significantly, how do these questions of ontology help us to understand the many and varied powers of the farm and its consequences in shaping modernity's social, economic and ecological worlds (its modernist 'political ontology')? This is a story that questions not only how modernity is made by farms, but also how it is unmade. How does the ontology of the farm help us understand the politics of how modernist farming worlds came to be, as well as what 'post-modern' farms might be in the future?

There are two important reasons for taking this unusual theoretical pathway into the study of farms. The first is that farms haven't received enough attention as sites where social, economic and ecological powers are enacted.[15] Farms are not simply the outcome of other more important social and economic processes under modernity; rather, they play their own role in enacting the ontology of modernity.[16]

This leads to a second reason: if we are hoping to promote and develop 'alternative agriculture', what is the political and material character of the thing that we are hoping to provide alternatives to? In other words, before we can understand the politics and powers of alternative agriculture and pose alternative futures,[17] we need to answer the ontological question: 'alternative to what'?[18] Once we have a means for posing questions about how to understand the 'centre' of modernist farming worlds, we have the opportunity to ask questions about how stable that centre is. How does it relate to the materiality[19] of farms and farmed environments, and do particular farming worlds[20] generate multiple potential worlds of action, or do they shut down options and suppress alternatives?[21]

Given the abstract tone of these opening pages, I want to spend some time considering two examples of how ontologies are enacted by farms.

Two farms, two ontologies

Let us walk through the gate of two farms in the Canterbury region of New Zealand that have very different ontologies. One is a 'mixed' organic crop and stock farm; the other is a nearby intensive dairy farm that was established on the site of an earlier sheep farm after the development of a large irrigation scheme. They aren't random choices. One farm sits in direct continuity with the great trajectory of modernist pastoral farming in New Zealand; the other is a very specific kind of 'alternative' farming. Both farms enact a very different kind of farm ontology.

Rendell Stream Farm

About fifteen years ago I was invited, along with several dozen local farmers and agricultural researchers, to visit a successful and innovative organic farm. Rendell Stream Farm[22] has been a participant in many research projects, and is known as a good exemplar of an established organic farm. It is also interesting because Rendell Stream itself is a tributary of Lake Ellesmere/Te Waihora[23] – a site of highly contentious environmental degradation partly resulting from excessive nutrient run-off from new intensive dairy farms in the catchment. Rendell Stream Farm is sometimes referred to as an exemplar of the kind of farm that, if it was emulated across the catchment, might reverse some of the ecological dynamics that have caused the eutrophic death of Lake Ellesmere/Te Waihora.[24]

Violet and Mike run it as a mixed farm, with multiple varieties of stock and crops, interesting rotations, other kinds of experimentation taking place with things like flame weeders (much debated in terms of sustainability by some attendees at the open day) and innovations in composting. Market linkages were diverse, ranging from local to national networks for organic products, with one product joining the growing stream of certified organic products arriving in UK supermarkets. We were sitting around under established trees. In fact, once you noticed them, the number and size of the trees on this farm set it apart from many of its neighbours, whose owners were cutting down trees to open up space for centre-pivot irrigators to roll. There were unusual and experimental activities: woofers (Willing Workers on Organic Farms), cute accommodation, eccentric homemade equipment that often failed and sometimes succeeded. Huge interest was focused on the restoration of Rendell Stream through riparian planting of native vegetation, as well as the creation of a weir behind which water was allowed to back up through a reedy water meadow that helped filter sediment out of the water. As Violet put it, 'We want the water leaving our farm to be better than when it arrived. Not the same. Better!' A generally happy throng of visitors gathered around a barbeque at the end of the day to sample home brew and eat home-killed meat. It was a slightly dusty and cheerful New Zealand variant of the kind of open day at Joel Salatin's Polyface Farm in the United States that is approvingly narrated by author Michael Pollan.[25]

The reason this farm was chosen for an open day was that it points towards different options for pastoral farming in New Zealand. Violet and Mike are well-known nationally in the organic farming movement and their approach to farming is interesting, experimental and based around a constant search for new information and techniques. But this farm is much more than just the sum of Violet and Mike's management decisions: it is a collaboration of human and non-human powers that provide a useful exhibition of what we might call 'farm powers'. The farm was succeeding in orthodox economic terms, but it also had impressive ecological dynamics, heterogeneity and vitality, sustaining trees, a stream, as well as fields of wildflowers and birds, along with the many domesticated species in the farming system. It was also a socially impressive farm, with social networks connecting to the local community through visits by trout fishers, school children learning about stream restoration, as well as participation in the farmer's market. It had networks of woofers from around the world, and it was a site of constant experimentation, with researchers from the nearby university, polytechnic and participants in organic organizations being welcomed to bring their ideas or experiments onto the farm. In sum, this farm was enacting material powers that influenced ecological, social and economic outcomes. It wasn't just a passive tableau for human agency: it brought human and non-human powers together.

This may seem like an odd observation, but many farmers understand this truth. When we walked away from the open day, some of the non-organic farmer attendees recognized this particular kind of farm power in an interesting kind of way: muttering that this farm was impressive, but some farms just didn't bring the key qualities needed to work in exactly this kind of way – particular soil profiles and reservoirs of fertility, rainfall patterns, the presence of a spring creek, the ensemble of skills and resources brought by the family, years of 'tuning' tricky products like organic onions to particular growing conditions, distance to a farmer's market among other things … 'In comparison,' they pondered, 'my farm can't do this.'[26]

There is another interesting way to think about this particular farm, because while it was a site of vital powers, it was also a place where many future options (and hopes) existed. This ran counter to the existential fear of many farmers in New Zealand – of 'uncontrolled ferality' that might ruin them at any moment. Rabbits weren't overwhelming this landscape, crops were produced in mixes that reduced risk from pest incursions, and organic certifiers allowed accommodations with some animal health remedies to maintain animal welfare standards. The soil was very lively, but that was the result of years of composting and working with key soil resources. It was, in short, a farm that over a twenty-year period was enacting complexity in particular and important ways: it had generated a lot of potential options, opportunities and futures. Many things had happened and could yet happen.

This farm was complex in ways that made it unable to be converted into a 'single plan' template for organic farming.[27] There is no standard plan (or single label) that can capture the multiple powers of a farm like this, and you can't just prescribe some categorical actions and objects to reproduce it across a variable landscape like Canterbury. Its activities align with ecological complexity and heterogeneity as well as being connected to wider ecological, social and economic worlds. It is a farm that has multiple potential futures and is rooted in an ontology of strong ecological and social networks and weak boundaries.

#370 Five-Mile Road

Compare this to a second farm nearby that we interviewed as part of a project on how to understand transitions from extensive sheep to intensive dairy farming systems.[28] This farm, unlike previous generations of pastoral family farms in New Zealand, doesn't have a name – it has an address on Five-Mile Rd[29] and is known by its 'rapid rural number': #370. It is a dairy 'unit' in an area that had previously been dryland sheep farming terrain. It could only support the kinds of pasture growth needed to sustain an intensive dairy unit because of its participation in a new irrigation scheme.

When walking onto this farm as a researcher, I encounter a simpler set of objects and relationships. The entire farm is densely pastured with high-growth ryegrass that is bred to turn water and nutrients into maximum production of 'dry matter'. It has also been re-fenced and trees removed to allow large centre-pivot irrigators to roll over the pasture. Water sensors have been placed under the ground in the paddocks to enable the farm operator to calibrate the distribution of water.

On these paddocks are grazing over 600 representatives of one breed of cow – the Holstein Friesian,[30] described by some as the 'industrial cow' – which are being milked twice a day in a large state-of-the-art rotary milking shed.[31] The milk is destined for the large Synlait factory down the road, which is a large industrial complex dedicated mainly to the production of milk powder for export to markets like China. The cows graze on scientifically perfected ryegrass, calculated to produce the maximum 'dry matter' per hectare under irrigated conditions.

This farm was converted from a dryland sheep farm by its owner Rob[32] (we never met his partner) with the assistance of a large loan from a bank. Securing that loan was possible because of a number of 'certainties' in the system. Rob purchased rights to water through a commercial irrigation scheme, which meant there was a predictable amount of grass that his farm could produce per hectare of land. That giant 'centre pivot' irrigator acts with considerable power to make a whole lot of things more certain and predictable on his farm.

Other things also help lock down certainties. The contract with Synlait secures a guaranteed buyer for every drop of milk produced on the farm, although the price is not entirely controllable. Consequently, Rob, his banker, Synlait and a couple of technical advisors follow a series of numbers very closely. They see the daily graph of how much milk is collected every day during the season (lasting usually around nine months of the year before the cows are 'dried off' for the winter and sent elsewhere for 'run off' grazing to allow the main pastures to recover). That graph should ideally show as rapid as possible an incline to high levels of milk production at the start of the season, maintaining its heights through the peak, and then holding on as long as possible before dropping when the weather turns colder. A dip in that line is a problem, and may require the purchase of external feed supplements like Palm Kernel Expeller, imported from Indonesia. A second number is the price per kg of 'milk solid' paid out by Synlait. Generally following the international price achieved in the Global Dairy Trade auction (established and managed by New Zealand dairy giant Fonterra), Synlait positions its price to gain contracts from dairy producers who want to supply someone other than Fonterra (which purchases over 80 per cent of New Zealand's daily milk production).

A third more slow-moving set of numbers is the interest rate on the bank loan and the current valuation per hectare of the farm, both of which are of particular interest to Rob's farm accountant. These numbers coalesce around the total number of hectares in production.[33] Combined, each hectare of the farm possesses its own notional formula of how much debt it is supporting, how much grass it produces and thus how many cows it feeds, how much milk it is producing, and how much profit/loss it is generating. There aren't a wide variety of risks in this system, but those that are there all involve big numbers.

One of the most compelling things about this farm is how similar it is to thousands of other irrigated dairy units across New Zealand. Rob could sell his finely calibrated intensive dairy unit and purchase another such farm and be able to competently manage it within a matter of weeks. There are a few local variations to navigate (like which major dairy company has a nearby factory, sources of extra fodder and the options for leasing 'run-off' grazing in the middle of winter), but most of the rest is standardized. The cows are identified by their numerical ear tags and have a metrological life in the software that elaborates production data, the dairy sheds are standardized, the technical inputs are equally standard and available, there is only a small number of well-known software packages that allow for control of parts of the system, and the key metrics are all the same.[34]

A crucial quality of this farm is that it sits inside some invisible but highly consequential ontological boundaries. It has far fewer social networks and ties than Rendell Stream Farm, and few would pick this farm to host an open day. Importantly, it has a close relationship with agricultural scientists at nearly Lincoln University, and its componentry is modelled, to a large extent, on the university's model intensive dairy unit where the system of perennial ryegrass, water, fertilizer and Holstein Friesian cows was perfected for Canterbury conditions. For this reason, an open day would be much more likely to take place at the research farm at Lincoln University that provided the blueprint for the farm at #370 Five-Mile Rd.

It is also situated in a highly contentious and fragile environmental position. Like Rendell Stream Farm, this farm also sits in the catchment for the eutrophically devastated Lake Ellesmere/Te Waihora. Consequently, a final set of numbers that is followed on this farm is the nutrient budgeting score created by the software package Overseer, which calculates the amount of nitrate fertilizers that can be applied while keeping run-off in acceptable limits for a highly sensitive freshwater catchment.[35] Some members of the industry are concerned as to whether they can make dairy units in a sensitive region like Canterbury more environmentally sustainable.[36] Discussion groups are forming and technical interventions are being scoped. Rob is not an enthusiastic participant in these and leaves his Overseer metrics to an advisor from his fertilizer company. He is more focused on what he can control inside the fenceline of his farm. One of our most telling quotes obtained from a farmer running a near identical farm was: 'My farm is a machine for producing grass.' The centre of Rob's ontology, and that of his farm, is keeping his 'grass-producing machine' running at maximum speed. What happens *outside* the boundary of his farm because of what happens *inside* the boundary is only of vague and abstract interest to him.

As a pathway into the theoretical discussions that will take place in this book, these farms are different in particular kinds of ways. #370 Five-Mile Rd is a machine made of technical components, fungible metrics, running on a template that is technically reproducible and able to be replicated on any landscape where fences can be erected, water obtained, fertilizer imported, the 'industrial cow' acquired, along with enough scientists and consultants on hand to fine-tune elements of the system. This is a farm of highly knowable parts that produces a single thing (well, two things: grass and milk). It also operates 'over the top' of landscape ecologies and for that reason, in this particular part of New Zealand, it is already ecologically unsustainable and might soon be politically unsustainable as well. It is a farm that exists inside one reality, a knowable technical world, which aligns it with a thousand other similar farms, united as participants enacting the 'universal reality' of modernity. It also sits inside a highly consequential ontological boundary. Unlike Rendell Stream Farm, this unit has tight technical networks, weakly elaborated wider ecological and social networks, and sits inside a tight boundary that encapsulates a small range of technologies, metrics, experts, financial measures and a simple relationship to an industrial processor of milk. How those ontological boundaries came into existence and how they are maintained will be a major theme of the rest of this book.

My argument in this book is that #370 is a farm that stands in direct lineage with a particular style of modernist farming in New Zealand. Like its predecessors, it is a farm that is doing a particular kind of work to homogenize the farming landscape and render key relations increasingly simplified. Unlike Rendell Stream Farm, #370 is converging on a narrowing set of future options. And those options are potentially catastrophic. A crisis is emerging because of the careful elaboration of a mechanistic, production-focused system inside the boundaries of the farm, while ignoring what is happening outside those boundaries. This crisis threatens the economic future of both this farm and the wider systems (ecological and social) that it resides in. Seen as an ontology, #370 has strong boundaries, weak wider networks and a mechanistic and uncomplex internal structure, all of which contribute to it having a narrowing set of future options.[37]

Explaining difference in farming worlds

I have described these two farms as being different in a range of ways. Their components, their boundaries, their networks and engagements are quite compellingly different. As examples of two kinds of farm *ontology*, they do useful work in bringing a lot of different elements of farming worlds into consideration, albeit with enough complexity that it will take the rest of this book to elaborate why this approach can be so useful for understanding much of the long-term trajectory and disruption of modernist farming. To start this elaboration, however, it is interesting to consider how other ways of explaining difference in political discourse and agrifood theorization might try to separate these two farms.

In activist terminology (and across a lot of casual attribution by academics), these farms fall into a binary between conventional and alternative.[38] The difficulty with this binary is that it usually struggles to satisfactorily answer the question, 'alternative to what?' This is a question that has challenged my research colleagues and me over many decades of research in New Zealand. While we have undertaken a great deal of research into characterizing the various ways in which farms and orchards might be understood as 'alternative' – and I'll return to some of the findings of those enquiries later in this book – we often have operated with only a shadowy, undefinable and, at times, invisible 'other' to those alternative farms. What was 'conventional' in an alternative-conventional binary? How might we characterize the invisible and powerful 'centre' of farming worlds? The farms in our studies that we conveniently labelled as 'conventional' often displayed such a wide variation in actions and outcomes that the category struggled to convey any meaningful information.[39] #370 Five-Mile Rd shares this problem as to where it fits inside the category of being 'conventional'. It is neither a completely industrial unit like the neighbouring beef feedlot to the south, nor the factory-farm producing chicken meat just further north towards the city of Christchurch. Neither is it the kind of extensive farm found in some 'conventional' parts of New Zealand's farmscape, where environmentally minded 'conventional' farmers preserve wetlands, conserve remnant native bush, plant ornamental trees and seek to reduce fertilizer inputs. As a category, 'conventional' farming is trying to contain too much variation and thus disguises much more than it reveals.[40]

For popular writers who aren't quite so burdened by these complexities – like Michael Pollan – this alternative-conventional binary assembles around some popular concepts in food activism: conventional farms are corporate, large-scale, and utilize industrial and factory[41] systems; alternative farms are smaller, family-owned and more likely to supply a local market. This doesn't work particularly well to distinguish this couplet in New Zealand. Both my exemplar farms are family-owned, and if one includes leased land the 'alternative' farm is slightly larger than the 'conventional' one. Rob might sell his milk to a big corporate company, but he could join over 80 per cent of New Zealand's other dairy farmers and supply the mega-cooperative Fonterra instead. Pollan's binary works well in the clearly bifurcated farming world of the United States, but is less well suited to explaining difference in the complex world of medium-sized family farms in New Zealand.

Others might see these farms as differentiated by the 'intensity' of their production systems. #370 Five-Mile Rd (and its thousands of close kin) is definitely highly intensive in that it uses a large quantity of externally derived technical inputs like fertilizer, stock food and irrigated water to produce a reliably high level of productivity. However, Rendell Stream Farm also has a highly 'intensive' management system, but the inputs are knowledge, expertise, and a variably sourced cornucopia of composts, sprays and simple machinery. Another comparison might be to describe #370 Five-Mile Rd as 'productivist' as it is highly oriented towards a single goal of producing the maximum amount of grass to produce the maximum amount of milk. But Rendell Stream Farm is also trying to produce a lot of high-quality organic products. Productivism and intensity alone don't capture all the differences between these two farms. We clearly need more complex ways to characterize the dynamics that are hinted at when we use the crude category of 'conventional' farming.

Critical theories of the farm:
Farming under capitalism and/or modernity?

If the activist literature has a tendency to fall into an alternative-conventional binary – which renders the conventional side of the binary unsatisfyingly uncomplex or simplistic – then the journey towards a more sophisticated theoretical understanding of these differences started for researchers like myself in a period of farming crisis in the 1970s and '80s. Briefly reviewing that moment in theoretical history reveals the emerging lines of fracture between scholars who are working in critical theory, and orthodox academic approaches to understanding modernist farming as enacted by agricultural scientists, economists and extensionists. It is a line of fracture that reveals different scholarly ontologies of the farm.

Critical social theorists started to take an interest in farms during the period after the 1970s known popularly as the 'farm crisis' in the Developed World. After decades of seemingly unbroken growth and expansion of farming during the boom years after the Second World War, farming in Developed World countries entered a period of crisis in the 1970s, out of which some might argue it has never fully emerged. A group of social theorists began to try to account for this period of farm crisis and found that existing modes of explanation arising from models derived from agricultural economics or agricultural science were highly limited in their capacity to explain the wider systemic dimensions of the crisis. Orthodox agricultural science, agricultural economics and, in many cases, their partner field of agricultural extension provided tightly bounded ontologies of what was a 'farm unit' or a 'farm enterprise'. They provided powerful explanations for dynamics inside their field of view, but seemed to exclude much else that was happening to farms – including, for those social scientists, the very reasons why so many farms were in crisis in the first place.[42] Breaking away from these orthodox (and, as I'll go on to argue, highly modernist) ontologies of the farm, this new critical spirit of social theorizing enacted a very different way to understand the ontology of farms: they could only be understood in terms of their operation and relations within wider relations of capitalism.[43] It was an approach that brought critical left-leaning scholarship into the academic study of agriculture, something that prominent radical rural sociologist Fred Buttel and his colleagues characterized as incendiary in the otherwise depoliticized, conservative world of agricultural research and education at most US universities.[44]

Taking shape under the banner of the New Rural Sociology,[45] the farm was retheorized according to a Marxist and neo-Marxist understanding of the deep relations, inequalities and structures of capitalist society. This was a dramatically new ontology: farms weren't neatly bounded enterprises following simple economic laws; neither were they purely technical systems following mechanistic and naturalistic laws of biological productivity, crop management and harvest.[46] The farm was simultaneously an economic *and* a social institution enmeshed in the wider relations of capitalist society. It was politically charged and politically inflicted with the kinds of economic inequalities that were intensifying under late capitalism, and the future of family farms was fraught in a world of corporatizing and industrializing agriculture.[47]

The New Rural Sociology (and its allies and successors) posed a dramatically new ontology of the farm to the prevailing orthodoxy of agricultural science, economics and extension. Over the subsequent decades of elaboration, debate and reconstruction of most of the elements of the New Rural Sociology and its theoretical kin, the significance of this original fracture point has now become lost deep in the origin stories of how critical scholars invaded one of the most conservative fields of scholarly life. But, as I'll argue in this book, the fracture point between radical, critical ontologies of the farm and the great body of academic, educational and techno-scientific elaboration of modernist ontologies of the farm is central to how we might understand the question: 'alternative to what?'

I'll return to the big critical-modernist ontological split shortly. However, the ways in which critical scholars might enact the ontology of the farm were starting to undergo significant changes. The more recent approach, characterized as 'agrifood studies', emerged from a dramatic ontological shift in the New Rural Sociology. The focus shifted from farms to commodities, with scholars beginning to 'follow' commodities out of the farm gate and across multiple sites of political, cultural and economic action.[48] Farms became linked via long chains to retailers; political pressures and conflicts were identified all the way from production to consumption; and larger political shifts like neoliberalism came into view. The agrifood approach was a highly sympathetic critique and elaboration of earlier studies of farming under capitalism.[49] Farms, plus commodities, plus global-scale labour relations, plus a new suite of corporate capitalists (ranging from processors to agrifood corporates to supermarkets) opened up wider fields of interest and generated new debates and alliances across wide terrains of academic interest, yet were usually grounded in reasonably familiar Marxist and neo-Marxist ontologies.

The New Rural Sociology (and to a lesser extent the early iterations of agrifood theory) was both enlivened and restricted by this adherence to a familiar ontology grounded in the critical characterization of capitalism. Numerous critiques arose that questioned some important silences created by this ontological framing. First, there was an important critique from feminist scholars that the New Rural Sociology had downplayed the importance of gender inequalities on farms and in food systems as both a characteristic inequity of farming worlds and a driver of changing approaches to farming.[50] Furthermore, as Actor Network Theorists went on to argue, theories grounded ontologically in the unfolding and contradictory structures of capitalism always prioritize social and economic forces as the drivers of social change. These approaches tend to ignore or subordinate other agencies and causalities of change – particularly those that might emanate from non-human agencies.[51] This had particular effects in dampening interest in ecological dynamics in agrifood systems – something that became increasingly difficult to sustain in an agrifood approach that was increasingly attracting a range of new scholars interested in sustainability issues. Another omission was a lack of attention to the powers of science and scientific knowledge production.[52] Finally, in the collective enthusiasm to wage war with the pernicious effects of late capitalism, family farmers, in all their conservative glory, became positioned as champions in a theoretical project of anti-capitalist politics. By inhabiting this position, potentially problematic histories of family farming were left unexplored. All these critiques challenged the kind of limited ontology of the farm being enacted in critical theory, and provided the impetus for further innovation in agrifood theorization: farms needed to be also understood as sites of gender, or include non-human agencies, to be understood in terms of their compromised ecologies, or, as I'll go on to argue, to have their crucial relationship with science elaborated, or to have the complex histories of their origins made visible – particularly in colonization.[53]

An alternative way to theorize the current character and future destination of farms, which tries to take into account some of these critiques, has been to academically situate farms as participants in wider transitions in *modernity*.[54] Drawing inspiration from classical theorists like Max Weber, the farm crisis was characterized by some scholars as a crisis of 'de-traditionalization', with farm culture being increasingly rationalized and de-humanized.[55] Theorists of modernity like Max Weber (or Jacques Ellul) saw dark futures for modernity, with the increasing rationalization of economic worlds, de-humanization of life, and technologically and bureaucratically dominated societies in which human 'enchantments' become subordinated to dystopian modernist rationalities and technologies.[56]

Over the last two decades, characterizing farms as drawing some of their ontological character from wider transitions in modernity (as well as in capitalism) has been the road less taken for agrifood theory.[57] The distinction between capitalism and modernity as different (yet linked) meta-theoretical tropes in agrifood theorization can be understood in two separate ways. First, the terms often distinguish between scholars operating within structural theoretical approaches, but who trace their inspiration from either Marx (capitalism) or from Weber (modernity). Lately, however, use of 'modernity' has also become a signifier of deeper theoretical differences between structural and post-structural theorizing – particularly through the embrace of actor network theory (ANT) and/or science and technology studies (STS).

My intention in this book is to travel down the road that bends towards positioning agrifood questions within a theorization of modernity. By using the idea of political ontologies, the questions of non-human agency, the power of science and the politics of colonization – and their relationship to the elaboration of modernist worlds – become central to my narrative. As James Scott argues in his influential analysis of the rise and demise of the modernist state, modernist projects that seek to control (and 'bracket') reality inevitably pitch modernity into reality-bending conflicts with wider networks of social and ecological vitality.[58] Modernity ends up in inevitable tensions and crises when it seeks rational ends, but ignores society and nature. This is where we can start to find answers to why my two farms in Canterbury, New Zealand, are so different in both their ontological composition and their many effects. It is a road that takes us back to the original fracture point in the 1970s, when critical theorization began to enact a highly different ontology of the farm compared to the modernist world of agricultural science, economics and extension. This is my theoretical launching point: what is the ontology of the *modernist* farm, and how did farms enact wider elements of *modernity*?

This question can only be answered by looking at the making and unmaking of modernist farming at its moments of origin. Rather than looking in the usual place for such answers – in the emergence of modern agriculture in the Old World, or the imposition of modernist systems into the Developing World during the Green Revolution – this enquiry searches for origins in the dynamics of colonization in settler states like New Zealand. That story takes shape around a series of colonial frontier conflicts.[59] These colonial frontiers were sites of both socio-political and ecological struggle and often farms were primary agents in these conflicts.[60]

Understanding the differences between farms like #370 Five-Mile Road and Rendell Stream Farm requires a deep dive into colonial histories of farming. It forces us to look at the creation story of the modernist farm and how its particular ontology was enacted, stabilized, defended and eventually disrupted. Telling that colonial creation story brings us into serious contemplation of the Promethean powers of science[61] in turning colonial worlds into modern worlds.

Agricultural science and modernity's beautiful machine

The way that we produce knowledge – through disciplinary science, expertise, situated knowledges and practices – enacts ontological worlds. In modernity, the enactive power of science to 'make' worlds, and to do so in very specific kinds of ways, is of particular importance. During the farm crisis of the 1970s, new radical approaches in rural sociology and geography thrived in part because orthodox academic modes of researching farming systems (and intervening as researchers into farming worlds) were (unsuccessfully) addressing a world through the limited lens of their own modernist ontologies. This wasn't due to inattention or failure of imagination. A separation between interior/knowable and exterior/irrelevant worlds of farming was a core element of the modernist ontology of these disciplines.[62] Agricultural science, and its companions in economics and extension, tended to practise their academic craft in ways that specifically created these boundaries around their object of interest.[63] That is the modernist way. It just shares, with much else in the modern world, the fatal flaw of failing to recognize the intrinsic connectivity of social and ecological worlds.

In this gap resides the perplexing mystery of why there has been relatively little scholarship on the relationship between farming, science and modernity. While much of the (not particularly extensive) literature on the relationship between farming and modernity is undertaken by historians concerned with transitions in the scientific understanding of farming processes that were taking place around 200 years ago in Europe,[64] the most immediately accessible clash between modernist agriculture (and agricultural science) and other ways of knowing and acting in farming worlds is in the Green Revolution. If one were to ask a leading scientist of the Green Revolution like Norman Borlaug what was the core componentry of the kinds of 'modern agriculture' that were being promulgated in the Green Revolution, he would likely have replied along the lines of new seeds, new fertilizers, chemical pest controls, elaborating particular types of farm machinery, scientifically educated farmers – all of which contributed to affirming a new rationale of 'good' agriculture in the form of more precise and predictable systems of farming, higher productivity and lower technical risk in production.[65]

Seen ontologically, what Borlaug and his scientific kin enacted in the mid-twentieth century was a segmented world of knowledge, securely lodged inside a powerful ontological boundary. Inside that boundary was a beautiful and powerful farm/machine, a miracle of modernist power and promise. It connected a series of technical elements into powerfully productive alignment and produced food like nothing that its predecessors could aspire to. Borlaug's machine-like modernist farm was revolutionary because it broke through some of the technical and biophysical limits of agricultural productivity inside the boundary of the farm. It's flaw, however, was its lack of capacity to manage (or even recognize) all its effects and consequences outside that ontological boundary.[66]

The enacting of an ontological boundary around a machine-like farm created exactly these kinds of consequences when the Green Revolution was extended into Developing World peasant farming worlds. Vandana Shiva is the most prominent critic of the Green Revolution's tendency to trigger exactly these kinds of consequential calamities for peasant farming. Shiva described the ways that peasant farming existed in an ontologically broad and more connected world of wider relations in comparison to Borlaug's machine-like, bounded, modernist farm. She argued that Borlaug's ensemble created 'monocultures of the mind' and caused Western agricultural scientists, aid bureaucrats, government officials and large-scale farmers to adopt a style of farming that prioritized techno-scientific rationales, narrow machine-like models of the operation of farms, and prioritized productivity above all other functions. At the same time these farms rendered invisible the positive connections and effects of the social and ecological dynamics of existing peasant farming systems and replaced them with nothing. The Green Revolution was, in this rendering, both highly creative and highly destructive. It generated the beautiful and powerful machine of modernist farming inside the boundary of the farm while decimating wider social and ecological worlds.[67]

A hypothetical debate between Norman Borlaug and Vandana Shiva held at Lincoln University in Canterbury would be an interesting event to attend.[68] Borlaug would likely make a stirring case for the powers and potentials of his farming machine wrapped in some vaguely abstract claims that any increase in food production would lead to a reduction in world hunger. If our dairy farmer Rob was in the audience, he would relate to the description of the perfect farm as a machine-like package of technologies, measures and techniques for maximizing production of wheat, rice or grass/milk. Vandana Shiva would likely then argue on behalf of all the other worlds that are annihilated and rendered invisible by Borlaug's machine. She would put the case for the wider social and ecological relations and different sources of ecological knowledge that are erased or removed from view by modernist farming. Violet and Mike would understand that what Shiva was describing is the reason why Lake Ellesmere/Te Waihora is dying. Historically, modernist farms with hard ontological boundaries haven't been required to take account of their wider social and ecological consequences, but those consequences happen anyway.

At the heart of their differences lie two radically different ontologies of how farms have been enacted in hard science versus soft/systems and/or social scientific disciplines. For Borlaug his technical machine needed no defence – it was simply a well-designed technical system that was delivering on its narrowly designed productivist goals. Understood through the lens of science and technology studies, this isn't the consequence of a particular worldview, or a carefully elaborated set of human assumptions: it is the effect created by the mundane day-to-day practice of science. Its discursive existence is preceded by a world of objects, measures, daily lab-based practices and relations that collectively enact a bounded, mechanistic farming world.[69] Scientists don't create unrealistically bounded farm worlds because they are bad scientists; they do so by enacting the day-to-day practices and relationalities of good science. For Shiva, in contrast, this wasn't good science: the difference between the two ontologies was a matter of life and death for the Indian peasantry. The daily lived experience of being an Indian peasant enacted a farm ontology that was intrinsically connected to wider social and ecological networks. The wider connectivity that modernist farming erased from peasant worlds was what had made that society viable.

Borlaug's ontology of the farm has hard farm boundaries and weak wider networks. Shiva's ontology of the farm has weak farm boundaries and strong wider networks. This book will provide a detailed elaboration of how these two different ontologies – which were in direct conflict during the Green Revolution – are also central to the dramatic history of colonization in many parts of the world.

Ontologies, colonization and invisible worlds

In turning towards colonization (as well as science) as the key anchors in the upcoming narrative, we can return to some of the originating terrain of the political ontologies approach. For scholars who have participated in the 'ontological turn' in the critical social sciences, one of their enduring themes has been how the 'unified reality' characteristic of modernity came to be enacted in processes of colonization. This book focuses on one very specific aspect of colonization: trying to understand how a particular kind of farming became powerful and assumed a hegemonic position as modernity's farm through much of the twentieth century. Such a narrative includes the ways that farms acted to homogenize landscapes and unify realities in ways that supported other effects of modernity.

For many critical theorists, the motions of colonization align closely to the formation of wider global capitalism and should be explained in such terms.[70] A political ontologies approach acknowledges that the birthing of capitalism was hugely significant, but examines the arrival of modernity into colonized worlds by talking first about indigenous people and environments, and their pre-existing worlds. One advocate of this kind of approach is Mario Blaser, who directs his attention at the political consequences of multiple elements of the ontological clash between modernity and indigenous cultures. He argues that theoretical approaches that conflate modernity with capitalism fail to grasp all the different types of power being enacted in modernity, and exclude the meaningful political and cultural worlds of indigenous people.[71] Such conflations are common in many historical accounts of colonization.[72]

This critique is highly influenced by ANT approaches: it is in the context of colonization that any tendency to downplay the agency of materials, objects, environments and other non-human actors has significant analytical consequences. Any silencing of other agencies potentially renders invisible other worlds that don't align with modernist ontologies. Processes of colonization have, in orthodox accounts, tended to be framed within a politics of contestation over land, labour and capital. These are, in most accounts, central elements of the way in which worlds are transformed, anchoring vastly diverging outcomes for peoples, environments and economies in the often-brutal dynamics of colonization. The political ontologies approach that I will elaborate in this narrative points towards a reframing of these to create a more nuanced and complex ontology of land, a reworking of the relationship between land and capital, as well as adding in the essential role of science in enacting particular outcomes during colonization. To do so, the orthodox study of capitalism, colonization and agriculture needs to be nudged in two important directions: towards a much more careful examination of the agency of farms in colonial history, along with a much more nuanced engagement with the powers of particular kinds of rationality and science as participants in enacting colonial farm ontologies.

A related, and highly consequential, insight from the political ontologies approach is the way that power is enacted not only through overt/visible coercion, but also through the power of silencing.[73] More specifically, part of the ontological power of modernity is the power to silence other worlds by extinguishing other realities.[74] This is one of the crucial dynamics enacted during colonization and plays out in the breaching of ecological frontiers, the erasure of ecosystems, and the extinguishing of indigenous ecologies, knowledges and cultures. Much of the historical narrative in this book will focus on two things: (1) how indigenous land-use practices – which were often enacting a multiplicity of different ways of using and relating to land – became vulnerable to marginalization or outright erasure; and (2) how vibrant, diverse and complex landscape ecologies were decimated and rendered invisible as farms breached key ecological frontiers.

Taking a political ontologies approach both opens up the larger consequences for indigenous people and environments of being rendered invisible, and also demands an examination of how these outcomes have been enacted in situ. What materials, practices, agents and processes combined to enact a politics of visibilization and invisibilization, and how did farms participate in or contest such processes? These are the key elements of the generally invisible history of farming under modernity.[75]

This approach is not intended to be an alternative to critical agrifood approaches to understanding worlds of food under capitalism. Rather, it opens out the categories and boundaries of the orthodox political economy approach, as well as seeking insight by looking for those sites and processes where new powers are enacted. In the rest of this book the political ontologies approach will be elaborated in ways that challenge us to think differently about how we approach parts of our agrifood scholarship. To orient agrifood scholars towards the kind of bridging discussion that will unfold, some initial points are worth noting about the kinds of theoretical dialogue enabled by a political ontologies approach:

1. It opens up the black box of the farm in important ways, giving a chance to think more carefully about the multiple human and non-human elements that enact farming ontologies. By recognizing these elements of the farming world as having material vitality and agency, we can start to move away from the kinds of mechanistic

and naturalistic ontological frameworks characteristic of some of the orthodox science/economy disciplines that tend to pacify the political dynamics of farms.

2. It suggests being open to the way in which farms are not only shaped by wider political dynamics but also contribute in their own ways to enacting political outcomes. Placing the modernist farm at the centre of larger historical narratives opens up terrain for examining both how the farms of modernity were assembled and stabilized in colonized worlds, and also how they have eventually been disrupted and destabilized.

3. The political ontologies approach demands openness to searching for wider ontologies and silences. How did the modernist farm act to silence colonized worlds, and how were science and modernist ontology central to such outcomes?[76]

4. By moving towards multiplicity, farms can be seen as a site of potentially generative politics and experimentation. If farms have vitalities and political agencies, then we need to make them, and their multiple worlds, a more explicit part of how we understand the enacting of alternatives.

5. A political ontologies approach implicitly brings researchers themselves into the picture as active participants in the worlds they are studying. As researchers and scholars we play our own role in enacting and disrupting worlds of modernist farming.

For agrifood scholars, this is a challenging but exciting extension of our traditional agenda. For other scholars who produce knowledge and enact techno-scientific and/ or economistic worlds of scholarship, this approach may be challenging on a more fundamental level. The agenda of this book, and the demands of a political ontologies approach, challenges us to be reflexive about whether we are creating knowledge about farming (or even acting as farmers ourselves) in ways that mean that we are able to enact and experiment inside multiple worlds, or whether we are constrained inside bounded and inflexible modernist farming ontologies, locked into farming inside invisible worlds.

Stabilization and disruption: The two halves of this book

The political ontologies approach provides the opportunity to tell a compellingly different story about farming in New Zealand and, thus, farming in other colonized worlds. It opens up the possibility of asking about long-term projects of both stabilization and disruption of modernist farming, and brings us to an interestingly different place to address the question that I posed at the start of this chapter: why has modernist farming lost its hegemonic position and how do we understand the search for alternatives?

In the rest of this book I want to look at the dynamics of this rising and falling of the great modernist project of agriculture: commencing in colonization, describing the multiple forces that stabilized one specific modernist ontology of land-use by breaching ecological frontiers and rendering the indigenous invisible, enacted through a convergence on pastoral family farming as the dominant new form of land-use in New Zealand, then moving into the contemporary era to consider the key vectors and moments of disruption of modernist farming, the conflict that has emerged around a recent act of 'frontier-breaching' by modernist farming, and the emergence of diverse alternatives.

The first objective is to dive into the great colonial encounter in New Zealand and look at the way in which a multiplicity of ontologies of land-use erupted around the disrupting forces and materials of those chaotic times. Chapter 2 examines the complex dynamics that emerged from the first moments of colonial encounter, through the multiplicity of worlds that were enacted, then followed by the closing down of land-use options through the stabilization of one model of pastoral farming that became hegemonic after the 1920s. In order to follow this historical drama in a manageable and situated way (as well as situating my own political and cultural origins as a researcher), I use a particular narrative device: telling the story of the establishment and life of some of my forebears' farms. These farms were protagonists in both collaborations and contests with Māori worlds, along with the frontier movement of ecological transformation – removing forests and draining wetlands – and provide insight into the complex environmental and social histories of landscape transformation in New Zealand.

In Chapter 3 I examine the transition from colonial to modernist farming. Emerging from decades of multiplicity and periods of chaos, the impressive stability of the new grasslands pastoral model – and its capacity to silence indigenous land-use and ecologies – provokes important theoretical questions about how farming systems stabilize. Using the ontologies approach, key elements of modernist farming are examined: the making of boundaries, the creation of 'exterior' and 'interior' relations around these boundaries, the elaboration of a narrowing world of legitimate knowledge and expertise, the populating of farm 'interiors' with particular social and material relations, and the consolidation of a 'productivist' rationality for land-use – all of which enact a particular modernist ontology of land-use and/or do political work in stabilizing frontier chaos and silencing other ways of using land in New Zealand. All these actions combined to turn farms into economic and affective anchors of previously chaotic colonized worlds.

Chapter 4 tells the story of how, after many decades of uncontested hegemony for modernist pastoral family farming, landscape-level conflict began to become more visible in the latter decades of the twentieth century. Commencing in the 1970s, the chapter follows a series of conflicts, each one describing a particular moment that forced farming in New Zealand out of its depoliticized ontological world. These conflicts reveal four kinds of forces of disruption of modernist farming: ferality, conflicts around science, the 'greening' of farming systems, and the rising political presence of indigenous protest and calls for de-colonization. In combination, these four vectors of disruption began to enable (and be enabled by) greater experimentation in land-use. These disruptions come into stark focus around a final frontier conflict of modernist farming with the shifting of drylands farming systems into intensive pasture through irrigation.

Chapter 5 turns in more detail to the farm level in New Zealand to examine specific farms that disrupted modernist ontological worlds of farming – all of them situated in key ecological frontiers. These 'post-modern' farms demonstrate how the key elements of modernist farm ontologies described in Chapter 3 have been disrupted and subverted at both the farm level and in new networks of social, ecological and economic action. Through this chapter, the possibility of a re-theorization of 'alternative' agriculture takes shape. The Epilogue to the book asks the question: how do we start theorizing farms inside visible worlds? How can a series of bridging debates in agrifood theory bring the ideas of ontology, frontiers, diverse agencies and de-colonization into mainstream debates in critical agrifood studies?

Making our own invisible worlds visible

In bringing the role of science (and wider worlds of research) into focus as part of the 'making' of modernist agriculture, our own position as researchers comes into question. To grasp the ontological politics of this, we need to be open to where and when our academic production of knowledge enables some worlds and silences others.[77]

The study of farming in New Zealand is heavily influenced by the character, history and cultural weight of that world – as I articulated in the Prologue to this book. I have a personal history that connects me in very particular ways to the world of farming and, equally significantly, to the invisible histories of farming in New Zealand. This is a complex history. By using some of my own forebears' farms to demonstrate the contesting and enacting of farming ontologies in colonial New Zealand, I am seeking a place to write from that neither denies the involvement of our own histories in our own scholarship, nor reproduces the fiction that scholars stand entirely independent of their worlds of research. But my farms aren't a neutral political venue; they brought to New Zealand diverse peoples and capitals and enacted very different outcomes. Real colonial histories are complicated and often compromised. While one key farm in this narrative was a site of cooperation and alliance between Māori and Pākehā worlds, two others inhabited land that was alienated from Māori owners. Some of the wealth that was used to buy one farm had its origins in a slave plantation in Antigua. Several farms took shape on landscapes that were ecologically devastated to make British-style farming possible. More mundanely, some of my forebears were just the usual run-of-the-mill migrants looking for a better life, a purer faith or an escape from the ill winds of the Industrial Revolution. All these things are the secret legacy that lurk in the background when I participate as a Pākehā researcher in worlds of farming. They are, in Māori ontology, important parts of my academic whakapapa (lineage/descent). The following account is partly my attempt to try and find a kaupapa (guiding rationale) for Pākehā researchers who are starting to look inside previously invisible worlds.[78]

Consequently, one of the most compelling reasons for me to take a political ontologies approach to understanding farming in New Zealand is not only that it might help resolve some important theoretical gaps and challenges in the field of agrifood studies, but also that it might render visible the ontological space inhabited by Pākehā researchers living with the legacy of colonial farming. Down that path lies more than just introspection; it takes us to both the beginning and the ending of the great trajectory of modernist farming, and does so in ways that characterize this destination as not so much a disaster as an opportunity to rediscover invisible worlds, holding out the promise of a new recognition of multiplicity, experimentation and hope for sustainable futures.

Notes

1   The terms 'modernity' and 'modernist' will recur throughout this text. It is an important term in social theory. For many, it simply signifies a particular historical epoch – everything that happened after the intellectual turn during the Enlightenment that ushered in a 'modern' world dominated by rationality and scientific enquiry. Others attach it as a descriptor to the emergence of industrial capitalist society and the untethering of human societies from traditional rurally based worlds in favour of 'modern' living in industrial cities with its much more divided worlds of class, space and politics. Significant social theorists like Ernest Gellner, Max Weber, James Scott and Michel Foucault pointed towards the need to theorize modernity as a collecting together of multiple threads and historical dynamics that created particular effects in society. For prominent theorists of modernity like Gellner and Weber, the mutually reinforcing power of capitalist industrialization and the rising central state was premised upon an increasing alignment of society around new norms and rationalities. For Gellner, capitalism was more than just a revolution in economic systems; it was a force that created a more socially homogeneous and categorized social world. In Scott's account, modernity rises as an effect of the modernist state, with implications for how science and rationality are deployed by the modern state to make society (and nature) more 'legible' and thus amenable to control. For Foucault, modernist worlds partly took their shape through the rising power of science, and the institutionalization of professional and educational bodies engaged in the pursuit of new scientific realities. These had the powerful effect of collectively gathering multiple realities under the umbrella of one singular reality – the material rational world – while, somewhat contradictorily, also breaking down the specialist pursuit of knowledge into separate disciplinary worlds, taking highly specialized and siloed approaches to how to obtain legitimate knowledge about specific segments of this unitary reality. I will borrow from all these approaches in this book: 'modernity' is strongly characterized by both the intellectual 'reality-building' projects of science and rationality, and the elaboration of new governing structures and social and economic forms and relationships under capitalism (or in this case, colonialism and capitalism). In terms of immediate predecessors, this task closely resembles the framing of Scott's (1998) classic *Seeing Like a State*, although the way in which science and rationality help to enact a particular state-agriculture configuration will be more post-structural in character in my narrative.

2   The arrival of these new farming 'realities' and the implications for the future trajectory of intensive, industrial agriculture were the subject of two book collections arising from academic reflection taking place during these crises (Rosin et al. 2012; Almas and Campbell 2012).

3   And then, as James Scott argues in his classic history of the modernist state, having devastated existing social and ecological worlds, these high-minded modernist farming ventures often didn't actually deliver what they promised across the Developing World (Scott 1998).

4   The character of 'settler states' where colonization was undertaken by European
    farmer settlers has been the focus of the early work of Philip McMichael (1984) and
    was foundational to the idea of food regimes (Friedmann and McMichael 1989;
    McMichael 2013).

5   The geographer was Kenneth Cumberland who was pondering, during the 1940s, the
    implications of the centennial of the British founding of the New Zealand colony in
    1840 (see Pawson 2011 for an extended consideration of the politics and implications
    of Cumberland's bleak assessment of the New Zealand environment in the 1940s).

6   Most directly comparable to a major agricultural exporting country like the
    Netherlands, and significantly exceeding similar ex-colonies like Canada where 'only'
    around half of total food production is exported.

7   This new world of social and political challenges to modernist agriculture which, as I
    will go on to describe, came to New Zealand much later than many other countries,
    has resulted in a new artefact in policy discourse – the 'social licence to farm' – which
    is now under discussion by many farming stakeholders in places like Australia and
    New Zealand (see Williams and Martin 2011; Edwards and Trafford 2016).

8   Given the breadth of possible discussions that could take shape around the idea of
    ontologies, it might be helpful to give some pointers of how I'm going to explore
    these potentials. There are two grounding points of the following theoretical
    dialogue. The first is the broad field of agrifood studies which critically engages
    issues in farming and food worlds (often in linked ways), often taking its theoretical
    inspiration from critical political economy approaches grounded in Marxist and
    Neo-Marxist framings of capitalism and how farming and food worlds are shaped
    by actors and institutions that conform with wider patterns of inequality, power and
    tension emerging from the capitalist structure of society. Within agrifood studies, a
    minority interest in post-structuralist theorizing has started to take shape and this
    book sits firmly within an emerging site of dialogue between orthodox agrifood
    political economy and new post-structuralist approaches to worlds of food and
    farming (for an elaboration of these emerging dialogues, see Lewis et al. 2013, 2016;
    Le Heron et al. 2016a; Pawson et al. 2018). The post-structuralist side of this dialogue
    is influenced by post-colonial studies, Foucauldian interests in governmentality,
    actor network theory, assemblage approaches and science and technology studies.
    While the two sides of this debate often have starkly different foci and methodology,
    I argue that they can come into a shared intellectual space via the concept of 'political
    ontology', particularly in relation to understanding the full gamut of relations
    and consequences that took shape during colonization, as well as in scholarly
    consideration of the emerging modernist farm and its role in the territorialization
    and de-territorialization of wider modernist worlds. This meeting place situates the
    modernist farm as a thing that is both an interesting material and economic object
    in its own right, but also participates in enacting wider economic worlds (that are
    characterized as capitalist by orthodox agrifood theorists) and silencing other worlds
    of action (particularly those of interest to post-colonial and indigenous scholarship)
    in the formation of a settled modernist farming world.

9   What Escobar (2007) described as the 'ontological turn' in the social sciences,
    emerged from a series of discussions in anthropology (Vivieros de Castro 1998),
    actor network theory and science and technology studies involving theorists like
    Bruno Latour, John Law and Annemarie Mol about the ontological power of
    modernity, and how to describe the disruption and deconstruction of the powers of
    modernity in ways that could open up new ways of understanding worlds of action.

They were particularly focused on the way modernity creates a single, universal view of material reality, with a hierarchy of human causality and intentionality acting upon material objects, processes and dynamics, along with a critique of both social scientific and natural science disciplines for reproducing these particular ontologies. The first important manoeuvre in actor network theory is to 'flatten' the ontological hierarchy between human and non-human actors and replace the modernist emphasis on hierarchies and categorizations with greater attention to relationalities and networks.

10   A useful example can be seen in discussion about the ontology of the state in political theory. The state is one of the core concepts that organize discussion and enquiry in political science, but what is actually being included and excluded when we use the term 'the state'? Is it only the formal system of governing and decision-making in parliaments and congresses (maybe just national, or maybe including regional and local?), or does it also include the apparatus and institutions of state bureaucracy, state-ordered and funded agencies, anything that is funded by taxpayer's contributions to economic and social life, or is it actually a set of discourses of governing and practices of governance that order social life in particular ways? What sits inside and outside the boundaries of what we mean by 'the state' has very significant consequences for how we conduct the study of political science. What is even more interesting is how the state itself 'makes reality' and 'brackets off the world' by re-ordering the internal sense of what is 'real' in state-governed worlds, as James Scott argues in *Seeing Like a State* (Scott 1998).

11   Bodies are, from the outset, interesting ontological subjects. We all inhabit a body but what is its boundary? Is there a hierarchy of importance that differentiates how we feel about our hair and fingernails? What happens to their status as part of our body when they are trimmed off? What about those billions of gut bacteria – are they part of our body or independent passengers in our bodily vessel? Or the status of recently ingested (and perhaps regurgitated) food in our stomach or the excrement we are about to expel? In ontological terms, bodies have messy real boundaries and complex material effects, yet also a clear ontologically constructed sense of what is inside or outside the body's boundaries in our everyday lives.

12   For many social theorists, this claim raises a question as to what value the 'ontological turn' represents, when we have already been examining many of these things under older social theoretical frameworks. For example, social constructionism makes similar claims about the socially mediated processes by which a sense of 'reality' is produced, and even the older notion of ideology incorporates the claim that reality is generated from class political actions and has political consequences. The ontological turn points towards a particular academic stance which, drawing on roots in STS, is interested in the way that realities are often generated relationally from mundane, day-to-day practices and objects (an outcome sought in Mol 2002), rather than created by the perspectives, attitudes or 'social construction' of only human agents. Its second pivot is that important 'world making' objects (as Woolgar and Leuzaun (2013) argue) can sometimes be mundane and thus overlooked (in the case of this book: the powers of the farm).

13   As Michael Carolan (2004) puts it, how can we undertake the study of 'environmental sociology' if we haven't given serious thought as to what is the ontology of the thing that we are talking about? Especially when the complex and intertwined thing we call the 'environment' has been separated under modernity into different and causally separate realms of action like 'nature' and 'culture'.

14   Blaser (2009, 2013) provides a useful summary of the emergence of the 'political
       ontologies' approach. Political ontology has emerged at the meeting place of a shared
       interest in ontology in actor network theory (particularly Annemarie Mol, Michel
       Callon and John Law), science and technology studies (strongly influenced by Bruno
       Latour), and new political theorization arising from political ecology, indigenous
       studies and post-colonialism (e.g. Escobar 2007; Blaser 2009, 2013, 2014; Ansems
       de Vries 2016). Recently it has also been intersecting with work emerging from
       Foucauldian-inspired governmentality approaches (e.g. Agrawal 2005, Li 2007a) or
       the recent interest in the idea of the constitution of the world in assemblages that has
       become a popular analytic device in anthropology and geography (Li 2007b, 2010,
       2014, 2017, summarized in Forney et al. 2018).

15   The term 'enact' is central to any ontological approach. I use it in the way that
       Annemarie Mol (2002) suggests: as a way of clearly demarcating the way that social
       and economic worlds are 'made', which explicitly includes the agency of non-human
       actors. This is in contrast to orthodox sociological methods that seek to uncover
       the effect of 'perspectives', 'attitudes', or 'social construction' by human actors or
       groups. The term 'enact' is used to clearly include the complex assembling of social
       phenomena via both human and non-human agencies.

16   Studying the ontology of farms has very few precedents. Early entrants into an explicit
       examination of ontology in food worlds took shape around the ANT critique of
       the modernist nature-society binary in social scientific study of agricultural change
       (notably Goodman and Watts (1997) with a summary of these debates in Goodman
       (2001)), or almost entirely concentrated on foods as objects, or worlds of consumption
       rather than on farms themselves. The most notable is Annemarie Mol's 'I eat an apple'
       (Mol 2008), with other examples being Forney's examination of 'cheese ontologies'
       in Switzerland (Forney 2016), Spiers and Lewis (2016) on the ontology of bees and
       beehive materials, and Burch's study of radioactivity and food in post-Fukushima Japan
       (Burch et al. 2018). The focus draws closer to the farm with Demeulenaere's (2014) use
       of ontology to elaborate the scientific and social movement politics of seed breeding
       and ownership, and Le Heron et al. (2016b) on soils and biological dairy farming.
       My own first foray into this world, prompted by Christopher Rosin, considered the
       role of researchers in alternative agriculture (Campbell and Rosin 2011), an idea
       that is also explored in a consideration of disciplinary research ontologies enacting
       'biological economies' by Erena Le Heron and her collaborators (2016). There is also
       an interesting wider debate looming about the ontological dynamics of food regimes,
       which is pre-figured by McMichael (2012) in his discussion of the ontological politics
       of the environment and food regime relations as enacted by La Via Campesina.

17   This orientation towards the politics of what is possible is fundamental to a political
       ontologies approach, as argued by Holbraad et al. (2014: 1): 'For purposes of
       discussion, then, we begin with a broad distinction between three different manners
       in which ontology and politics are correlated in the social sciences and cognate
       disciplines … (1) the traditional philosophical concept of ontology, in which
       "politics" takes the implicit form of an injunction to discover and disseminate a single
       absolute truth about *how things are*; (2) the sociological critique of this and other
       "essentialisms", which, in skeptically debunking all ontological projects to reveal their
       insidiously political nature, ends up affirming the critical politics of debunking as its
       own version of *how things should be*; and (3) the anthropological concept of ontology
       as the multiplicity of forms of existence enacted in concrete practices, where politics
       becomes the non-skeptical elicitation of this manifold of potentials for *how things
       could be* … '.

18 For agrifood scholars, this should be a familiar question. Are we searching for alternatives to capitalist agriculture or productivist agriculture? The first requires the search for more just social and economic worlds; the other involves searching for greater 'sustainability' in agriculture. While there are creative attempts to align critiques grounded in capitalism with those grounded in sustainability, they aren't necessarily the same thing.

19 The idea of 'materiality' carries a lot of weight in actor network theory and indicates the 'flattening' of research approaches to give more agency to non-human actors and objects. For example, Jane Bennett (2010) uses the term 'vital materiality' and ascribes objects with 'vitality' to re-frame them away from being simply passive objects and inert matter upon which humans act. Bennett redirects focus towards the way that materials act and have influence on the world. Hence, farms and environments are not causally inert, they have 'vital materiality'.

20 A further brief clarification on theoretical terminology might help here. Scholars in this theoretical genre tend to avoid the term 'realities' and instead use the term 'worlds' to reflect the multiplicity of realities and their constitution in more than just human perception. The term 'worlds' opens up more possibilities and recognizes the constitution of 'reality' in human + non-human assemblages.

21 A key concern in this style of theorizing is a contrast between 'multiplicity' and 'unitary reality'. Modernity is characterized by the enacting of unitary reality – something that is fundamental to the objective-subjective binary, or contrasting of unitary material reality with variable human perceptions of it – while multiplicity describes how the world is enacted in situ through many practices, materials and relations, thus resulting in a 'multiplicity' of different worlds of action. The ontological turn in the social sciences was strongly influenced by Annemarie Mol's classic 2002 book *The Body Multiple*. It is an extended examination of the human body in the context of medical treatment for atherosclerosis in Dutch hospitals. Mol opened her observations by noting that the bodies of her patients, the sites of their pathology, the diagnosis, the ensemble of actors and objects that gave meaning to both their bodies and their disease, differed dramatically in different parts of the medical system – even differing between different rooms in the same hospital. She argued that the explanation for such differences could not be found in the orthodox idea that the body was a fixed material entity experiencing a unitary set of effects called a disease, around which different people assembled different perspectives. To distinguish from 'perspectivalism', she turned to her philosophical training to borrow the word 'ontology'. This allowed her to distinguish her method from the social constructionist approach of much social science, thus allowing space for the inclusion of both human and non-human actors into the mix. Aligning herself with actor network approaches, she examined each setting where the disease atherosclerosis was being enacted – by an ensemble of patients, doctors, bodies, arteries and veins, diagnostic machines, metrics, and medical notes and records – to argue that the disease was not the same in each place. Each site enacted its own disease ontology. Hence, a seemingly stable thing – a well-known disease – was actually being enacted in multiple ontologies. It had the quality of multiplicity. At the same time, some elements in the actor-network of the disease – scientific names, medical notes, textbooks – enacted the modernist tendency to universalize the reality of the disease. They enact a unitary sense of reality that is one of the characteristic claims of modernity – despite the multiplicity of realities that actually characterize worlds of bodies and diseases. Thus, by focusing on ontology we can explicitly engage with the contest between those things that enact a unitary modernist reality and those that enact multiplicity.

22 A pseudonym.

23 The reason why many locations in New Zealand now have two names will be explained later in the book.

24 The escalating environmental crisis that both these farms participate in is summarized in Joy (2015) and succinctly reviewed in a recent article (Warne 2017). Both tell of the incompatibility of Canterbury's freshwater systems with intensification of dairy farming in the region.

25 Pollan (2006).

26 This is an interesting way in which some farmers acknowledge the agency of their farms. My highly successful farming uncle commented to a reporter, upon being awarded the Hawke's Bay Farmer of the Year Award, that it was 'the farm that won, not anything he did to it'. (*Dominion Post*, 'Dyed-in-the-Wool Farmer', 27 May 2004: p C5).

27 In fact, Mike and Violet grumbled that organic certification was 'too prescriptive' and locked down too many options that they wanted to experiment with.

28 This (pseudonymous) farm is actually a compilation of several farms, and incorporates observations gained from studying its many near-identical partners around the newly intensifying dairy landscapes of the South Island.

29 A fictitious address and thus not to be confused with Five Cross Roads, Five Gully Stream, Five Jagged Peaks, Five Mile Creek and Five Mile Saddle which are all real locations in Canterbury.

30 Often referred to in New Zealand as simply 'Friesians', a cow that is suited to industrial production systems, as against the earlier preferred breed of high cream-producing Jersey cows.

31 A slightly larger herd than the national average of 413, but not huge by South Island standards.

32 Rob earned his pseudonym from Mike Bell's very similar American exponent of intensive farming strategies in his 2004 book *Farming for Us All*.

33 This need for the maximum possible amount of grass under irrigation has driven some dramatic changes to the ecology of the farm. When they took over the farm, they bulldozed multiple lines of trees to allow space for the irrigators to roll. This reflects a wider shift in the landscape ecology of Canterbury with a significant reduction in trees to make space for irrigators, and contributes to another environmental crisis in farming – biodiversity loss.

34 Despite all this standardization, Cassie McTavish still found enchanting levels of agency among the cows themselves, which disrupted and altered even the most finely tuned industrial milking systems (McTavish 2015).

35 The key freshwater problems generated by an intensive dairy unit are nitrates, phosphates, soil sediments and pathogens. This metric-generating tool is becoming an essential 'technical fix' for dairy farms enmeshed in Canterbury's water quality crisis. According to many farmers whom we interviewed, it can't possibly leverage the level of change needed to bring nitrogen back under required thresholds, but it is important that it exists to at least show they are trying something (Hale et al. 2019). For a review of the technical components of the crisis, see Joy (2015).

36 Or less optimistically, in the words of one local professor: 'Decisions which seemed justifiable to many at the time, now, with hindsight, look decidedly flawed. The consequence is that we have the wrong cows, the wrong dairy systems, the wrong product mix, a raft of environmental issues, and too much debt' (Keith Woodford in Joy (2018: 3)).

37 These two examples usefully demonstrate particular ontological orientations: modernist industrialism versus complexity and multiplicity. As this book will show, however, even within these ontologies the potential for the other exists. Rendell Stream Farm chafes against the unifying and homogenizing power of organic audits, while Rob goes home and wonders whether it will all work out or whether he should consider the unthinkable and change direction. How one ontology is locked in place, or loosened, is a key question in this book.

38 A well-cited exemplar of a simple academic elaboration of a binary between conventional and alternative is the work of Beus and Dunlap (1990, 1991) who posit the existence of Alternative Conventional Agricultural Paradigms (ACAP) that they then test with various social measures to differentiate farmers on either side of an alternative-conventional binary.

39 See Fairweather et al. (2009), Campbell et al. (2009b).

40 The same limitation with the explanatory value of the alternative-conventional binary was articulated by Goodman et al. (2011) in their examination of alternative food networks.

41 The idea that 'bad' farming is 'factory farming' is pervasive and has its roots in early critiques like Ruth Harrison's *Animal Machines* (1964). All of these mobilize the kinds of 'factory' or 'machine-like' metaphors that point towards the kind of dynamics that this book will investigate (and significantly expand and elaborate) at their moments of historical origin.

42 Such approaches have often been characterized as 'reductionist' by those taking a more systemic or connected view of the world. The most poetic elaboration of the difference between technical scientists who think that 'everything that is important resides inside the technical system of the farm' versus those that think that the 'things that are important lie outside the boundary of the farm' is by Wendell Berry in his classic work *The Unsettling of America* (1977).

43 For me, that 'ontological break' occurred when reading a copy of Geoffrey Lawrence's *Capitalism and the Countryside: The Rural Crisis in Australia* (1987) in a farmhouse in rural New Zealand in 1989. I was working at one of New Zealand's bastions of orthodox agricultural science and economics – Lincoln University – but surrounded by dozens of family farms in crisis. How to explain that crisis and the responses of farm households became my PhD question (Campbell 1995).

44 See Buttel and Newby (1980) and Buttel et al. (1990).

45 The New Rural Sociology was my gateway, as a sociologist, into these debates – although there was a parallel New Rural Geography, and these two disciplinary threads become deeply intertwined within the same intellectual venture.

46 In these orthodox ontologies, if 'social' dynamics entered consideration, they tended to use simple psychological models to explain 'adoption' of new technologies, a prominent example being the 'diffusion of innovations' model of Everett Rogers in the 1960s (see Rogers 1962) that became foundational to much of the disciplinary ontology of agricultural extension.

47 Classical German theorist Karl Kautsky posed the 'agrarian question': why hadn't farms become 'factories in the fields' as Marx had predicted? This question animated the iconic 'survival vs subsumption' debate in the New Rural Sociology – contemplating whether family farms had particular characteristics that would allow them to either outlast, or eventually be subsumed into, more corporate and industrial styles of capitalist agriculture.

48 Agrifood approaches were strongly influenced by 'commodity systems analysis' stemming from the work of Friedland (1984) and Friedland et al. (1981), and began

to 'follow' key food commodities from production, through food chains, out to end consumption points (paralleling similar changes across other areas being studied in economic geography). In this act of 'following', agrifood approaches began engaging with food chains, processing and distribution industries, the politics of retailing, finance, agrifood chain governance and trade politics, eventually joining with the established worlds of both the sociology of food and geographies/sociologies of consumption.

49   This was further solidified in the rising popularity of what became known as the 'food regimes' approach. Commencing with a seminal paper by Friedmann and McMichael (1989), Food Regime Theory in its early form posited that periods of capitalist growth were underwritten by a conjuncture of multiple key relationships that combined to create a stable 'regime' of food relationships. These relationships elaborated beyond the orthodox neo-Marxist canon by including: a specific style of land-based production, particular political structures, key technological inputs, and the organization of trade systems aligning the production and consumption of specific food and fibre commodities. This ensemble of relations in the food regime was later elaborated further to include more explicit discussion of cultural and consumption dynamics (Campbell and Dixon 2009) and ecological dynamics (Campbell 2009) stabilizing regime relations.

50   This is an omission that informs this book, but can't be entirely resolved in it. Some early participants in the New Rural Sociology questioned why gender wasn't playing a more central role in understandings of rural inequalities (e.g. Gasson 1980; Sachs 1983) or, similarly, dynamics of sexuality and heteronormativity (Little 2003). The silence around gender is addressed in parts of the upcoming narrative, but as a wider project, the re-centring of worlds of gender and sexuality would require a slightly different body of historical work and style of engagement to that required for this book. Put simply, the emergence of modernist farming has implications for how men and women were authorized and legitimized to act in farming worlds (as the upcoming narrative will show), but there is much more going on in gendered farming worlds that this book doesn't have the scope to address. (These were the core focus of Law et al. 1999 and Campbell et al. 2006.)

51   The initial entry of actor network theory in these debates was via a collection by Goodman and Watts (1997), which was followed by a series of articles by David Goodman and others about the need to bring more 'bio-power' into agrifood theorization (e.g. Goodman 1999). While this was the source of considerable conflict between new ANT-inflected approaches and the neo-Marxist political economies of much of the New Rural Sociology, more recently there have been some important attempts to bridge these two styles of academic ontology. Useful examples of those bringing more bio-power into their accounts of the political economy of agriculture are the work of Jason Moore (2000, 2015) on the intrinsic relations between capitalist dynamics and ecological dynamics, David Goodman's attempts to reconcile these two theoretical worlds in relation to biotechnologies (Goodman 2001), the work of the Biological Economies group in New Zealand (Le Heron et al. 2016a), and Julie Guthman's recent study of the bio-socio-economic crises of the strawberry industry in California (2019).

52   There were moments when agricultural science was scrutinized (see Buttel 1993, 1999) – particularly in relation to debates about GMOs (which will be discussed in Chapter 4). But science and technology studies has not been as influential in agrifood scholarship as it might have been, with only a select body of work being produced by scholars like Jack Kloppenburg and Neva Hassanein (Kloppenburg 1991; Hassanein

and Kloppenburg 1995; Hassanein 1999), David Goodman (1999, 2008), the group
of scholars who have been nurtured by Larry Busch (e.g. Busch et al. 1994; Juska and
Busch 1994), and the recent work of Julie Guthman (2011, 2019).

53   While the absence of many longer histories of farms as agents of colonization is an
      important gap in agrifood theorization, there was one notable exception: the 'food
      regimes' approach. Friedmann and McMichael (1989) identified particular 'food
      regimes' as structuring capitalist relations in food and farming during particular
      moments in history. The 'First food regime' or 'Imperial food regime' specifically
      identified some characteristics of food and farming relations that acted to stabilize
      a global food order around 'settler states', which then became disrupted during the
      twentieth century. The food regime account of colonial farming worlds does point
      towards decisive moments in which agriculture was central to the political dynamics
      of colonization. It did not, however, undertake the kind of deep dive into colonial
      farm worlds that this book will attempt.

54   Examining farms in the context of modernity has, for the most part, been an exercise
      for historians rather than social theorists of contemporary society. There are plenty of
      historical accounts (like Jones 2016) which trace the emergence of specific scientific
      approaches to farming and locate the transformation of the character of farming with the
      emergence of specialist disciplines like agronomy in the 1800s (e.g. Jones 2016: 29–31).
      Other more critical histories have placed farms at the centre of larger transitions in
      modern political and socio-legal history – particularly around the emergence of private
      property (e.g. Linklater 2013; Fuglestad 2018). The most compelling example of this kind
      of approach is Scott's (1998) *Seeing Like a State*, which used agriculture as an exemplar
      of a particular set of rationalities and controls enacted by the modernist state in order to
      render nature (and farming) legible and thus amenable to state control. For Scott (1998),
      in important ways that this book will explore, agricultural rationalities, agricultural
      science and the modernist state have a close and mutually reinforcing relationship.

55   For example, see Gray (1996) on 'de-traditionalization' in Australian farming and
      Holmes (1989) on the 'disenchantment' of peasant farming in Italy.

56   The darkest expression of this is Ellul's (1963) classic *The Technological Society*.

57   There are some excellent examples of this kind of re-framing of theoretical
      understandings of food worlds in terms of post-structuralist engagements with
      modernity – for instance, Melanie DuPuis' (2002) historical exploration of the
      perfect and imperfect worlds of milk in the United States.

58   The modern state loves to demarcate and thus control reality: 'Certain forms of
      knowledge and control require a narrowing of vision. The great advantage of such
      tunnel vision is that it brings into sharp focus certain limited aspects of an otherwise
      far more complex and unwieldy reality. This very simplification in turn, makes the
      phenomenon at the center of the field of vision more legible and hence more susceptible
      to careful measurement and calculation.' Scott (1998: 11). However, in using the case of
      state-controlled forestry (and the nurturing of a narrow 'forestry science') in Germany
      as a historical exemplar, disastrous tensions with social and ecological processes begin
      to mount: 'Utilitarian simplification in the forest was an effective way of maximizing
      wood production in the short and intermediate term. Ultimately, however, its emphasis
      on yield and paper profits, its relatively short time horizon, and, above all, the vast array
      of consequences it had resolutely bracketed came back to haunt it.' (Scott 1998: 21).

59   The idea of 'frontier' as a site of colonization is one that I will use throughout this
      book, so a moment of clarification is necessary. This is a term that has been used
      flexibly in many academic and popular culture settings, yet, as Patricia Limerick

(2000) chides, has very specific meaning for historians of the American West. New Zealand history has not tended to use 'frontier' as a descriptor to the same extent as the United States, due to the absence of a neatly defined line of political control moving across the countryside in the way that excited Frederick Jackson Turner. Cronon (1987) provides a useful review of the use and critiques of the foundational Turnerian idea of frontier in the American West. As Limerick (2000) argues, 'frontier' should really be understood as having two opposing meanings in the context of colonization in America. Historically, the white American usage is universally positive, describing a borderlands of freedom and economic opportunity, mythologized as a zone of conquest that brought progress. In contrast, the Spanish term *La Frontera* as it was used historically in the American Southwest always understood frontier as describing a zone of cultural and economic struggle and dispute. In academic usage, classic histories of the American West understood frontier as a demographic, socio-cultural and cartographic term, but did not tend to use it to describe frontiers between colonized and non-colonized ecosystems. Academic consideration of 'ecosystems frontiers' became more visible after the publication of William Cronon's *Changes in the Land* ([1983] 2003), which made the seminal argument for understanding colonization as a political *and* ecological process; and Alfred Crosby's *Ecological Imperialism* (1986), with subsequent debates starting to focus on the kinds of messy socio-ecological conflicts, entanglements and agencies that shaped ecological frontiers. In the New Zealand context, I am borrowing from multiple strands of this thinking: frontier is intrinsic to colonization, and does involve actual geographic borders between political, social and ecological assemblages, but does also recognize some of the politically vexing popular American discursive usage that associates frontier with ideas of 'progress', 'modernity' and 'virtuous conquest'. Consequently, the use of frontier in this book recognizes the freighting of modernist meaning as intrinsic to the idea of frontier as it was politically and ecologically enacted in New Zealand. More importantly, the New Zealand frontier can only be understood as deeply ecological, with the political and economic projects of colonial expansion being both made possible by ecological conquest and yet unleashing chaotic consequences that echo through subsequent political, social and economic dynamics in these colonized landscapes.

60   There are some interesting precursor projects that inform this book. The most obvious is William Cronon's *Changes in the Land* ([1983] 2003), which signalled the emergence of a significant body of work in environmental history in colonial settings. His setting is the political, economic and ecological colonization of New England, and his frontier account creates much of the template for that which follows in this book. Another can be found in Jason Moore's characterization of 'commodity frontiers' and the subsequent discussion emerging around the idea of the 'plantationocene'. Using the island of Madeira as his example, Moore (2000, 2015) seeks to bring environmental dynamics into a more central role in World Systems theorizing. In identifying the role of new commodities and their frontier-based sites of production, Moore points towards an interesting dynamic: these commodity frontiers expanded not just because of the internal dynamics of capitalism, but also because there were specific ecological powers that were unleashed that drove the expansion of these frontiers. This kind of interest in commodity frontiers based around extractive industries or plantation systems has become a site of new scholarly discussion (e.g. Harraway's (2015) summary of an emerging new interest in the 'plantationocene'). My project is to pursue such insights in those frontier settings where modernist family farms, rather than plantation systems, were the agents of change.

61 To forestall possible misunderstanding, 'science' is not used to simply denote a particular method (especially if that method is understood to exist in some kind of independence from its socio-econo-material worlds). It is used throughout this text in its STS rendering: as an assemblage of relations between humans, non-human materials and various relations of action that establish socially authoritative ways of knowing the world. Science is a central concern for theories of ontology because it is a 'reality-making' venture; it just does so through a complex web of relations – including the relationship between formal science institutions and education, and the modernist state (as Scott 1998 argues).

62 The creation of boundaries between disciplines is, in Bruno Latour's account, one of the great hallmarks of modernity. In his extended essay *We Have Never Been Modern* (1993), he poetically articulates both the separation of disciplinary epistemes/ ontologies and the unthinkability of reuniting them, even when the subject matter under discussion – like climate change – clearly moves across many such areas and renders disciplinary boundaries inherently non-sensical: 'Let us not mix up heaven and earth, the global stage and the local scene, the human and the non-human. "But these imbroglios do the mixing" you'll say, "they weave our world together!" "Act as if they don't exist," the analysts reply. They have cut the Gordian knot with a well-honed sword. The shaft is broken: on the left, they have put knowledge of things; on the right, power and human politics … In the eyes of our critics the ozone hole above our heads, the moral law in our hearts, the autonomous text, may each be of interest, but only separately. That a delicate shuttle should have woven together the heavens, industry, texts, souls and moral law – this remains uncanny, unthinkable, unseemly.' (Latour 1993: 3–5).

63 While I will concentrate in my narrative on the practices of agricultural science as enacting modernist farm ontologies, this idea is also elaborated in STS in relation to the boundedness of the practice of economics. Callon (1998; Caliskan and Callon 2010) is particularly arch in his critique of the 'world narrowing' practices of many economists, whereby boundaries are drawn around a sphere of activities called 'economy' and, in order for many epistemological techniques to work, it is necessary to exclude many other social or ecological worlds by placing them into an outside space called 'externalities'. The result might be excellent economics, but it is also enacting an ontologically bounded world that enacts a modernist framing of the separation and categorization of what are actually complex inter-related worlds. It is no surprise, therefore, that radical economic approaches from celebrated economists like Eleanor Ostrom tend to disrupt exactly this kind of boundary. (An excellent example is the 'wellbeing economics' approach of Dalziel and Saunders (2014) and Dalziel et al. (2018), or the recent exploration of terms like 'inclusive economy' and 'complexity economics'.)

64 With some very notable exceptions, particularly Scott (1998) and the corpus of work of van der Ploeg (e.g. 2008), who has produced important insights into the politics and tensions of the contemporary Dutch peasantry in the face of the 'modernist paradigm'.

65 For a formal tabulation of these qualities of modernist farms in Developing World settings, see Scott (1998: 262–306).

66 As Scott (1998: 20) characterizes it, the modern state and its scientists 'bracket off' much of reality in order to govern it, and 'a whole world lying "outside the brackets" returned to haunt this technological vision'.

67 Her critique of the Green Revolution is summarized in Shiva (2016).

68   Remarkable, in particular, given that Borlaug passed away in 2009.

69   Here is where I part company slightly with Scott's (1998) approach. In his masterwork, scientific forestry or agriculture is deployed as part of the *statecraft* of the modern state in order to generate legible, controllable worlds. My account will follow STS by giving space for many other agencies (as well as those of the modern state) in enacting these kinds of outcomes.

70   An interest in the relationship between capitalism and empire was fundamental to much of classical Marxist theory and the subsequent elaboration of 'world systems' theory by Immanuel Wallerstein and his successors. For example, influential Marxist theorist Eric Wolf in his celebrated 1982 book *Europe and the People without History* created a compelling picture of a colonized world increasingly drawn into the drama of capitalism through the elaboration of global-scale trade in key commodities to supply the Industrial Revolution (Wolf 1982).

71   He opens his argument (in Blaser 2013) with a critique of Eric Wolf. Wolf had argued that all global history is connected through its participation in the elaboration of global capitalism, and that a great academic omission, to that point, had been the exclusion of indigenous people's colonization and resistance to capitalism. Blaser responded that while this is true from the perspective of a Marxist ontology, it also reduces the ontological world of the indigenous other to simply that which is subsumed by or resists capitalism – an act of modernist universalism that excludes and subordinates the potential for other worlds and other politics. He also argued that the sole focus on capitalism was limiting because modernity has other powers – like the universalism of science and the ability to monopolize reality – which are central to struggles between indigenous and colonizing ontologies (see also Blaser 2009, 2014).

72   Taking a political ontologies approach to colonial history differs in some key respects to an approach grounded in Marxist and Neo-Marxist ontology, but doesn't exclude the operation of capitalist dynamics and relations. It just argues that these have a tendency to explain the many indigenous stories and struggles solely from within the terms set by Marxist ontology, remaining less observant of other fields of struggle. For Blaser (2013: 548) this leaves out modernity's hegemonic scientific culture, which continually displayed a tendency to annihilate and silence other worlds of knowledge along with other non-materialist and non-reductionist ontologies.

73   Ansems de Vries (2016) and Ansems de Vries et al. (2017) argue that this is an important dynamic in post-structuralist understandings of power in relation to indigenous/colonization struggles. Working from Foucault (but inverting his argument about the power of constant visibility), they argue that the ability to ontologically render particular worlds invisible is a crucial dynamic in disempowering indigenous ontologies. In their account, indigenous ontologies don't so much get contested and debated as simply rendered invisible and thus powerless in modernity. Such an account of the modernist power to silence indigeneity resonates strongly in New Zealand. In her influential work on indigeneity, research and colonization, Linda Tuhiwai Smith opens her argument with the observation that colonization and its world of knowledge-creation are being countered in indigenous worlds with a push-back against: 'the knowledge claims of disciplines and approaches, about the content of knowledge, about absences, silences and invisibilities of other peoples, about practices and ethics, and about the implications for communities of research' (Smith 2012: X). It is an insight that will prove useful in much that follows in this book, and provides a strong hint towards the theoretical intentions of the book's title.

74 Ansems de Vries et al. (2017: 95) argue: 'Being seen and recognized is a constitutive aspect of being political in the modern sense. Post-structuralist scholars like Judith Butler … reproduce this image by describing movements against precariousness as the exercise of "a plural and performative right to appear." This raises the questions: what does making visible leave out of sight and, what other tactics of invisibility are at play? In addition, it provokes the question of whether this economy of visibility and invisibility is the object of politics *per se*.'

75 In seeking to write an account of the invisible histories of farming in modernity, there are choices that I have made in structuring the content and narrative of this account that do require some defence – especially for post-structuralist readers. First, I have chosen to place *ontologies* at the centre of my narrative when a more widely taken pathway into the interface between post-structuralist theorizing and economic worlds has been to follow *assemblages*. Following assemblages has been a core element of the elaboration of a new economic geography of New Zealand by the Biological Economies Group (see Lewis et al. 2013, 2016; Le Heron et al. 2016a; Pawson et al. 2018 as well as Forney et al. 2018). This book is strongly influenced by assemblage-thinking which is, in my reading, intrinsically compatible with ontologies thinking. My foregrounding of political ontologies, however, recognizes the challenge of researching inside colonized worlds. The political ontologies approach emerged from anthropological engagements across the boundaries of indigenous-modernist conflicts during colonization. Colonization was a 'world-making' venture, and an approach framed by political ontology provides me with significant purchase on the world-making power of modernist farms and the new, bounded, reality they enacted. Furthermore, prior political ontologies scholarship points towards the role of science in colonization, and this appears to be both a clear gap in prior work in critical agrifood traditions yet also a key element of the story I am seeking to tell. Second, by choosing to follow a long historical trajectory – the rising and falling of modernist agriculture – the narrative bends strongly towards the kinds of big historical claims and patterns that are characteristic of critical political economy. There is more than just a hint here of the food regimes narrative of farming under capitalism that I have used in previous work. The focus on large trajectories of modernity provides a clear bridge to structural approaches in critical agrifood theory, but may leave assemblage-thinkers less enthused – the most significant omission simply being the subtlety of small moments and dynamics of change and stabilization. Intrinsic to any theoretical discussion founded in Deleuzian thinking is that assemblages are constantly territorializing, de-territorializing and re-territorializing. My 'rising and falling' trajectory, played out over more than a century of farming change, threatens to render opaque the many specific resistances, conflicts and experiments that took shape during its 'rising', and likewise a downplaying of all but a few of the most obvious instances of the re-territorializing of modernist farming powers during its 'falling' trajectory. My response can only be that a fully elaborated assemblage approach to the long sweep of farming history of New Zealand could never be achieved inside the confines of one book. By signalling an approach via political ontologies, I openly surrender the specific detail of multiple elements of my grand narrative to other scholars who wish to use assemblage-informed approaches.

76 Put in stark terms, has agrifood studies faced its moment of de-colonization? The question is increasingly asked by a new generation of scholars like Reid and Rout (2016), and Mayes (2018).

77 The turn towards 'enactive approaches' to scholarship was strongly influenced by Law and Urry (2004), who argued for a clearer recognition of how the day-to-day actions of scholars and researchers help 'make' the worlds they study. Philip Lowe (2010) elaborated this idea specifically in the context of how rural sociologists had helped 'make the rural'. The enactive turn in scholarship is a key discussion in Le Heron et al. (2016a).

78 This clearly isn't a straightforward political space. The following narrative is strongly concerned with colonization and its consequences, including the way in which my forebears and their successors participated in the silencing and erasing of Māori worlds of land-use. As the descendent of those colonizers, my intention is not to speak for Māori, it is first to reflect on how the Pākehā farming world that I grew up in has enacted an ontological world – grounded in the invisibilization of other worlds – that now needs to be deconstructed; and second, to play my own part in making these invisible worlds visible again. At the same time, I am arriving in a conversation that is already well underway. The great 're-visibilization' of marginalized worlds has already animated generations of Māori scholars who have worked to render visible other ways of knowing land and cultivating alternatives. Building on important political statements like that of Sir Ranginui Walker's exhortation to engage in struggle without end (Walker 2004), and Linda Tuhiwai Smith's influential call to decolonize methodologies (Smith 2012), Māori scholars are generating both critiques of past land-use practices by modernist farming and enacting alternative ways forward. They are the first and most legitimate voices in articulating a future pathway for Māori land-use and I rely greatly on their work in the upcoming chapters. The following narrative is my response to their work.

2

The colonial farm and its powers

In Chapter 1, a different way of understanding the power of farms was introduced using the idea of political ontology. In the next two chapters, this relationship will be elaborated in a quite specific way: how do *farms* enact ontological politics? Great worlds of action are at stake when we consider the power of farming ontologies, and this can be demonstrated using one of the most compelling sites of clashing and fracturing powers: the colonial encounter between indigenous and European worlds.

This chapter follows the consequences of such a meeting – which took place in New Zealand from 1642. It cannot provide a complete history of the subsequent colonization of the Māori world of Aotearoa by Europe to create a new thing called New Zealand, although there are very important conflicts and transition points in this history that need some deeper examination. Rather, it is a history of the emerging multiplicity of how land is used and people are fed – how the collision of Māori Aotearoa and colonial New Zealand created a moment of chaotic multiplication of the possible ontologies of land-use in New Zealand. This didn't then trigger a linear process of colonization and consolidation into a capitalist world order. Rather, ontologies of land-use were shaped around important frontiers and multiplied in various spaces and salients in New Zealand as the tidal surges of colonization enacted new realities and worlds: unleashed disruption, disease, contests over resource extraction, land negotiations (followed by dubious land acquisition), war, and responded to changing global conditions and circuits of trade that prioritized new commodities. At the centre of this drama are farms themselves. They are one of the primary agents that first pushed back the frontiers of indigenous land-use and indigenous ecologies, unleashed chaos, before starting to create enclaves and then entire new landscapes within those chaotic ecological and social crises, eventually elevating one particular model of farming to dominance over the colonized landscape.

This set of conflicts, transitions and periods of stabilization reveal a particular political ontology of farms. The narrative in this chapter will trace how farms acted in multiple ways – both as agents of cooperation and alliance with indigenous worlds, and also, in other cases, as agents of colonization – erasing indigenous land-use and pushing through key ecological frontiers in New Zealand by destroying forests and draining wetlands in order to enact grasslands-based family farming. The major part of this chapter will tell this story of collaboration and colonization using the case of four colonial farms and their successors (which all were established by my own ancestors). Each one demonstrates the enacting of elements of a modernist pastoral farming world which had profound ontological effects, and collectively they describe how colonial farms simultaneously created and erased ecological, social and economic worlds.

Undiscovered lands

Aotearoa came into existence because of a frontier problem. New Zealand also came into existence because of a frontier problem. Both problems were variations on the question: what exists outside the knowable world?

It was apparent to the seafarers from greater Polynesia around a millennium ago that some kind of land existed in the southern reaches of the Pacific Ocean. Historians give significant credit to the remarkable powers of Polynesian seafarers[1] to read the semiotics of sea and sky and to pose the question: does something exist to the south? Sailing into the unknown in order to answer that question would create Aotearoa[2] – one of the most significant outposts of Polynesia, at its southernmost boundary.

The arrival of Polynesian voyagers breached a series of ecological frontiers in Aotearoa. Their early pursuit of easily available food sources would trigger a series of ecological crises, the extinction of major fauna and land-use strategies that are characteristic of the exploitation of new frontiers. As a new Polynesian frontier, Aotearoa presented different ecologies, resources, landscape forms and weather patterns, and its long islands did not mimic the island clusters of central Polynesia. Michael King summarizes the work of many prior prehistorians in suggesting that out of chaos, something new emerged in Aotearoa.[3] The first Polynesian phase breached frontiers – particularly the burning of forests to hunt the large flightless moa – and then went through a process of nomadic transition as easily available resources (like moa) were hunted to extinction, before settling over several centuries into permanent tribal regions. As King recounts, a post-frontier world emerged, with the land colonized and devastated by Polynesian exploitation eventually becoming something new, more stable and more in tune with the limits and capacities of Aotearoa. The Polynesian frontier world receded, lessons learned and something new emerged that was unique to this place – a Māori world. By the time of European contact, 'classic' Māori society had been ecologically and geographically settled for many centuries and had developed ways of living that were uniquely their own. This settled new home was the prologue to the great second colonization of Aotearoa that is the main subject matter of this book. It would remain this way for many centuries before the frontier question began to be posed by other seafarers and traders.

The possible existence of Terra Australis Incognita – the Great Southern Land that would balance the landmass of the Northern Hemisphere[4] – provided an intriguing question for the Dutch East India Company. In commissioning Abel Tasman to sail from Batavia in search of the land-that-must-exist, this great agent of European mercantilism was not searching for new homes for settlers. Rather, the company's vision was of a potential frontier of new resources and commodities that might exist at the outermost bounds of their mercantile empire and that could be brought into South East Asian and European trading circuits.

Nothing reveals the cataclysmic meeting and rupturing of ontological worlds quite like the moment of first contact – the first moment when a frontier erupts separating ontological worlds.[5] The dominant world is *Aotearoa*, the homes, villages, kinship networks, politics, landscape, culture and ecology of classic tribal Māori society. The (then) much smaller world is *New Zealand*, a potential site of extractable resources, tradeable goods and commodities.[6]

Tasman didn't find gold, silver or spices in New Zealand, discoveries that would have triggered an immediate and dramatically different future for New Zealand. More importantly for the narrative of this book, as Tasman searched for valuable commodities he gazed from within an ontological world that didn't enable him to see what was plainly evident: the extensive gardens spreading from every village. Māori were prospering as a result of their ability to exploit marine resources and engage in productive horticulture.[7] Aotearoa was a settled land of cultivation and food gathering, of villages and tribal organization, and of land-use that had already been modified in response to catastrophic ecological mistakes made during early Polynesian settlement.[8] Aotearoa was a garden.[9]

In a book about the ontology of farms, this lapse of vision by Tasman is important.[10] When James Cook and Joseph Banks gazed at New Zealand 130 years later, they would immediately observe the potential for cultivation that Tasman missed. But they envisaged a dramatically different form to that being practised by Māori. They saw the future potential for settlement by European farmers. Cook, on his numerous visits to New Zealand in the late 1700s, frequently noted in his journals the potentially farmable nature of the land.[11] While he definitely did appraise the resources that were available for extraction and immediate trade, he also saw New Zealand's potential for European settlement. The evidence of what Māori were achieving in cultivating the land suggested that this could be a site for permanent settlement, specifically including farms.[12]

From this point on, multiple potential futures start to elaborate and there are many possible colonial New Zealands that might emerge.[13] Tasman was searching for New Zealand as a site of resource extraction and tradeable commodities. Cook saw the same potential, but also saw a site for permanent settlement and farming: a new British frontier that might be appropriated. Other competing futures were also in play: New Zealand could be French, it could be a penal colony, it could eventually be a land with no Māori at all or it could be shared between Māori and Pākehā.[14] Among this multiplicity of possible futures, Cook's arrival triggered the one particular frontier contest that is central to the narrative of this book – the contest between multiple ontologies of land-use. Even at the point of his first arrival, we see two contesting worlds starting to be enacted: if Aotearoa was a garden, New Zealand had the potential to be a farm.

Cooperation: Aotearoa feeds New Zealand

An eventual fracturing and enacting of different ontologies between Pākehā farming and older Māori land-use did not happen immediately, and the first phase of colonization was actually premised on a highly cooperative network of economic, social and sustenance relations between Māori and newly arriving Pākehā. The creation of a hard frontier between Māori and Pākehā worlds was, in fact, not an inevitability. From the period immediately after Cook's voyages until the 1830s, cooperating economic networks emerged based on the highly developed ability of Māori to feed and trade with the arriving waves of adventurers, opportunists and outcasts who were searching for tradeable commodities like seal pelts.

The emergence and expansion of this cooperating economy created the opportunity for one kind of future for New Zealand: a collaboration and sharing of Aotearoa New Zealand between Māori and Pākehā. From the outset, this exchange and collaboration took place around food and gardens. One item became highly consequential – the potato.[15] Within forty years of Cook's arrival, Māori gardens had both an array of Polynesian crops – particularly kūmara (sweet potato) – along with new arrivals like potatoes, turnips, cabbages and maize.[16] Later successful arrivals, according to Helen Leach, were watermelons and peaches.[17] Building on the fertile gardens of Aotearoa, and adapting new crops with speed and skill, Māori generally welcomed new Pākehā whalers, sealers and traders; many Pākehā men married locally, and were certainly fed, in major part, by Māori.[18]

The first waves of Pākehā colonization arrived in search of commodities and extractive resources: seals, whales, flax, timber for spars, kauri gum and eventually gold. The food and trading dynamics of the early encounters became stable and mutually profitable, and this period represents the highest level of cooperation between Māori and Pākehā. The potential for a collaborative future existed and was being enacted in a thousand meals. However, while this relationship between Māori and Pākehā was prospering, dire consequences were being unleashed inside Māori Aotearoa.

From the first moments of European contact, the arrival of muskets and potatoes increased leverage within the jostling power relations between iwi (tribes), with devastating consequences. Early contact opened up strong trade links to Australia, where potatoes (and later flour) were traded for muskets. The grim period of early colonial history known as the 'musket wars' (1820–1830)[19] ensued, as tribal war parties, using muskets and fed by potatoes, engaged in a more mobile and deadly form of what had previously been a more geographically circumscribed and ritualized form of inter-tribal warfare. Potatoes broke the geographical boundaries constraining military ambition and fed roving war parties.[20] The result was a brutal period of ascendancy by musket-owning tribes, and the displacement, enslavement and absorbing of smaller tribes. By the time of the first moves investigating formal British settlement in the 1830s, Māori society was politically and geographically transformed.

While the musket wars were devastating the internal fabric of Aotearoa, they also spurred economic trade and collaboration with Pākehā, and this only intensified collaborative economic networks between Māori and Pākehā – especially around food and cordage from flax.[21]

The signing of the Treaty of Waitangi in 1840 formalized the relationship between Māori and the British Crown, establishing New Zealand as a British colony.[22] The political dynamics and consequences of the signing of the Treaty form a centrepiece of New Zealand history, and shaped action in both the nineteenth century and then again from the 1970s as the Treaty returned as an active document of law and political intent. Of particular significance for this book, the Treaty granted the Crown the sole right to purchase land from Māori, effectively placing within British hands the means to establish political arrangements to purchase or otherwise alienate Māori land and transfer it to Pākehā settlers.[23] With the signing of the Treaty, possible futures change and new contests in the colony emerged: between trading and extractive economies in collaboration with the Māori world that had been feeding them, and a new settled economy that would eventually converge on pastoral farming as the dominant form of land-use. The extractive economy had a soft frontier (if at all); the settled economy enacted a hard frontier that would be the site of significant conflicts. Belich argues that from 1840 forward, at least three kinds of economy and society were operating: what he calls Aotearoa (the considerable part of the colonial world where Māori still dominated), Old New Zealand (the extractive/collaborating economy) and New New Zealand (a society increasingly organized around settler farming).[24]

While the looming frontier contests over ontologies of land-use and farming are the central concern of this book, it is important to recognize those other potential futures for New Zealand. Fishing was important at the outset of trans-Tasman trade and remains an important economic venture to this day. Kauri gum[25] found in the forests and swamps of Northland became Auckland's major export in the second half of the nineteenth century.[26] The seemingly inevitable moment when gold was discovered in the 1860s prompted new waves of immigration. Harvesting of hardwood from native forests initially met the needs of the Royal Navy and the commercial shipping industry and then began to supply timber to build the towns and cities of New Zealand and Australia, all of which continued to solidify New Zealand's key economic relations with some wider imperial circuits of trade.[27] Kauri gum digging eventually died out, but mining and forestry never disappeared, and continue to fracture and enact particular kinds of colonial ontology. All of these might have become more dominant in New Zealand's economic future, but eventually receded to more marginal status in the face of the new powers of settler farming.

Establishing Britain's 'Farm in the South Pacific'

When Cook gazed across the fertile and productive gardens surrounding Māori villages in the 1770s, much had changed since Tasman's time to shape the way he looked at the potential of a new world.[28] Cook was voyaging during the first decades of the Industrial Revolution and food supply was becoming a subject of interest. In the 1770s British farming systems were becoming increasingly productive, but already the British industrial food system was importing goods like sugar from the Caribbean,[29] tobacco from the United States,[30] grain from Ireland[31] and beef[32] from mainland Europe. While the early decades of the Industrial Revolution stimulated trade in food, the reliance on new sources of food from outside Britain began to escalate dramatically, and by the time the colonial settlement of New Zealand was formally commenced in 1840 the demand for food (and farmland to produce it) was a major concern for the British Empire. From the outset, New Zealand was the first colony to be politically understood, in Britain, as fulfilling the urgent need for new sources of familiar British foodstuffs.

Within the British Empire, the 1840s sit at the cusp of what Friedmann and McMichael call the 'imperial food regime'.[33] One element of this new regime was a surge of potential farmers circulating through the empire. The second phase of the Highland Clearances, effectively pushing Scottish crofters off their land, was taking place.[34] During the 'hungry forties' in England, the capacity of local English farming to feed new industrial cities was reaching exhaustion point,[35] and this was massively exacerbated by the Irish Potato Famine (and the collapse of potato farming across Europe) in the mid-1840s.[36] All of these crises displaced small and sometimes middle-class farmers, creating a pool of potential farmers/settlers. Many of these potential settlers weren't farmers at all, but – like two of my own ancestral families – were escaping the collapse of small businesses and industries that were exhausted (like Cornish tin mining) or being swamped by the industrialization of manufacturing (like wooden boat-building). It was a moment in which the British Empire was awash with potential farmers desperately looking for land.

Successors to the British East India Company began lining up to establish new circuits and connections, no longer trading in seal pelts but instead moving large quantities of wheat and wool (and later butter, cheese and meat) around the Empire. These circuits passed through other nodes of empire. Australia's goldfields receded, and a focus on colonial economy and new lines of global economic integration emerged around sheep farming in the great river valleys and plains of the interior.[37] The peasant grain-producing regions of India were re-ordered by the creation of railways.[38] Canadian prairies, Argentine pampas, temperate regions of South Africa, the Russian steppes and the vast expanding potential of the American Midwest[39] were transformed by these new circuits of trade, coalescing around durable foods, new transportation and preservation technologies like refrigerated shipping and canning, new communication technologies and trading organizations, and an emerging food culture in the Industrial Revolution forming around wheat, sugar and animal proteins.[40]

These wider trade circuits, a horde of desperate farmers, the pressing need for food to sustain the workers of the Industrial Revolution and a new conceptualization of colonized spaces as having cultivatable potential, all provided clear reasons for the settler explosion around the colonial world. What was revealed was the power of farms as agents of settlement. As Belich argues, 'settlement is more powerful than empire' because it establishes a range of stable and ordered outcomes that outlive the specific political arrangements of much of empire and the predominantly directly exploitative economic networks that empire enacted.[41] Settler farming had many powers, and while they were often contested, in New Zealand they were pursued with vigour. Out of chaos and contest at the frontier would emerge a pacified, hegemonic order of land-use. The story of how this new farming frontier was enacted is not uncomplicated.

Prior to the signing of the Treaty of Waitangi in 1840, there were only around 2,000 Pākehā in residence in New Zealand. Only eighteen years later (and before a gold rush in 1861), this number had swelled to 59,000, surpassing the estimated Māori population for the first time.[42] The key dynamic underpinning this surge in colonial in-migration was the opportunity for ownership of farmland. The founder and amateur philosopher of organized settlement in New Zealand, Edward Gibbon Wakefield, placed farming at the centre of his imagined political economy of successful colonization. Wakefield calculated such important measures as the size and cost of farms, ensuring that land was scarce (and thus retained a strong market value) but was not placed out of reach of those who had arrived in the colony as labourers and aspired to become farmers.[43]

At the same time that the cultivatable quality of the New Zealand landscape was being boosted, a parallel project of ideological erasure of indigenous uses of land was starting to be circulated in the colony. One of the central elements of this erasure was the Lockean discursive duality of 'land improvement' in contrast to 'wasted' or 'unproductive' land.[44] Brooking and Pawson argue that this idea was central to the colonizing venture and became a standard legitimizer for a range of activities that attacked indigenous Aotearoa – both its people and its landscape ecologies.[45] Central to this was the idea that areas of native forest and the fern and bracken landscapes left by ancient forest burning, both important areas for Māori food gathering, were 'unproductive' or 'wasted' land. This disparagement varied in tone from the philosophically high-minded appeal to Lockean philosophy, to the purely politically instrumental, or to the notion that unproductive land was a symptom of the absence of Christian converts to bring the land closer to God's productive plans.[46]

Sites of settlement after the signing of the Treaty varied in tone, political intent and religious character, but they all were founded on the premise that settlers would be able to acquire farms. The first planned settlement was undertaken by Wakefield's private company – the New Zealand Company – which, in 1840/41, surveyed, sold plots and arranged transport for settlers to New Plymouth, Nelson and Wellington. Church-based settlements in Otago (Free Church of Scotland) and Canterbury (Church of England) followed a similar model of organization to the New Zealand Company. Standing well north of this piety and (semi)organization and situated between two navigable harbours, Auckland emerged as a chaotic, commercial entrepôt.

Over the next seventy years, the pastoral farming experiment in New Zealand would go through many contests and face competition from other land-uses, but eventually stabilized around what Pawson and Brooking describe as a 'one-model-fits-all' regime, which enclosed much of the landscape and would dominate New Zealand farming for most of the twentieth century.[47] How this conquest-by-farms happened is the subject of the rest of this and the next chapter. The great conquest will take shape around a two sets of frontiers. First, the Treaty of Waitangi enacted a hard frontier between Māori land and the expanding horde of Pākehā settlers wishing to lease and purchase farmland. The second frontier is ecological. Between Pākehā settlers and potential farms lie vast ecologies of forests, wetlands and native grasses. The role of farms in breaching these two frontiers would enact the chaotic transformation of the entire landscape of New Zealand.

Colonial farm histories

Orthodox histories provide a useful general pattern to the shape of New Zealand history, but tend to rush past those things that might be more central to the interests of a political ontologies approach. In more orthodox political economy accounts of the dynamism and growth of the colonial economy in places like New Zealand, the interaction of land, labour and capital is central. In the following account, farms play more of a central role in enacting outcomes. They are frontier-breaching agents that enact huge political and ecological change, but they also eventually become a new stable order, covering the land in bounded units of private property that establish a new culture, erase the indigenous and assemble in a way that make farms a stable item of economic capital.

My approach to this task involves narrating the stories of my own forebears' farms. This narrative is strongly influenced by two wider bodies of scholarship in New Zealand: environmental history and post-colonial history.[48] This body of work – on the transformation of the environment and periods of crisis and stabilization into a hegemonic regime of pastoral farming after 1920 – forms an essential part of the narrative to follow.[49] Their work has culminated in a 'grass-centric' narrative of New Zealand history, which covers over the silences that sat at the centre of historical narratives of change in New Zealand and in other colonized landscapes that became nodes of a great imperial regime of pastoral farming in the second half of the nineteenth century.

My narrative places particular farms inside these environmental histories of colonization, focusing on the way the farms did particular kinds of political work: building collaboration or breaching frontiers, erasing pasts, settling landscapes and channelling futures.

Telling this story in any kind of comprehensive detail is a near-impossible task.[50] To give some pathway through the complexities ahead, as well as situating myself as a Pākehā scholar and beneficiary of multiple generations of pastoral farming families in New Zealand, I want to concentrate on two clusters of colonial farms and their immediate successors, which belonged to my own forebears. Their creation as farms, and the way they created my predecessors as New Zealand pastoral farmers, tells the story of how some colonial farms not only became powerful to the point of ontological annihilation of all alternatives: they also helped enact those erasures.

1840s–1860s: Heather's Homestead/Marotahei, beside the Waipa River, Waikato

Heather's Homestead (its Pākehā name) or Marotahei (its Māori name) was established in the heart of the early collaborative economy between Māori and Pākehā. As a colonial trading post and farm, it straddled and melded two worlds for around fifteen years, before being destroyed in the climactic moments of the colonial invasion of the Waikato and the great conflagration over the potential for Māori sovereignty.

The Heather of Heather's Homestead was my forebear, Dennett Hersee Heather, who left a farm on the outskirts of a fishing community on the south coast of England, most likely because he was the youngest son, and migrated to New Zealand twice at the outset of colonial settlement, His first arrival into Auckland, with wife Mary Anne and three infant children in 1840, ended in fear and disaster. They were participants in the first wave of actual 'settlers' and clearly intended to farm, purchasing twenty-three acres in the first government offer of farm lots in July 1841.[51] Unlike settlements elsewhere around New Zealand, Auckland was wedged between two great centres of Māori Aotearoa: Northland to the north and Waikato to the south. Despite the new Treaty, reports began arriving in 1845 of a Māori uprising in Northland, of fighting, of the deaths of settlers and soldiers, and of imminent danger to Auckland.[52] The family decided to return to England and boarded a doomed ship in 1845. Mary Anne and two of the children would drown when their ship – the *Mary* – foundered in Bass Strait. Dennett and one child (my ancestor Arthur) survived in a lifeboat and were returned to Sydney, where they awaited a colonial commission of enquiry into the wreck, an event that contributed to changes in maritime law regarding the seaworthiness of passenger vessels.[53]

Dennett Heather returned to New Zealand in 1847. This time, however, he left Auckland and set off into the heart of Aotearoa, journeying up the Waikato and Waipa rivers deep into the interior of what was still Māori-controlled land – the Waikato, which would become the great site of conflict over the potential for a united Māori political response to colonization.[54] Dennett entered this other world and within a few years had established a trading post at the junction of Waipa River and Mangaotama Stream. He married his second wife, Unaiki, with whom he had a son called Stanley, and purchased a sizeable piece of land around his trading post.[55]

This land had consequences, not least that the trading post called Heather's Homestead now also had a Māori name – Marotahei – which named the wider body of land that was initially leased and then purchased from the local tribe.[57] This farm was an act of integration between the aspirations of the new settler and an existing, highly productive and profitable Māori farming economy.[58] This important Māori farming region in Waikato had been commercially active within colonial trading circuits for many decades and provided an abundant supply of food to new settlers in Auckland.[59] Heather's Homestead/Marotahei was not a farm that enacted a frontier. Rather, it was a small Pākehā arrival into the Māori economy, in which the farm was incorporated as an element of the existing Māori economic order. Dennett, his Pākehā son Arthur, his Māori wife Unaiki and son Stanley in effect farmed and traded as a hinge connecting two worlds. This is why Heather's Homestead/Marotahei was a site of both hope and doom. Dennett and Unaiki Heather's farm was situated at the very site where the next great colonial fracture was about to happen.

As an actor in this drama, the homestead fixed in place a complex network that enacted a hinge in colonial worlds (in important ways the opposite of a frontier). It existed in close association with the local Māori, who had made it available for sale. This sale came with important kinship obligations and a new whānau (extended family). The farm fixed this new alliance in a particular place inside the Māori world. Yet it was also a remarkably distant terminus in the transport systems of empire. Out here, the homestead was barely noticeable in the formal governing of the colony. It first appeared in 1854 at the creation of its first simple surveyor's map (see Figure 2) and deed of sale (although the land may have been leased by Dennett well before then), and it appeared again in 1861 in a Crown grant of land retrospectively recognizing that Dennett Heather owned the land.[60] This area of the Waikato had taken up production of wheat, fruit (peaches and watermelons), cattle, horses and sheep, as well as the long-term staples of potatoes and pigs, and the produce that passed through the farm as a trading post was mostly foods desired by Europeans. Heather's Homestead/Marotahei brought a farm boy from Sussex into this arena of highly productive and adaptive farming. Within ten years, the homestead was producing a wide variety of goods on 170 acres.[61] By 1863, on the eve of colonial

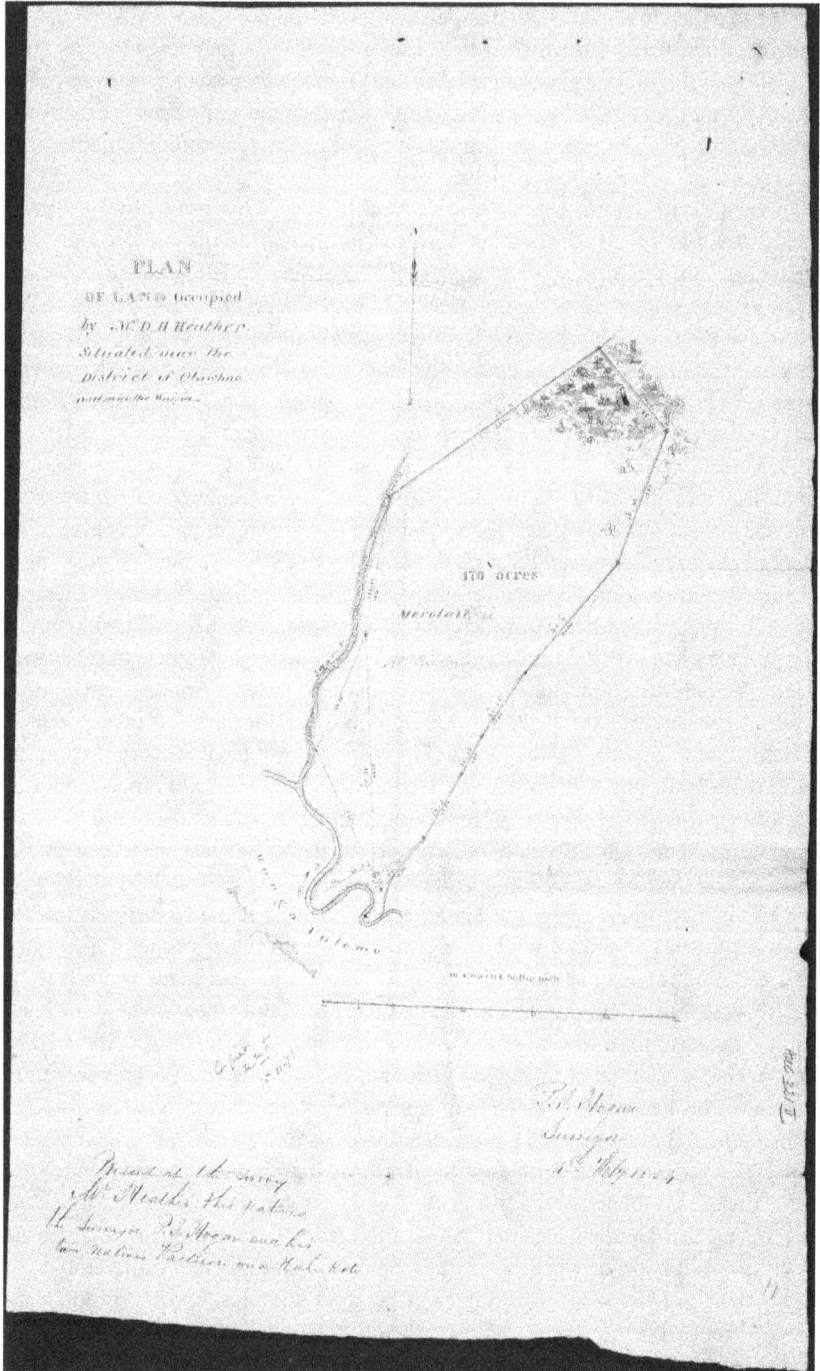

Figure 2 Original surveyor's map of Marotahei[56]
Source: Archives New Zealand *Te Rua Mahara o te Kāwanatanga.*

invasion of Waikato, it was a highly productive farm with many assets, timber, crops, stock and future potentials.[62]

Dennett's name then appeared in a couple more registers and attempts by regional authorities to keep track of Pākehā settlers in Māori-controlled territories, although in these the nature of his second marriage and offspring is vague. More fatefully, the name 'Heather's Homestead' eventually appeared as a landmark, along with a handful of other Pākehā settlers, among the Māori villages, sites of defensible ground, swamps and the mission station, on an 1864 map used by the invading army of General Cameron.

The farm was not only the farthest tentacle of colonial influence, it was also a site of demonstration of Māori power. Dennett arrived in the Waikato to find emerging (albeit complexly contested) political power, a thriving economy and a culturally strong and well-defined world. His farm was not a site of colonization of Māori by Pākehā. It was a site of collaboration between Pākehā and Māori, and its dominant rationale and components resided clearly within Aotearoa, not New Zealand. The farm made this collaboration a reality and anchored it in place. The human inhabitants who lived together there for over ten years became bilingual, and were contributors in negotiations between the Crown and the King Movement.[63]

The ontological effect of Heather's Homestead/Marotahei was that it assembled all the ingredients for different possible futures. While it existed, a different future was possible. Here the new colony was being fed by Māori food, and two cooperating bases of cultural and political influence were co-producing an outcome that was potentially both Māori and Pākehā. The Treaty of Waitangi created the legal potential for this, and Heather's Homestead/Marotahei was the kind of place where that potentially collaborative future was actually being enacted.

But history ran down another path.[64] The next official mention of 'Heather's Homestead' was in the account given by journalists travelling with the invading forces of the colonial army, which had been sent to destroy the rival power of the Kīngitanga in 1863. The farm was sited exactly between the encampment of the invading General Cameron and the heavily fortified pā (hill forts), Paterangi and Pikipiko.[65] Militarily embedded journalists tell of the soldiers arriving at Heather's Homestead and watching as the 'Māori rebels' torched it and retreated.[66] I am more agnostic about the various motivations for destroying this physical site of Māori/Pākehā collaboration, as the invasion made its existence an intractable anomaly to both sides.[67] Either way, the result was the destruction of the complex network of relations that Heather's Homestead/Marotahei enacted. Dennett and Stanley had already retreated down the river;[68] Unaiki stayed behind and took shelter with her family.[69] The all-important Māori kinship bond to land was ruptured. The claim to legal ownership of the land then became a subject of complex negotiations (with questions of compensation at stake). Dennett received compensation for lost stock and possessions, and retained formal title to the land until it was sold after his death in 1866.[70] Auckland had a new frontier made up of 'safe' farms feeding it, to the south. Māori sovereignty was tested and conquered.[71] The Pākehā world ascended. The farm was no longer situated inside Aotearoa, but was now legally and politically British territory enacting an expansion of the frontier of 'substantive sovereignty' of the British colony of New Zealand.

Dennett pursued compensation for the loss of the homestead[72] and re-established his trading post closer to Auckland. Later, this was lucratively absorbed into a colonial trading company. He died soon after while still relatively young. Dennett and Mary Anne's only surviving son – my forebear Arthur Heather, who was plucked from the seas in Bass Strait as most of his family died around him and spent some of his youth in Māori territory with his Māori stepmother and stepbrother – rose through the trading company and became a prosperous businessman in Auckland. He made himself busy with many acts of settlement in the transition to stable colonial society in Auckland, helping to establish schools, sports clubs and charities. Having achieved great respectability, he lost his fortune in the collapse of the kauri gum industry (one of the last vestiges of the older extractive colonial economy) and returned to die in England. Dennett and Unaiki's son Stanley also worked in colonial trading and acted as a company agent in the Cook Islands. He married Rangitai – the granddaughter of a famous Tahitian missionary, Papeiha, who was also the great-granddaughter of the paramount chief of that district Tinomana – and founded a dynasty (Ngati Tanere) in the Cook Islands and Samoa that still celebrates his memory along with that of his adventurous father and mother who traversed two worlds. All of this was partly enacted by the existence of Heather's Homestead/Marotahei – a farm that made different futures possible, but was destroyed along with the wider collaborative moment between Māori and Pākehā in regions like the Waikato.

1840s–1860s: The Fencible's Gift, Howick Village, Auckland

Heather's Homestead/Marotahei poses a strong contrast with a parallel farm from my family's history, a farm just south of Auckland that was gifted to a retired soldier and his family.

The destabilizing crisis of the northern Māori 'rebellion', which drove Dennett and Mary Anne Heather away from the new settlement of Auckland in 1845, posed an existential threat to a colony, but New Zealand was just too small and remote to justify the stationing of permanent troops. Its original Pākehā settlers – sealers and whalers who were often refugees from British rule (particularly the significant number of escaped convicts from Australia) – were reluctant recruits. Farms lay at the heart of one proposed solution to this problem of inadequate security. Rapid plans were made to settle four villages (Panmure, Onehunga, Howick and Otahuhu) to the south of Auckland, which would become a military buffer between Auckland and any potential invading threat from the powerful Māori alliance in the Waikato to the south. The key drawcard was the promised gift of small farms to military veterans (of at least fifteen years of service) to lure them into settling the more threatened fringes of the new colony. This group was known as the 'Fencibles', and over 700 Fencibles came to New Zealand with their families between 1847 and 1852 to form a 'militia' on Auckland's southern border: they and their families made up one third of Auckland's population. The cottage and freehold land offered to each Fencible was an essential part of the arrangement; after a period of seven years of faithful service – which seemed mostly to involve public displays of military discipline and colour along with a considerable amount of public labouring works – they were rewarded with private title to the house and acre of land they were inhabiting.[73]

Although small, Fencible farms were still attractive to ex-soldiers, who originally came from peasant communities in England or Ireland in the early decades of the nineteenth century. One acre of land was small for a colonial farm, but large for those raised in the Irish 'conacre' system.[74] And the farms were a free gift contingent only on a period of military duty.[75] Furthermore, for many Irish soldiers who had served their time in the army, their home communities in Ireland had been devastated by the Potato Famine; death and outmigration had decimated their home communities and made return a less certain prospect.[76]

The Fencibles and their lands enacted a particular rationale for the settling of New Zealand. These settlers and their farms were explicitly intended to build a frontier. My own forebears in this particular story – Thomas and Mary Bailey – arrived in the first wave of Fencibles. Thomas was known subsequently by some bureaucratic markers. His footprint in official documents is traced through recruitment in Somerset (listed as a 'labourer') and twenty-four years of service in the 17th Light Dragoons; he spent most of his army life in India. Fencible families are identified by which ship they arrived on – the Baileys arrived on the *Minerva* in 1847 – and to which of the four villages they were assigned – the Baileys went to Howick. Their son William was the first Pākehā child born in Howick. Thomas and Mary took up residence on their acre and then bought a further five acres (a pre-emptive option available to Fencibles). Their farm was too small to have a name.

Fencibles were given the option of guaranteed public works employment by the colonial government to help build roads, houses and fortifications, and in 1857 Thomas's occupation on the electoral roll was again 'labourer'.[77] Thomas and Mary Bailey were poor; they had arrived with no capital and only an army pension, and the Fencible's Gift of a cottage and piece of farmable land changed their status in a small but significant way. Thomas and Mary died quite young, having sold off their six acres of land in Howick as soon as Thomas's seven years of service were up, but their son William went on to build on that early gift of land and became a prosperous farmer.

Fencible farms and villages took on particular material dynamics. Cottages were built and vegetables planted and Fencibles were given the option of being awarded 'depasturage' leases on nearby Māori land, where cattle could forage on native grasses.[78] Settlers in Howick complained that unlike the settlers in the other three villages, which were situated on fertile volcanic loam, they had to contend with clay soil that was hard to work into useful cultivation.[79] Because of this, the settlers had to rely heavily on the staples – pork and potatoes – of the collaborative Māori/Pākehā food economy to survive, and it was several years before any significant amount of food from Fencible allotments in Howick travelled north to the emerging settlement of Auckland.[80] The historical society that celebrates their achievements (which, given the tone of some of their writing, 'disappointingly' did not include many actual moments of military confrontation) talks of their collective desire to build redoubts and connect the villages with roads to enable more rapid mobilization and reinforcement in moments of attack. While never required to actually fight, the settlers established the roading infrastructure that would later be used for the rapid elaboration of farming and other commerce southwards from Auckland. They also created roads through a crucial geographical land bridge, bringing Auckland into easier contact with the Waikato river system – and again, bringing the settlement much closer to the great world of Māori life in the Waikato. In doing so, the Fencibles fuelled the pressures for new land that would eventually lead to the invasion of the Waikato and the destruction of Heather's Homestead/Marotahei. As a martial exercise, then, the Fencibles and their villages and farms were almost entirely counter-productive.[81] They failed as a military perimeter, but succeeded in extending a farming and commercial frontier south of Auckland.

Heather's Homestead/Marotahei and the Fencible's Gift enacted two very different colonial ontologies. The first sat inside and helped enact a strong collaboration between New Zealand and Aotearoa; the second was founded in the martial intent to magnify the boundary between the two. They reproduced the American frontier dynamic of trading posts and army forts that expressed the contradictory politics of collaboration and conquest in that setting. In James Belich's timeline, they sat inside the crucial period from 1840 to 1865 when the newly arrived settler society progressively contested land ownership, expanded the settled frontier and eventually both subdued the older independent Māori world of Aotearoa and dismantled the collaborating economy and society of what Belich terms 'Old New Zealand'.[82]

The two pieces of land demonstrate some key materialities that influence the trajectories and outcomes of that time of contest and transition. Heather's Homestead/Marotahei emerged in collaboration between Pākehā and Māori. Its title transitioned through various forms until it was absorbed into the land court system. Eventually, after the invasion, it ended up in the hands of a 'normal' Pākehā settler, and the world of collaboration it was enacting was extinguished. There were no successor collaborative farms to Heather's Homestead/Marotahei. Its moment passed.

The Fencible's Gift performed another kind of work. It enabled a poor soldier from a modest background to become a landowner. These powers then accumulated. Thomas's son William Bailey went on to prosper in the colony and eventually ended up acquiring a farm of his own and set up his only child – his daughter Reine – and family on a second farm in the first decade of the twentieth century.

Reine married Ned Roberts, and in doing so brought together the capital from two farms. Just behind the Fencible's perimeter was a larger farm called Clovernook, farmed by Joe and Jane Roberts and their son Ned, who had fled the failure of their farm in Cornwall probably as a result of the economic crisis caused by the collapse of tin mining. Combining the capital of Clovernook and the Fencible's Gift, Reine Bailey and Ned Roberts' new farm was purchased in the first decades of the twentieth century. It had an interesting name– Te Rahui – as we'll go on to discover.

This farm will be particularly revealing of the kinds of destination that Pākehā farms are travelling towards. Te Rahui sat in exactly the same kind of setting that Heather's Homestead/Marotahei once occupied: it was deep inside a strong Māori area (the East Coast of the North Island), across a lane from a Māori marae and village, on a highly fertile river flat that was once central to the local Māori food economy. But the Māori world was now devastated and in a state of economic collapse. Te Rahui was purchased by Ned and Reine Roberts from a local Māori family who were in desperate straits. The Roberts had access to credit from the state and a new option for success, producing butter and cheese for export to England. Te Rahui would lead the establishment of the local dairy cooperative and the Roberts family would discuss rationalism and science.[83]

They were the successful and rational inheritors of the kind of farming world that took shape after the frontier had been settled: Pākehā farmers took ownership of lands to farm, and Māori worlds were pushed back to the margins.

A final kind of work performed by these two farms is cultural. The farms became sites of the creation of new stories and histories. By the time Te Rahui was flourishing in the 1920s, the last vestiges of a collaborating farm space in New Zealand were all but gone. The Māori ownership of the land became the subject of historical amnesia, the translation of the farm's Māori name was incorrectly understood by its new Pākehā owners and a new history (the one that I grew up with) was being written.[84] The new history of Te Rahui made its contribution to the narrating of the colonial economy, progress and science, and when it was sold, the capital was used to set up six children in new economic ventures (including the purchase of Windsor Lodge, where I grew up). From Heather's Homestead/ Marotahei to Te Rahui, the farm as a site enacting a particular collaborative frontier ontology of Māori/Pākehā relations and collaboration had been completely reversed. All of the cultural ways in which early farms performed acts of cooperation around food, culture, language, economy, politics and kinship had now become sites of fracture and separation.

Both these farms did the work that Belich argued was at the core of the consolidation of empire in the farming colonies – they settled the landscape – but they did it in ways that were not pre-determined or inevitable.[85] Understanding their role means embracing the work of both the farmers and the farms in making things happen – after all, the landscape was settled, in crucial respects, not only by farmers but also by farms. Humans come and go, but the farms settle. Each farm enacted and anchored new ontologies, and each carried the potential for different futures to happen. By the mid-1860s many of these possible futures had started to disappear, and one trajectory began to coalesce around one style of farming and one kind of economic, cultural and political relationship between Pākehā and Māori. The alliance between Heather's Homestead and Marotahei failed, its hybrid status and culture supplanted by a 'normal' Pākehā farm, and the collaborative world it potentially enacted shrank by the size of one parcel of land. The Fencible's Gift did its work of extending a frontier into Māori worlds. Clovernook and Te Rahui became firmly embedded in the new landscape taking shape behind this frontier. Their world grew and swelled and consolidated.

While these farms tell the story of one crucial period in the narrowing of options for what kind of land-use (and socio-economic) future New Zealand would have, this tells only half the story. Two other farms provide the second half of this narrative and complete the picture of the ontological politics of farms in the colonization of the New Zealand landscape. If the first great impediment to establishing the modernist pastoral farm in New Zealand was indigenous society and its potential political control over land, the other impediment was the landscape ecology of Aotearoa. Between settlers and their dream of grassland farms lay significant ecological frontiers composed of vast wetlands and towering forests.

1860s–1880s: Ashburn Estate, Dunedin, Otago

The first two farms that lay on different sides of the frontier between Māori Waikato and Pākehā Auckland existed during a crucial moment when particular futures were being made and unmade in New Zealand. They both made things happen: one enacted collaboration and the other enacted a frontier. The next two farms – Ashburn Estate and Glenn Rd – may be understood as doing the opposite: they act to make things disappear.

Ashburn Estate was situated on one of the hills flanking the settlement of Dunedin, in the religious colony of Otago in the South Island. The rim of hills around Dunedin are remnants of volcanoes and are rocky terrain. This, combined with a preponderance of heavy clays, a pluvial climate and a windy aspect, makes the area a challenging prospect for farming. The original Pākehā settler taking on this misty hillside, Jacob Wain, spent a lot of time collecting volcanic rocks out of the fields and piling them into walls ('dry-stone' or 'drystane' dykes) and making foundations for a house.

The Campbells arrived to live behind these dry-stone dykes with a strong sense of persecution and misfortune. They had a lot of history to leave behind. John and Elizabeth Campbell were both leaving the Isle of Bute in Scotland for compelling reasons. Her family had been deeply involved in religious schism[86] in the Presbyterian Church in the 1840s and her father had surrendered a two-century-long lease on his farm (Ambrismore Farm) in 1851.[87] John's family were carpenters and boat-builders in the little town of Rothesay and their business was in decline as a powerful industrial centre of shipping manufacture was taking shape across the Clyde, in Glasgow. John and Elizabeth brought five children with them, three of whom were already adults and had worked in the family business.

The extended Campbell family arrived in the first year of the Otago goldrush in 1862 but, surprisingly, didn't take their engineering skills inland to the goldfields. Instead they engaged in construction and engineering in the growing settlement of Dunedin, contributing to the building of bridges, roads and houses and later trading as Campbell Bros. After six years of success as engineers, the daughter of a religious dissident who surrendered his farm lease and her husband (who had no prior experience of farming), purchased Ashburn Estate, became farmers and owners of land and elevated themselves up the ladder of colonial society.

Having picked up too many stones, the original owner of Ashburn Estate had departed for the goldfields in 1862, leaving his misty farm in the hands of a relative who commissioned a large house to be built, secured on the promise of future wealth from gold. The unpaid architect eventually forced him to put it up for sale. The future would show, however, that sometimes farmhouses have better future prospects than their farms.

Ashburn Estate becomes the Campbell property in 1868 and did important work in service of its new owners. Crucially, however, it didn't work particularly well doing the narrow range of tasks that are usually prioritized in farm narratives: it wasn't a 'good farm' that turned out lots of produce and stock. It had ninety acres of stony ground, a nice house incorporating some solid 'locally sourced' volcanic stone and a stream with enough volume to drive a waterwheel. It was well situated on the outskirts of Dunedin beside one of the roads leading to the goldfields, and it had a decent view (on a clear day) with bracing airs and, if one wasn't being too fussy, an atmosphere that seemed almost redolent of a Scottish hillside – misty, stony, cool, with mānuka as a substitute for heather.

But farms that are bad in some important respects sometimes do other kinds of significant work. Calling the farm Ashburn Estate was important for the daughter of the recently lost Ambrismore Farm, whose forebears had spent two centuries toiling on behalf of the Marquis of Bute. The word 'estate' clearly worked as a cultural signifier for the new Campbell owners.[88]

For the three sons who were now in their twenties, the stream on the farm proved much more useful than the stony pastures. They set up water wheels to drive various items of machinery that could be used for threshing grain, processing flax and running two 'bone stamping' mills that produced fertilizer out of bones from the local abattoir. They extended the main farmhouse substantially until it had ten rooms, and built stables, a coach house and numerous other buildings and worker's cottages that allowed them to run the various engineering activities of Campbell Bros. The farm provided all that they needed for this, as well as an orchard. In search of better use for the pasture, they expanded the previous owner's plantings of scotch firs and pines.[89] Taken together, this combination of ninety acres of 'productive' farmland and multiple other ventures was somewhat polycultural. This one farm was the site of many economic practices. It was also becoming, as a later newspaper article described, a 'residence that is not to be surpassed', a site where a gentlemen might arrive and take up a satisfactory situation in the new colony. Just not for actual farming.

John Campbell died after only sixteen years living in this 'gentlemen's residence'. None of the Campbell sons wanted to take on the farm, and some had already left by the time he died. But the timing of the resultant sale is interesting: it was 1882, and Elizabeth sold Ashburn Estate just as new ways of farming were emerging in New Zealand. The first key change was that the farm was sold in April 1882, two months and five days after the SS *Dunedin* set sail from a nearby harbour with New Zealand's first consignment of frozen meat for England. This event would provide a massive stimulus to the development of a pastoral farming economy, although it is uncertain whether Ashburn's ninety stony acres could have succeeded as a sheep farm even in those newly improved economic conditions. The second change taking shape in the 1880s was that Dunedin had been reaping the economic harvest of the gold rush. There wasn't much interest in buying Ashburn Estate as a farm (it sat on the market for four years before selling), but it had developed a varied array of physical and cultural assets that made it suitable for other purposes. When two doctors purchased Ashburn Estate in 1882, they developed it into a private psychiatric institution,[90] which it has remained to this day under its modified name, Ashburn Hall.[91] The sale liberated a significant quantity of capital, which, along with the success of various earlier Campbell Bros ventures, sent the four sons out into the world each with a significant amount of capital to invest. They headed for the North Island to the opening of a great new frontier of farming that was being created with the conquering, burning and draining of the Taranaki region.

In only fourteen years, Ashburn Estate successfully made things disappear. It resolved the shame of the loss of a tenant farm and provided an escape from religious schism. It created a site where the disadvantaged situation of a small family of boat-builders and engineers could escape being absorbed into the great maw of Clydeside, and instead could run small and profitable activities in the new colony. It gave them the title of owners of an 'estate', with a view over Dunedin and plenty of Scotch firs.

It imprinted on the landscape a particular pattern of farming enacting a multiplicity of new activities and rationales. And it built up capital that would then make other worlds disappear.

1880s–1920s: Glenn Rd, Kaupokonui, Taranaki

After the sale of Ashburn Estate the two eldest sons, Archie and James Campbell, headed north and made the transition from engineers to land speculators. This reflected a wider movement in the overall economic dynamics of colonial New Zealand, as the end of the gold rush and the declining relative fortunes of the great sheep runs that dominated the landscape in the South Island began to give way to new economic opportunities in the North Island. After 1882, with the advent of refrigerated shipping, the extent to which farms (and the scale of such farms) could participate in global networks of food commodity production and consumption was amplifying. At the same time, the final brutal acts of the Taranaki conflict between Māori and Pākehā, the confiscation of extensive lands, and the operation of the Native Land Court were facilitating the flow of large tracts of Māori land into formal markets. From this point, the only barrier to new farmland entering global circuits of economic activity would be how quickly the great bush and extensive wetlands of the North Island could be transitioned into grassland. In effect, a new frontier was opening up – not, as was the case between 1840 and the mid-1860s, simply a political and cultural boundary between Māori- and Pākehā-dominated landscapes and economic worlds, but two ecological frontiers: trees and wetlands.[92]

The most senior of the Campbell brothers, Archie, led this transition. Even before the sale of Ashburn Estate, he took his capital from the successful ventures of Campbell Bros in Dunedin and began to borrow and invest in new areas of farmland. In the early 1880s his interest increasingly focused on the newly exposed fertile soils of the Taranaki region on the North Island's west coast.[93] In cooperation with his younger brother, my direct ancestor James Campbell, he undertook significant volumes of land purchasing and mortgage lending for farmland around Taranaki. At different times his name would appear on over forty property titles around Taranaki.[94] While Archie travelled the path towards the time-honoured New Zealand profession of land speculator, his brother James did not find this so enticing and, perhaps motivated by his conversion to the Brethren faith, cashed out of some of their many property leases and bought a farm for himself on the southern coast of Taranaki in 1882.

Glenn Road, in the vicinity of Kaupokonui, was named for an earlier settler and became the name of the first major Campbell farm in the Taranaki region. Around it, multiple blocks of land were initially leased for cattle grazing further up the slopes of Mt Egmont,[95] and from this farm three sons and two daughters would also attain farms around Hawera and Eltham. Of the early farms that inhabit the narratives in this chapter, this is the only one that has a photographic record, showing a handsome wooden farmhouse with a distinctive prayer-tower in its centre, testimony to the strong religious sentiment of the Campbells. The earliest photo (Figure 3) is taken in the late 1880s, with infant children evident, and shows the rough quality of the emerging pasture, with mixed pasture grass species and some 'scrub' around the edges. It is clearly flat (albeit still showing some bumps from felled trees) and producing enough grass to

Figure 3 Glenn Rd, *c.* 1880s
Artist attribution: Marion Familton

Figure 4 Glenn Rd, *c.* 1890s
Artist attribution: Marion Familton

account for some healthy-looking Hampshire Down sheep, which are proudly posed in the foreground. There are trees, outbuildings, fences and gates. It is productive, but still slightly 'messy'. In the background is a small sawmill surrounded by a fence of split wooden palings and, looming in the background, a significant stand of native forest.

The second photograph (Figure 4) is likely taken around ten years later, judging by the ages of the children. It tells a significant story: the farmhouse sails like a ship in an ocean of deep pasture, large haystacks stand plumply by, the fences are now extensive and secure with multiple battens spreading wires between the major posts. Most tellingly, there are no longer any trees in sight – either close to the house or in the now-absent stand of native forest behind. The margins of scrub have disappeared. The farm is almost entirely composed of uniform grass pasture.

These photos show that this is a 'good' farm, and history bears out the claim. Glenn Rd produced five new farms for the next generation of family members, and was notable in all the ways that Ashburn wasn't, winning prizes for agricultural produce and stock breeding. This partly emerged as a collaboration between the farm, James Campbell and his most famous animal, the bull Hatter, around which the future wealth of the Campbells was anchored (see Figure 5).[96] When James Campbell eventually died, his obituaries celebrated him for all the right kinds of farming reasons: his approach to modern farming ideas, his bountiful increase in the share which he was given in farming life and his success in establishing farms for the next generation. So, in key farming terms, Glenn Rd was a good farm. But it was also a farm that, along with

Figure 5 The bull Hatter
Artist attribution: Marion Familton

its leased partners and subsequent successors, would only be successful after making other things disappear. The great farming estate of Taranaki existed because a war had been fought which extended the Pākehā frontier deep into Māori lands, and two highly significant ecological frontiers had been breached and colonized.[97]

When Archie and James Campbell were venturing forth from Ashburn Estate to make their fortune in the North Island, they arrived, in the late 1870s, at the start of a revolution by fire. The meaning and potential use of land in much of the North Island, including the heavily bush-clad majority of Taranaki, were in the process of being transformed by axe, saw and flame. What had previously been 'waste land', home to native bush and wetlands, was being moved into a marketable state as farmland through a combination of the Native Land Court and various brutal techniques for removing forest cover and draining wet ground.

Graeme Wynn narrates the history of the clearing of the forests of the North Island as taking place in three phases.[98] From the signing of the Treaty of Waitangi in 1840 for around three decades, milling of timber ate into the great bush from its coastal margins.[99] These incursions built on the centuries-earlier burning of bush by Māori to hunt moa. These ancient burned-out areas had regenerated, but left gaps in the previously dense ranks of 'old forest' in New Zealand. Settlers distinguished between 'scrub' and 'bush' – each posed a different set of barriers to establishing pasture. Wynn's second phase, from the 1870s, is described as a transition from the frenzy of milling to an urgent need to uncover the kinds of fertile land that Joseph Banks had earlier prophesied as lying under the soaring forests of the North Island. Milling simply wasn't moving with sufficient speed to clear enough potential farmland, and so a great burning commenced. For the next decade, a 'fire storm' engulfed much of the North Island.[100] This decade is the period in which the ecological frontier of forested lands was dramatically pushed back and colonized with a new ecology of grasslands farming systems.

Wynn's third phase of forest history is signified by a Royal Commission on Forestry in 1913, which recognized that the removal of forest cover from the landscape had overshot by some margin and too *much* forest had been cleared. The commission recommended that land which had been cleared but was unsuitable for farming should now be replanted with stands of fast-growing exotic trees. In a material sense, the indigenous forest frontier had been pushed back and then fixed for what would turn out to be much of the twentieth century.

The 1880s, in the middle of Wynn's second phase, were the climax point of the fevered burning of bushlands, and farms were key agents in this frenzy. Rollo Arnold's perceptive historical account commences with Taranaki at the epicentre of the inferno, and narrates the great fire that swept through the village of Stratford in Eastern Taranaki in the long hot summer of 1885–86.[101] Aligning with a global El Nino event in 1884–85, the great burning of that particular New Zealand summer was the culmination of many years of progressive clearing and felling that left timber lying on the ground unmilled, followed by a hot dry summer, to create perfect burning conditions. The results are evident in the statistics of land characterization in the colony. In 1861 there were 158,000 acres of 'improved pasture' in the colony, but by 1926 this had increased to 16.5 million acres,[102] much of which had been achieved by the burning of forests in the 1880s alone.[103]

The processes by which farmer settlers used fire to attain pasture were contingent on multiple other objects and materials.[104] Diaries of farm life in settler Taranaki show how, on obtaining ownership of bush land, early settlers progressively cut and laid woody vegetation to dry out on the forest floor. Debates surrounded the exact mix of undergrowth, drying time and month for optimum ignition.[105] Burning took place over summer, followed by stump pulling ('stumping') in winter. Animals had to be able to roam and graze through gradations of bush and new pasture, so fences were the next essential item, followed by the subdivision of paddocks and sowing with numerous rounds of grass seed: cocksfoot, ryegrass, timothy and clover.[106] Early photographs of the Taranaki farmscape taken five to ten years before the first photograph of Glenn Rd show these pastures taking hold among the bones of large trees, stumps and fallen charred limbs.[107]

While the original Glenn Rd farm was situated in land that had previously been partly burned by Māori, where forest had been replaced by a combination of scrub and bracken (also good material for burning[108]) among original stands of bush, the leased blocks for cattle grazing from the main farm were further towards the mountain inside these kinds of heavily burned bush zones. Glenn Rd had enough open land to burn off the scrub and bracken and then mill rather than burn the main stands of bush. The successor farms, however, out east from Glenn Rd, were right inside the epicentre of the great burning of the summer of 1885–86. James's two eldest sons took ownership of those farms between 1900 and 1920 when the landscape was still littered with the largest of the big tree stumps and charcoal was regularly ploughed up in the pasture.

My grandfather was the youngest and least reputable member of James Campbell's offspring. He enjoyed the pub and having various adventures, which earned him the nickname 'Black Jack' Campbell. The farm that he took up near his two older brothers was considered by the wider family to be so poor as to be a rebuke from his pious father. His farm incorporated the second great natural frontier acting as a barrier to grasslands farming: wetlands.

Geoff Park wrote of the loss of New Zealand's wetlands as one of the most dramatic features of ecological colonization. Commencing in 1840, roughly 670,000 hectares of wetland were reduced to around 100,000 hectares by 2000, a decline of 85 per cent.[109] This sets New Zealand apart as a world leader in wetland drainage. It had grievous impacts on both the abundant ecosystems in wetlands and on Māori, who relied on wetlands as a major source of food and fibre. Two potential futures of New Zealand land-use – the commercial production of eels, and the production of high-quality linen from New Zealand flax – progressively disappeared with every acre of wetland that was drained to make pasture. Settlers who arrived from the fenlands of England had the advantage of already knowing techniques for draining wetlands, and Park argues that their skills (which had to be learned by other settlers, like my Scottish forebears in Taranaki) were just as damaging as the chaos unleashed by axe and flame.

My Campbell grandfather Black Jack's poor inheritance eventually helped create his reputation as a 'good farmer'. He was the first in the district to purchase a D2 Caterpillar tractor,[110] which worked in alliance with a prototype of what would later be called 'giant discs', which could simultaneously slash and plough in woody regrowth vegetation. He also made ingenious use of the old sawmill at the back of the farm to produce hardwood shingles to line drains in his pasture/wetlands. He 'tamed' part of the Ngaere wetlands near Eltham and Stratford and turned it into pasture. His ingenuity enabled him to push back the ecological frontiers of wood and water, turning forests into grasslands and making wetlands dry, to join with the ranks of already assembled pasture-based farms in the Taranaki.

The Glenn Rd farm and its successors did everything that good farms should. They pushed back ecological frontiers, produced excellent grass and helped make James Campbell and his sons into farmers who were celebrated for their productivity and their roles as leading exemplars in new 'scientific' farming techniques. They were also lauded for the simultaneous devotion of economic and political capital to building up local farming infrastructure, such as the formation of local dairy cooperatives, the establishment of a box factory to pack dairy products, directing a meat processing company and service on local government organizations improving roading infrastructure. Local histories sing their praises in exactly these terms.[111]

Futures that never happened and the one that did

All this work that resulted in the pushing back of forest and wetland frontiers to create grasslands for grazing sheep and cattle might, with the benefit of hindsight, seem to have sent New Zealand down one deterministic path to the stable farming world that emerged after the 1920s. But colonization is an exercise in multiplicity: many other futures were possible.

The Māori world of land-use had already adapted once to its own chaotic earlier period of colonization and frontier exploitation. The resulting world of stable land-use had no frontiers and prioritized marine resources, forests and wetlands. Their cultivation systems took some slopes in fertile river valleys and terraced them into gardens, but the abundant productivity of the other landscapes meant that there was no logic in removing forests and wetlands.

The arrivals of Tasman and Cook set many things in motion. There were many possible futures for New Zealand, roads that were never taken and opportunities that were never grasped. Governor Grey advocated from the mid-1840s that New Zealand had the potential to support citrus, olives, silkworms and wine production in its sunnier northern regions. Others contemplated the potential of tea. Māori use of wetlands supported several other options: trade in flax had the potential to meet huge market demand for marine cordage around the British Empire at that time. An alternative use of flax, producing linen and linseed, was also available. Eels, which thrived in the wetlands, were a feature of British diets and could be preserved for transportation. New Zealand also had abundant forest resources that were initially milled and felled for lumber and shipping spars, until the point at which land hunger by settlers turned forests from a resource into an impediment that had to be felled and burned. Finally, around New Zealand's abundant coastlines were enormous marine resources that were only being narrowly exploited for seal pelts and whale oil. The teeming blue cod of New Zealand's southern shoreline alone were abundant enough to create the potential for New Zealand to become established as the salt cod supplier to much of this part of the globe.

All these alternative futures never happened. They fell by the wayside as grasslands farms, one by one, conducted their frontier work, both enclosing the landscape and taking over New Zealand's economic future. By pushing back the ecological frontiers of wetlands, indigenous grasslands and forests, many potential futures could no longer happen, and convergence on a future based almost entirely on exotic grasslands became an increasingly singular reality.[112]

My narrative of two clusters of colonial farms shows how these farms contributed to enacting particular kinds of futures and particular kinds of farmers, eventually converging on a specific kind of farming reality. They all initially enacted a multiplicity of possible futures, ranging from cooperation with Māori to outright resistance to indigenous New Zealand. They produced a variety of new crops, some of which didn't last; they didn't persist with other seemingly obvious options like linen from flax or cultivating eels in wetlands; they created farmed spaces, homes, new reputations and histories; and they moved through highly unstable zones of settlement like the Waikato and Howick during wartime, Dunedin in the gold rush and the opening of bushland around Taranaki during the great burning (and draining). By the 1920s, however, all these farms were becoming more similar and, in hindsight, had similar effects. They had breached frontiers, colonized the resulting spaces, stabilized many outcomes (if not, as yet, ecologies) and converged on one particular future.

At this point, it is appropriate to pause and consider how the agency of farms during the chaos of colonization can be understood as enacting an ontological politics. As articulated in Chapter 1, scholars like Mario Blaser elaborated the ontological politics of colonization in Latin America as a clash between indigeneity and modernity played out at the level of reality itself. They question what became invisible and what became visible in the expression of ontological powers during colonization. In my account, the colonial farm in New Zealand became an 'engine of destruction'[113] – making some things take shape while causing the disappearance of other worlds.

This happened in two highly significant and inter-related ways: through the marginalization of indigenous land-use and the decimation of indigenous ecology. These were not the only erasures and silencings taking place, but they were the two that are most revealing of the ontological power of farms in colonized landscapes.

Erasing indigenous land-use

Heather's Homestead/Marotahei participated in the collaborative economy and for fifteen years enacted an alternative collaborative future for New Zealand. In contrast, the other farms in this narrative had amazing powers of erasure; enacting not only the erasure of Māori as the original users of the landscape, they also erased much of the unsatisfactory past of the new Pākehā owners.

This ability to magically erase indigenous land-use has profound ontological effects and, once the collaborative economy is in decline, is central to all that follows. There is a cultural depth to Māori relations with land that is hard to translate, by which kinship is deeply central to both Māori social organization and human connections to the land.[114]

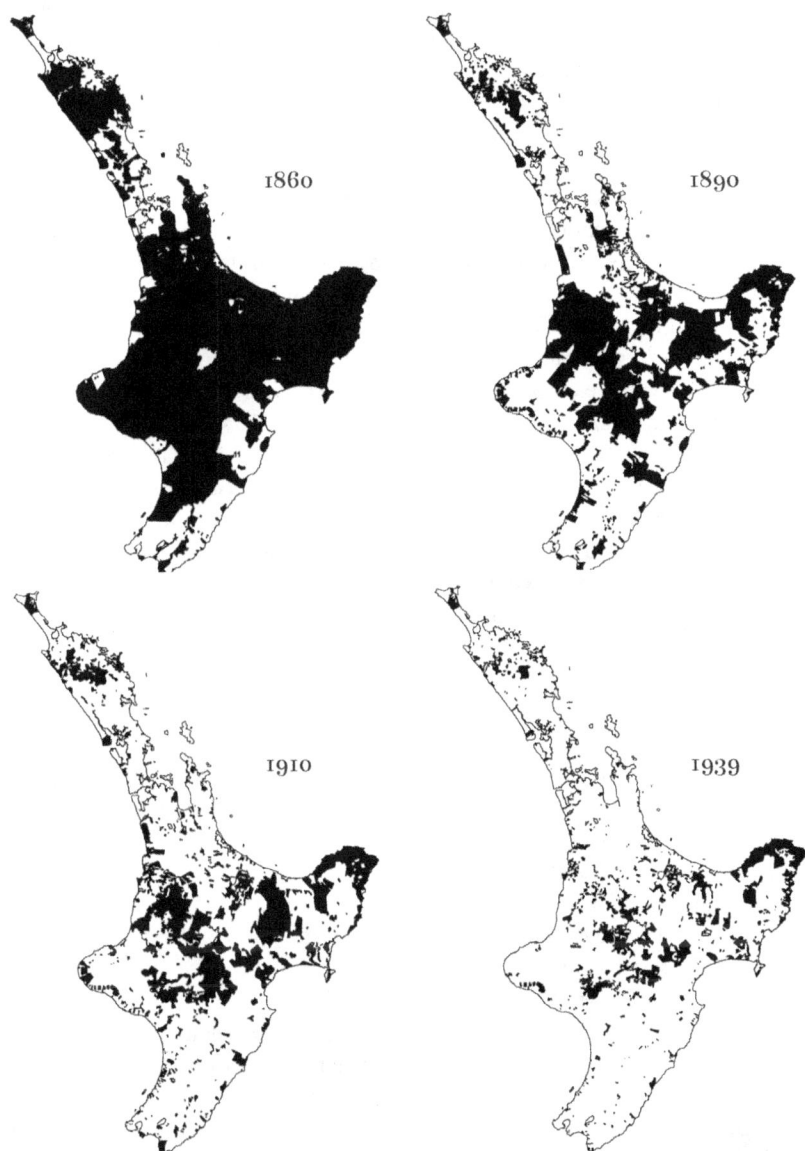

Map 3 Māori land loss, 1860–1939
Source: Waitangi Tribunal

In the next chapter, I will examine at length how this broad and complex relationship between humans and the land was ruptured, segmented and bounded by Pākehā land-use patterns, and in particular, the way that Pākehā farms acted to ontologically divide the landscape.

This leads directly to a second element of erasure of indigenous land-use – the transformation of formal property rights. While Māori land-ownership was unable to be entirely eradicated, Māori were left, by the 1920s, on a tiny residuum of land held in fractured titles under multiple ownership (see Map 3).[115] As I will show in the next chapter, even this remnant was hounded for most of the twentieth century to come into conformity with 'normal' modernist land ownership and practices. Parcel by parcel, fenceline by fenceline, name by name, the great interior of New Zealand was encapsulated into privately owned farms. This transition into private ownership created an uncontestable outcome. Once the frontier had been extended, the private ownership of land replaced older styles of human kinship with land, breaking the boundaryless ties of social and kinship obligation stretching from immediate family (whānau) to sub-tribe (hapū) to tribe (iwi) and beyond, with principles of utu (balance) that balanced gifting, obligations and the need for restitution and revenge.[116] This deeply interconnected social and ecological world, that situated land as a participant within much wider systems of connection and obligation, was incrementally replaced by Pākehā farms that rendered invisible the older ties and bonds.[117]

Decimating indigenous ecology

Alfred Crosby's classic work of environment history, which traces the global expansion of 'portmanteau ecologies' from Britain during colonization, devotes an entire chapter to New Zealand.[118] He considered New Zealand to be the perfect colonial exemplar of an ecological 'neo-Europe'.

The story of the Campbell farms told in this chapter captures the pivotal moment when ecological frontiers between indigenous Aotearoa and 'neo-Europe' were breached through the agency of farms. These farms are the frontier agents that turn forests into grasslands and make wetlands dry, anchoring those changes in semi-permanent form (see Map 4).

Looking back from the high perch of modernity, the colonial history of New Zealand, if it became visible at all, was written at the time as demonstrating progress from unproductive and 'wasteful' pre-modernity to productive, rational and controlled modernity. This backward glance edits out a fundamental truth of ecological colonization: it is chaotic, de-stabilizing and triggers consequences that are never fully resolvable.[119] As Nigel Clark argues, the colonization of New Zealand was not a linear or predictable process. It actually involved unpredictability and 'ferality'.[120] Some of the parties didn't behave as intended. Grass seeds may have been the agents of 'improvement' that transformed burned forests into farmable grasslands, but within a couple of decades the new de-forested landscapes proved to be highly unstable, undermined from below by collapsing soil structure and threatened above ground by rampant introduced pests, such as rabbits. The early history of colonial farming is not

Current extent   Pre-colonization extent

Current extent   Pre-colonization extent

Map 4 The wetland frontier
Source: Manaaki Whenua - Landcare Research

cool and rational progress; it resembles a rapidly nailed-together and rickety bridge of grass perched over an ecological abyss of its own creation.

This insight brings us to a turning point in this argument. The first set of dynamics exposed within the ontological politics of farms during colonization is the extent to which they push back frontiers and render invisible indigenous worlds. The second is to grasp what is then assembled into those voids and silences. Each time an ecological frontier is breached, it unleashes ecological (and at times political and social) chaos and disruption. Frontiers are both sites of new value creation and of unstable ferality. The transition from colonial to modernist farming in New Zealand rises from an imposition of systems of control and boundary-setting, attempting to impose order and coherence in these chaotic spaces. In the next chapter, I will explore how the triumphant dawn of a 'golden age' of pastoral family farming is not the result of a rational evolution of cultural order over unpredictable nature: it is the creation of 'order' in delimited spaces, inside defended boundaries, with careful circumscribing of responsibilities and obligations. It is a narrow and mechanistic world composed of that-which-is-able-to-be-stabilized within the chaos of ruptured ecosystems, unstable soils, rampant pests, and wider social inequalities and conflicts. In essence, modernist farming becomes dominant because farms create boundaries that can (albeit temporarily) stabilize this chaos; they become a site of self-mythologization; they assemble a newer, simpler order of knowledge, objects, relationships and potentials; and they do so by rendering invisible the multiplicity of other indigenous worlds (both past and future) while assembling a new, more homogeneous, object in their place.

If I reflect on where this enquiry began – in my own lived experience of a pastoral family farm in the early 1970s – this was the invisible world that surrounded the visible world of my daily farm life. The historical silence and amnesia around indigenous land-use and decimation of landscape ecology in colonial New Zealand are the secret chapter in the nation's history that, once opened, renders visible other worlds that actually needed to remain invisible in order for modernist farming to exist in a politically settled state. The most singular achievement of the 'golden age' of New Zealand farming, as narrated in the next chapter, is that it managed to maintain exactly this kind of settled and pacified state for most of the twentieth century. And the agent at the centre of this pacified world is my enduring object of interest – the modernist farm.

Notes

1   Te Rangi Hiroa (1938) dubbed them 'Vikings of the Sunrise', thus recognizing Polynesian seafaring and navigating as one of the remarkable achievements of all humankind.

2   As a name, 'Aotearoa' was not universally used, and has only relatively recently become generally accepted as the generic Māori name for the new land.

3   King (2003) writes that by the sixteenth century, the importance of hunting had diminished and gardening and foraging had increased – particularly around the key root vegetable crop kūmara – and became the anchor of settled, more tribally organized society: 'Like colonisers elsewhere, the East Polynesian ancestors and their immediate descendants had learned, by trial and error and committing some major

mistakes, to turn New Zealand's natural environment to human advantage. They thus managed to survive as a viable population and ... to convert an imported culture into a tangata or indigenous one with recognisable antecedents in East Polynesia but now connected inextricably to the roots and soil of New Zealand' (2003: 76–7).

4   Belich (1996: 117).

5   This meeting of worlds lies at the heart of the extensive historical work of Dame Anne Salmond – ranging from *Between Worlds* (1997) to *Tears of Rangi* (2017).

6   This ontologically fracturing moment is the subject of some important histories: notably by Salmond (e.g. 1997, 2017) as well as the less well-known but superb meditative ecological history by Geoff Park (1995).

7   The extent to which Polynesian styles of horticulture were successfully adapted to create a successful base for Māori settlement is recounted in Leach (1984) *1000 Years of Gardening in New Zealand*.

8   A useful summation of the major debates over early Māori settlement, deforestation and the extinction of the moa can be found in Anderson (2002).

9   As Leach (1984) elaborates, the distinction between horticulture and agriculture implies a division of activity that is inappropriately Euro-centric when applied to land and resource-use by Polynesian societies. Villages had extensive gardens, but also tended to be at river mouths, and a combination of marine abundance and cultivation of tubers provided the twin pillars of Māori existence. The metaphor of the 'garden' is used to deliberately signify that Māori are fed by a poly-culture (as distinct from the separations implicit in the terms agri-culture and horti-culture).

10 As historian James Belich quips: 'Tasman found, but he did not look very hard nor tell very well, and in discovery the telling is as important as the finding' (Belich 1996: 120).

11 Historian J. Beaglehole, best known for his examination of Cook's copious journals, indicates that these observations were apparent from the first weeks of Cook's arrival in New Zealand. When they sailed away after his first visit, Beaglehole noted that the encounter left Cook 'with admiration, not merely for the face of the new country – its timber, its evident fertility, its promise for settlement – but for its inhabitants' (1974: 223).

12 The voice of Cook's famous naturalist Joseph Banks was equally influential. Brooking and Pawson (2011: 14–15) recount Banks's logical interpretation of the lushness of the New Zealand forest signifying highly fertile soil that: 'promisd [*sic*] great returns to the people who would take the trouble of Clearing it'. Banks directed his gaze towards this forest in a crucial voyage into the Waihou River mouth in the Hauraki Gulf – and event that is recounted extensively for its importance in the accounts of both Park (1995: 33–5) and Salmond (1997: 241–51).

13 One important ontological transition is how to name the two peoples in this place. Before colonial contact, the indigenous inhabitants of Aotearoa identified themselves as members of different tribes. The generic term 'Māori' only arose as a result of the necessity to create a collective identity due to the arrival of a new people. At the same time, the generic name Pākehā created a term for all the variety of non-Māori emigrés arriving to create New Zealand.

14 Belich (1996: 121–9) surveys these other possible futures. Along with King (2003) he argues that the signing of the Treaty of Waitangi was directly spurred by the possible claiming of part of New Zealand by France. Another option was that New Zealand could form an extension of the Australian penal colonies (an idea that was abandoned due to the political strength and fighting abilities of Māori). Another dire

possibility was that introduced diseases would kill most Māori (and the survivors would be seamlessly assimilated into European society): Europeans would eventually have to 'smooth the pillow of a dying race' (Belich 1996: 174). As the following narrative will show, New Zealand is a colonized space where many potential futures would eventually fail to happen.

15 It is a source of slight sadness that in his magisterial review of the role of the potato in world history, Redcliffe Salaman was not aware of the transformative, and at times dreadful, role of the potato in New Zealand history (Salaman, 1949).

16 Leach (1984: 98–101).

17 Leach (1984: 102). Every other successful introduction involved plants that were either immediately suited to Māori gardening practices, or fitted the cultural patterns of Māori diet. Cultivating wheat began to enact a new farming ontology. It required a new cropping system and new technologies to be processed, and it had the one quality that would make it central to Pākehā farming in the second half of the nineteenth century – it was durable for long distance transport and would eventually become the centerpiece of a global-scale regime of trade (Friedmann, 1978). It will also become, for half a century, New Zealand's second most important plant in Pākehā farming systems. The first will be grass.

18 King (2003: 115–30); McAloon (2002).

19 Belich (1996: 156–69); King (2003: 132–5).

20 As Belich (1996: 159) characterizes it, potatoes could be grown over a wider geographical area and weren't subject to the same cultural sanctions and constraints as kūmara.

21 Stokes (2002: 41–3); McAloon (2002); Belich (1996: 130–4).

22 The signing of the Treaty, as with some of the retrospective analysis of James Cook, holds out the possibility that there can be a shared colonial space with a partnership between Māori and Pākehā (Belich 1996; King 2003; O'Malley et al. 2010; Salmond 2017). The failure of New Zealand to take that path is implied to be a lapse in Enlightenment intellect, national character, trust and political integrity. Taking a more ontological and material view, these events are consequential, but their results are mediated by many parties and objects.

23 As Dame Evelyn Stokes argues, the Treaty is usually understood as transacting citizenship and sovereignty. In reality, it was just as important that it legally established transaction of land (Stokes 1992, 2002).

24 Belich (1996: 192).

25 A tree gum/resin (copal) that was used for jewellery and varnishes.

26 Wynn (2002: 108).

27 Roche (1990).

28 Nowhere is this new gaze more compellingly narrated than in opening chapters of Park (1995).

29 Mintz (1985).

30 Goodman (2005).

31 Ó'Gráda (1993), Salaman (1949).

32 Tannahill (1973).

33 Friedmann and McMichael (1989).

34 Brooking (1996: 16–17).

35 Gurney (2009).

36 Ó'Gráda (1993), Salaman (1949).

37 Lawrence (1987), McMichael (1984).

38 Davis (2002).

39 Belich (2009), Cronon (1991).

40 There is a solid lineage of important histories of food tracing the emergence of global-scale production and consumption of food for the Industrial Revolution. Foreshadowed by Wolf (1982) the template was established by Sid Mintz's (1985) study of sugar. Later followers in this tradition like Moore (2000), Davis (2002) and Cronon (1991) widened the focus to include environmental transformations and/or the power of new technologies of transportation and communication for creating a world of trade. Friedmann and McMichael (1989) bring these together in their concept of historical 'food regimes'.

41 Belich (2009: 23): 'Settlement, the third form of European expansion, emphasized the creation of new societies, not the control of old ones. It had no moral superiority over empire. Indeed, it tended to displace, marginalize, and occasionally even exterminate indigenous peoples rather than simply exploit them. But it did reach further and last longer than empire … It was settlement, not empire, that had the spread and staying power in the history of European expansion, and it is time that historians of that expansion turned their attention to it.'

42 King (2003: 169).

43 An idea that had enough intellectual currency that Karl Marx saw the need to consider and then dismiss it in Volume 1 of *Capital*.

44 Salmond (2017: 326–7).

45 Brooking and Pawson (2011: 8–9).

46 As my colleague Anaru Eketone reminded me, this was entirely pointed in the specific direction of Māori land, since land that was occupied by Pākehā was automatically considered productive even if left idle.

47 Pawson and Brooking (2011: 12).

48 By moving the centre of gaze from the human actors, agents and institutions to the biophysical environment, a radically and creatively different way of understanding colonization appears (e.g, Crosby 1986; Pawson and Brooking 2002; Brooking and Pawson 2011). This aligns with a wider shift in post-colonial history (see Ballantyne 2011) away from human agencies and towards inclusion of the agencies of environments, objects and materials (e.g. Cooper et al. 2015).

49 Two key collections are Pawson and Brooking (2002) and Brooking and Pawson (2011), which incorporate the work of their close collaborators including historians (Paul Star, Vaughan Wood), historically inclined geographers (Graeme Wynn, Michael Roche, Peter Holland), and indigenous scholars and prehistorians (Jim Williams, Athol Anderson, Helen Leach).

50 Even one farm can become a life's work of writing and reflection. Environmental historians celebrate as foundational to their trade the story of a single farm in colonial New Zealand: *Tutira: The story of a New Zealand sheep station* (1921) by Herbert Guthrie-Smith. It is a lovingly detailed tale, but takes nearly 500 pages to tell!

51 In 1843 the census records him as a farmer, with a return of produce for the same year showing him having a quarter of an acre in potatoes, three-quarters of an acre in wheat, one acre in crops and three acres being grazed. He had two horses and cattle and it is recorded that he produced 201 bushels of wheat and two tons of potatoes. He had engaged a 'horse-breaker' and applied for a publican's licence (pers. com. Peter Wakeman).

52 Belich (1986: 37) describes this is a scene of unbounded panic.

53 The mid-1840s were important to the emerging regulation of (post-slavery) passenger transport as the global shipping trade began to absorb the flood of outmigrants from Britain, particularly from the Irish Potato Famine, including the infamous 'coffin ships' to North America.

54   The emergence and attempted consolidation of the King Movement in the Waikato after
     1858 – the Kīngitanga – is an important moment in Māori history and attempts to create
     alternative, more autonomous, political powers and stop sales of land. It is recounted at
     length in King (2003: 212–15), Belich (1996: 230–45) and Stokes (2002: 48).

55   Unaiki is known only by her first name as declared in Dennett's will. But local Māori
     genealogists are sure that she is Unaiki Te Watarauhi of Ngāti Tamainupo.

56   The original of this map is held at Archives New Zealand *Te Rua Mahara o te
     Kāwanatanga*. Among the notes on the map is the statement: 'Present at the survey
     Mr Heather + his natives'.

57   The name Marotahei doesn't have an obvious translation but may mean 'the place to
     snare birds'.

58   The farm is on the edges of Rangiaowhia, which Belich (1986: 160–5) describes as
     one of the three most important Māori agricultural regions in the Waikato.

59   Belich (1996: 215) recounts that in 1848, Māori were the largest purveyors of foodstuffs
     to Auckland; in 1853 there were around 2,000 canoes bringing goods into Auckland.

60   It is a big farm of 170 acres, according to this title, which would likely have been issued
     retrospectively under the terms of the highly contentious 'Waste Lands Act of 1858'
     (Brooking 1996: 41). This Act was the first attempt to legally classify Māori land as
     'wasted' or 'unproductive' and thus eligible for sale by regional governments to arriving
     settlers (Stokes 2002; 48–9), which would have made the pre-existing (non-wasteful and
     highly productive) Heather's Homestead/Marotahei an exception – even an anomaly.

61   Some good insight into what was being grown on the farm comes from later war
     correspondents accompanying the invading army of British troops, who noted of
     the area around Heather's Homestead: 'There was a fine paddock of wheat here, and
     extensive patches of Indian corn, which afforded abundant food for the horses of the
     mounted artillery, Colonial Defence Force, etc … There were but few peach trees,
     and the fruit far from ripe. The same may be said of the watermelons. Extensive
     pieces of ground appeared to have been used for growing potatoes, and though the
     best seemed to have been carried off by the Maoris, a pretty moderate quantity were
     collected by those of the soldiers who felt disposed and had the leisure to engage in
     potatoe digging. The soil, though somewhat light, appeared of very good quality for
     root crops.' *Daily Southern Cross*, 4 February 1864.

62   In the later compensation hearing to assign value to what was lost in the subsequent
     destruction of the farm, Dennett provides this account of his farm: 'Claimant
     stated that he was a settler at Waipa, and was obliged to abandon his homestead in
     the month of August, 1863. His farm consisted of 170 acres, 70 of which were in
     grass. He claimed £100 for non occupation of house and farm; £500, destruction
     of dwelling-house, furniture, books, pictures, linen, etc …; £100, detached kitchen
     and utensils; £140, value of outbuildings; £27, sawn timber; £19 10s., posts and rails;
     £300, destruction of orchard, containing 500 trees; £176 25., 557 rods of fencing;
     £30, crops and stores; £30, 3 bridges destroyed, £120, cattle and sheep; £15, poultry;
     £8, pigs; £80, for compulsory non-occupation; £35, cost of removal of family; £200,
     forest of 30 acres of kahikatea trees destroyed by fire; and 2 canoes, £15' (*Daily
     Southern Cross*, 12 April 1865).

63   Dennett became a regular correspondent with the Colonial Secretary and the
     Governor, passing on his advice and other important information both prior to and
     after the invasion, and his letters signalled that his information came from deep
     inside the Kīngitanga – almost certainly via Unaiki and her kin. The *Cyclopedia of
     New Zealand* (1902) also mentions that his son Arthur Heather attended a later

meeting of government and 'disaffected natives' in order to assist with translation and understanding between the parties.

64   While the causes of the invasion of the Waikato by British troops are an area of significant discussion by historians, Belich (1986: 76–80) cites 'land hunger' as an important cause (as do Wood et al. 2008). However, he also identifies a less clear-cut set of problems that war was intended to solve. Until 1860, the Crown did not enjoy 'substantive sovereignty' over most of New Zealand, even if the Treaty of Waitangi gave it 'formal sovereignty'. Belich (1986: 778) records that after 1848, British sovereignty over Māori districts remained 'more nominal than real … The Treaty did not, in hindsight, wave a magic wand and achieve substantive sovereignty. It had to be achieved piecemeal and by multiple means and contests. Including outright war in the Taranaki and Waikato.'

65   For the martially curious, the military engagement at Paterangi is discussed at length in Belich (1996: 160–5).

66   'At last a hill was reached facing Mr. Heather's house which gave us a good view of Pikopiko where the rebel flags were waving. As the troops came up in single file, they were formed into a column. The nature of the country could be divined and steps were taken to see if the enemy was lurking in some advanced position to intercept the further progress of the force. As the General and his staff rode up to the top of the hill a few Māori scouts became manifest. Mr. Heather's house was quickly set on fire by the enemy, who must have been stationed there on the lookout. The flames burned with a strongly lurid glare as seen at a distance, under such a broiling sun' (*Daily Southern Cross*, 4 February 1864).

67   Dennett was distraught at the loss of his farm and recounted that Māori in the area had promised not to torch the farm as long as General Cameron did not use it to shelter troops. In a letter, his affective bond with his farm is clear: 'I have been favoured the perusal of a letter from an army officer (illegible) at the front to a friend of mine, wherein he states the distressing news that not only my dwelling house has been burnt, but all the outhouses including a detached weatherboard house of two rooms, with loft over head, that all my fences have been taken away from their (illegible), stockyards in fact everything they could lay their hands. My fine orchard which has taken nine years to bring to perfection and all the trees having fruit have been cut down or otherwise destroyed. I may here remark that only a month back the natives informed me that if the General did not approach by my farm it would not be burnt. Their reason given that they will leave no buildings for him to occupy, however this may be – my loss is a severe and (illegible) – not having the health and strength to face it again, to do as I have hitherto. In fact I am quite an invalid.' Correspondence, D.H. Heather to F. Whittaker, Onehunga, February 1864.

68   The sundering of Pākehā-Māori marriages attacked what Belich (1996:249) describes as the 'marriage alliance' that had been a core element of the collaborating Māori-Pākehā world in the nineteenth century. Belich (1996: 254) describes the invasion of the Waikato as fracturing many such marriages.

69   Her father Watarauhi was a leading member of the Christian Pacifist community of Karakariki nearby, which sat as a Waikato variant of the better-known 'peace village' of Parihaka in Taranaki (Eketone 2020). Unaiki Te Watarauhi was named as a petitioner to the Native Land Court in 1889, and her death was recorded in 1925, meaning that she lived to around ninety years of age. She also married twice more.

70   His later correspondence suggests he had plans to return to the Waikato which keeps open the possibility of a return to Unaiki. Local Māori elders consider it unusual,

at that time, that she was named in his will which potentially signals a strong attachment between them.

71 Amongst his many claims, Belich's (1996) most influential revision of New Zealand history is that the wars of the north in the 1840s did not really result in victory for the British Crown (as was generally claimed) but established large concessions and facilitated compromise with Māori from 1847 to the early 1860s (not coincidentally, a close match to the period of existence of Heather's Homestead/Marotahei).

72 *Auckland Weekly News*, 19 August 1865, to the sum of £767.

73 The specific terms of the Fencible's Gift in relation to their farm were: 'On arriving in New Zealand each Pensioner [Fencible] will be put in possession of a cottage of two rooms with an acre of ground, one fourth of which will be cleared and made ready for cultivation … An advance of money to provide articles … and stock as may be required.' (Blake 1983: 13).

74 Salaman (1949) describes many of the subsistence peasant farms of Ireland in the early nineteenth century as comprising eleven-month leases of one-eighth of an acre – enough to grow a sufficiency of potatoes (until the famine) and a pig. In their history of the Fencibles, Alexander et al. (1997: 9) specifically identify the appeal of owning land for retired soldiers from peasant backgrounds – particularly those from Ireland.

75 This set an important precedent for one of the main attractions of serving in the colonial armies in New Zealand: the subsequent gift of farmland. 'Soldier settlement' schemes commenced with the Fencibles, continued through the wars of the 1860s (hundreds of General Cameron's troops were rewarded with farmland in the conquered Waikato), and continued through the First and Second World Wars. Members of my own family accessed farmland this way.

76 Various ships bringing Fencibles and their families departed from different regions of Britain. The tale of famine is mutely witnessed in the arriving passenger manifesto of the *Sir Robert Sale*, which sailed from Cork in August 1847. The ship experienced heavy loss of life due to the dire health of the passengers from Ireland in the year immediately after the famine (Alexander et al. 1997: 52).

77 Alexander et al. (1997: 9).

78 Alexander et al. (1997: 67).

79 An observation that was also made by William Fox in his account of colonial life, *The Six Colonies of New Zealand* (Fox 1851).

80 Joining the flow of goods into Auckland from the south, including, by the time the Fencibles were settled in Howick, goods flowing down the rivers from Heather's Homestead/Marotahei and the Māori farms of Rangiaowhia.

81 Criticism of the unsuitable location of the villages, the drunkenness of the retired soldiers and the fact that they never really provided a military use are recounted both in the local newspaper (*Daily Southern Cross*, 6 November 1874, reported in Alexander et al. 1997) and by future politician William Fox: 'Whether viewed in a military or a colonizing aspect, they are costly failures, affording a most decided warning against the continuance of the experiment' (Fox 1851: 43).

82 Belich (1996: 187–93).

83 Ned and Reine Roberts were strong proponents of the Rationalists movement. They didn't attend church and did believe in science.

84 It was not uncommon for Pākehā farms to adopt Māori names, but often in entirely de-contextualized form. 'Te Rahui' is literally (and prophetically!) translated as a place that has been captured by force, or placed under a ritual ban (often stemming from spiritual pollution, death, risk to conservation, or political sanction). It is a name that, for Māori,

signifies capture or warning of potential danger – depending on context. In my family history Te Rahui was, until recently, incorrectly thought to mean 'The Meeting Place'.

85   Belich (2009) spends considerable time considering this powerful dynamic in colonization, while not paying quite as much attention as I do to the material contribution of the farms themselves.

86   Dunedin is one of only a couple of 'Free Church of Scotland' colonies founded to provide refuge for the dissidents.

87   Respect is paid to her father James Jamieson in his obituary: 'The deceased was a man of great strength of mind and fixedness of purpose, which were strikingly evinced during some of the political and religious struggles in Bute, when he resisted very strong pressure, brought upon him to change his views … he gave the use of his barn for … meetings in spite of the threat that if he did so he would be ejected from his farm.' *The Buteman*, 18 March 1871.

88   At which point, the named farms in this narrative begin to accumulate: Clovernook, Te Rahui, Ashburn Estate, and it would be remiss to ignore the delightfully named (but likely equally stony) neighbouring Laing farm beside Ashburn called Overhillus which was felicitously situated for my Gt Grandfather James Campbell (Campbell Bros #2) to marry Isabella Laing.

89   These assets are all listed in the advertisement for sale of the property (*Otago Witness* 30 November 1878).

90   Clearly Ashburn worked as a site for enacting a particular style of psychiatric care. Stock and Brickell (2013) examine the nearby (and much larger) institution of Seacliff as being part of a move in the 1880s towards creating a healthy farm-style environment as a site of therapeutic care.

91   The setting is intrinsic to its claim as a therapeutic site. As one approving correspondent wrote a few months after the sale: 'The view from Ashburn Hall is very fine, embracing as it does all the principal suburbs of Dunedin, the harbour, the Peninsula, and a vast expanse of ocean. The back grounds are interlaced with the evergreen shrubberies peculiar to New Zealand, while underneath their shaded boughs the Ashburn [Stream] wimples past to lend her aid in the manufacture of flax carried on at the same estate' (*The Clutha Leader*, 13 October 1882).

92   Or, in the South Island, of indigenous tussock grasslands.

93   This new land also existed because of the drama of colonial land acquisition revealed in the first couplet of farms. These lands were becoming available because of war. The crushing of Māori resistance at Parihaka in November 1881 was the key event required to consolidate the confiscation of Parihaka and Waimate Plains lands in Taranaki and ended an important moment of Māori resistance to their rapid disposal by the Crown into the hands of settler farmers (and speculators like Archie Campbell).

94   He died relatively young in 1896, leaving a considerable estate of £27,000 – around NZ$5 million in contemporary prices. Enough for the rest of his siblings to carve up and fight over.

95   Later renamed Mt Taranaki.

96   James purchased an expensive polled Angus bull called Hatter (descended from the distinguished Erica family of Angus cattle bred by Sir George McPherson-Grant of Ballindalloch). According to local newspaper reports from agricultural shows in the early 1900s, Hatter stood at the head of a prizewinning string of polled Angus cattle. The J.J. Campbell prizewinners were the bulls Hatter, Cupbearer, Cavalier, Captain, Colonel, Cronje, Black Don, Darky, De Wett, Duke of York and the somewhat

eccentrically named Electrician. Prizewinning cows were Grand Duchess, Daisy Girl, Amy, Barbara, Baroness, Amelia, Countess, Cornelia, Chuddy, Cherry, Camellia and Belly Bawn.

97 The Taranaki region (like the Waikato) played a central role in the wars (Belich 1986).

98 Wynn (2002).

99 Wynn (2002: 106).

100 Rollo Arnold's (1994) history of the 1880s, *New Zealand's Burning: The Settlers' World in the Mid-1880s*, makes the great fires the centrepiece of his narrative.

101 This was close to some of the five family farms that would succeed Glenn Rd.

102 Holland et al. (2002: 72).

103 Arnold (1994).

104 Two of these were: the great difficulty in suddenly producing enough grass seed to sow all the newly burned land, and the difficulties in ploughing land full of tree roots, which meant that pasture was the only viable option rather than earlier farming styles based around vegetables and crops (recounted in Brooking and Pawson 2011: 23). The decay of those remnant forest root systems over the ensuing decades would help contribute towards a significant crisis of soil stability in the early-twentieth century. Through this whole transition, grass became the crucial agent of transformation and stabilization (worthy of an entire book – Brooking and Pawson 2011).

105 The following sequence is laid out in more detail in Brooking and Pawson (2002: 29–30).

106 Arnold (1994: 170) uses importing of wire for fencing as a key indicator of elaboration of pastoral farming systems. He estimates that in 1885 alone, enough wire was imported to provide 3765 miles of fences.

107 Star and Lochhead (2002: 119) open their chapter with Blanche Baughan's 1908 poem 'Burnt Bush': 'Naked, denuded,/Forestless, fernless,/Mute, now, and songless,/Sharp on sheer sky gape the lips of the gully;/Burden'd with black is the grass of its pasture;/On whose long slopes/The sheep in their browsing/Must leap o'er a million,/Strewn, helter-skelter, headlong and helpless/Burnt bones of the Bush …'.

108 Here, farm histories enter current memory. My father describes his early childhood involving Sunday lunches in which the post-lunch entertainment would be the chance to roam the farm with a box of matches and a roll of newspaper provided by his mother, burning scrub and gorse.

109 Park (1995, 2002). More recent estimates have updated this loss at over 90 per cent.

110 My father recalls as a nine-year-old, doing shifts driving the D2 Caterpillar bulldozing 'scrub' in long lines. He dozed off at the seat and drove the D2 into the swamp where it sat for several months, taxing the engineering ingenuity of multiple assembled scions of Campbell Bros to retrieve it.

111 Obituary of James Jamieson Campbell in the *Hawera and Normanby Star*, 18 April 1923: 'for many years he was one of Taranaki's best known farmers. A man of great public spirit, he was a prime mover in the formation of the Kaupokonui Dairy Company (the largest in New Zealand), and was chairman of directors for seven years. He was also one of the originators of the Egmont Box Company, being a director for many years, and a director of the Patea Freezing Company … He was particularly well known as a breeder of stock and cattle, and his house is adorned with many trophies won by him, one of the most valued being a magnificent cup presented by the president of the Egmont Agricultural and Pastoral Association in 1908 for the highest points in sheep, cattle and horses.' His wife Isabella Campbell didn't get quite so much recognition for her role in

the success of the farm. The *New Zealand Herald* (26 June 1925) noted simply in her later obituary, 'Mrs Campbell arrived in New Zealand about 67 years ago and during her married life resided for 30 years in Taranaki, where Mr Campbell was engaged in dairying.'

112 By concentrating on my family farm histories, one geographical gap in this narrative is the other great ecological frontier that was breached and colonized by colonial farming: the great uplands of indigenous grasses and, in particular, tussock ecologies. There is an entire literature on the indigenous grasslands (reviewed by Holland et al. 2002) and the chaos that resulted from the breaching of the indigenous grass frontier.

113 A phrase that was used by Sir Hugh Kawharu to characterize another great colonial destroyer – the actions of the Native Land Court: 'a veritable engine of destruction for any tribe's tenure of land' (Kawharu 1977: 17). The idea that land laws and legal processes became key agents of destruction of indigenous land-use is an important one in colonial history across the globe. For the United States, the Dawes Act (1887) is attributed with similar powers to those which Kawharu identifies in various stratagems in New Zealand in the same period, with its overt intention to move Native Americans towards 'normal' land-use as farmers of privately titled land (and 'surplus' land redistributed for sale in the same way that 'waste' land was in New Zealand). The further elaboration of these legal systems and frameworks to 'settle' Native American's into 'normal' farming is described by Brewer and Stock (2016) (see also Brewer and Dennis (2019)).

114 This level of connectivity to land (and its expression in Māori ontology), constituted in relations of kinship across human and non-human worlds, is a core element of Anne Salmond's important revisionist account of New Zealand history (Salmond 2017).

115 Brooking (1996: 131–56).

116 Salmond (2017).

117 This is also an important dynamic in the wider rise of environmentalism in New Zealand. There was mounting concern in Pākehā New Zealand about the environmental costs of colonization, but, as Star and Lochhead (2002) describe it, there was an almost total focus on preserving the 'indigenous remnant' during the decades around 1900 rather than critiquing the farming estate. This indigenous remnant would become the subject of considerable concern and provide the platform for the creation of national parks, but, as Geoff Park recounts (Park 1999) even as some of the landscape was being 'reserved and preserved', the farms that took over the majority of the landscape remained immune to criticism – a state of affairs, as the next chapter will show, that held until near the end of the twentieth century.

118 Crosby (1986).

119 As Australian anthropologist Deborah Rose describes it: 'A further consequence [of colonization] is catastrophe. New World settler societies loosen moral accountability from the powerful constraints of place and time … In detaching people from continuity in place they also loosen people from the feedback of time … Detached from organized moral accountability in two of the most fundamental domains of human life, New World settler societies generate catastrophe' (Rose 2004: 5–6).

120 Clark (1999: 136): 'European expansion, both in its own self-understanding and in critical confrontations, has tended to be understood as the imposition of a new order, the linear expansion, for better or worse, of a regime of intentionality, intelligence, gathering and control. What we might draw … is the germ of another history: one that takes account of the unruly side of this outward movement – the viral, the profligate, the uncontainable effects.'

3

From colonial to modernist farming

Chapter 2 described the particular powers and agencies of the colonial farm, particularly in its role as the key site of interface between European and indigenous worlds. In some places, the farm was a site of collaborative experimentation, holding out the prospects of collaborative futures between Māori and Pākehā. As the nineteenth century unfolded, however, the farm increasingly became an agent of destruction of indigenous worlds, breaching political and ecological frontiers, and eradicating the possibility of those other futures. This colonial story is a tale full of drama and destruction. Conquest and chaos reside in close proximity, and farms are a key agent forging through the burning fires and drained wetlands to converge on one political and economic future.

From this crucible of colonial destruction and de-stabilization, something remarkable and curious emerges: a passive world of pastoral farms, seemingly devoid of politics, characterized only by its technical components, its scientific rationalities and inhabited by a seemingly increasingly homogenous culture of white family farmers. This transition from chaos to passivity is challenging to narrate. It demands answers to questions such as: How did such a world forget its history? How did it rapidly become so politically settled and uncontested? And how did all thought of alternatives disappear? It is, in short, the story of how farming transitioned from being colonial to being modern.

This transition lies at the heart of New Zealand's farm history and sets a compelling challenge that I will attempt to address in this chapter. In becoming modern, much of what had previously been seen as important to farms began to be erased as insignificant, backward or irrelevant. At some point around the 1920s, farms in New Zealand began to be narrated in both popular discourse and more academic discussion in ways that ceased to recognize any deep colonial past. Instead, farms and the farming economy were 'rendered technical' and 'rendered economic'. They were increasingly represented by an academic narrative about the technical triumphs of the emerging discipline of agricultural science. Farms were accordingly celebrated as the providers of an endless stream of food and fibre products that collectively underpinned the rising economic prosperity and political success of the new nation state of New Zealand.

This growing technical and economic narrative of the farm also played a role in a particular, and highly selective, characterization of New Zealand's national history. Farms became modern in ways that reflected the wider creation of a modern capitalist world, but also, in crucial ways, helped to enact that modernist world in places like New Zealand.

Invisible worlds: Narrating the 'golden age' of farming in New Zealand

In my childhood, my parents and grandparents' generation would talk of a 'golden age' of New Zealand farming. This self-narrating of farm history stretched from the origins of our own family's farms in their modern form in the decades either just before or after the 1920s (leaving anything prior to that moment as a casualty of historical amnesia), surviving the Great Depression, and then assisting the world and the 'mother country' with farm-boy soldiers and food to support the war effort (and subsequent rationing). Having passed through this passage of trial and tested virtue, farming entered its golden age in the decades after the Second World War, experiencing prosperity and legitimacy in measures that lived long in the nostalgic memories of farmers during later periods of trial. This nostalgia strongly permeated my own on-farm education in the 1970s and is recognizable across many narratives generated in farming worlds in New Zealand. In this telling, the virtuous, scientific and economically successful family farm became both central to a rising narrative of a successful nation state and an exemplar to other farmers around the British Empire.[1] The story also came to what seems to be an abrupt halt in 1973 with the 'great betrayal', as Britain entered into its first major trading relationship with Europe and ended New Zealand's privileges as an ex-colony.

There are varying emphases in the many academic narratives that tell the story of this golden age of modern farming, which stretched from the early twentieth century to the betrayal of 1973. Some emphasize the rising power of the pastoral farming economy (see Table 1),[2] others a rising political class of family farmers.[3] Still others tell a resounding narrative of the triumph of agricultural science in rendering farming both highly productive and profitable after the 1920s,[4] and most of them note the strong relationship that was forged between the state, the farming economy and science institutions.

This is an important sweep of New Zealand's history and deserves a more considered history of the modern farm, particularly in ways that bring the status of New Zealand as a colonized countryside back into view. And the first place in which such a considered history should begin its narrative is in briefly considering the popular history of farming during its golden age.

In a farming world where historical amnesia was operating to such a profound level, the opportunity presented itself for a new cultural narrative to emerge among pastoral family farmers. Through the mid-twentieth century, Pākehā family farmers became excellent self-mythologizers. My grandparents were not alone in telling a particular kind of story about their origins and virtues. Commencing in the 1950s, a specialist genre of 'farm autobiographies' became popular in New Zealand. They were usually first-person accounts of people's lives on pastoral farms set in the key decades of the golden age.[6] Rural sociologist Alison Loveridge is struck both by the popularity of these tales and by the strong thematic similarities across the genre.[7] Repeated themes were as follows: living on farms was tough and challenging, but ultimately rewarding. Farms became worthy by becoming productive and the productivity of new farming systems demonstrated their worthiness as farmer occupants of the land.[8]

Table 1 Pastoral power: 1895–1967

	Pastoral export value[5]	Pastoral export earnings as a percentage of total exports
1895	£6,008,314	70
1899	£8,009,736	67
1903	£8,804,868	64
1907	£15,243,728	77
1911	£14,750,558	77.5
1915	£26,534,608	83.6
1919	£48,611,240	90.7
1923	£41,902,411	92
1927	£44,207,037	93
1931	£32,112,634	91
1935	£42,509,660	91
1939	£53,725,433	93
1943	£60,989,458	86.8
1947	£120,342,000	94.2
1951	£239,137,000	97.1
1955	£246,093,000	95.7
1959	£273,271,000	93.9
1963	£289,850,000	93.5
1967	£322,790,500	90

Source: New Zealand Yearbook

But farming was also intrinsically social; it created and relied upon deep bonds of family and also nurtured great farming skills and ingenuity. Farm women (the usual authors of these books) were intrepid, undertook multiple roles, cooperated with other farm women, and helped their dynamic farming husbands make their farms into special places, full of scenic beauty and replete with high levels of farming skill, while being excellent stewards of the land.[9] A key theme suggested that pastoral family farming was the right use of the New Zealand landscape – a destiny unlocked by a combination of progress, intellect and honest endeavour.[10] Implicitly, these accounts suggested that pastoral family farming provided an exemplar of a good life to the rest of the modern world. The authors were often highly educated, scientifically literate and great advocates for the world that farm families inhabited. They were the literary embodiments of my own enculturation on a farm in the early 1970s. They were also, almost without exception, entirely white.

In self-narrating the cultural history of Pākehā farming during its golden age, these personal histories are acts of both creation and exclusion. While the iconography of the successful family farm is lovingly reproduced across the genre, there are some alarming absences. First, these are tales of specifically pastoral farming, with the key variant being whether they are mainstream sheep farms, or the special high country farms of the upland South Island that have been particularly well mythologized in the popular culture of Pākehā farming.[11] Even dairy farming doesn't feature very much, and other kinds of land-use like viticulture will have to wait until the end of the twentieth century for any self-narration. Second, there is a major absence of some important ecological dynamics. The lived environment is challenging, but only as dictated by the semi-predictable vicissitudes of 'mother nature' – climatic events, storms, floods, etc. The underlying crisis of a destabilized ecosystem that was central to Guthrie Smith's remarkable farm autobiography in the 1920s is entirely absent. No one writes about how their own deforestation has accentuated a dramatic flood, or narrates their dynamic husband's struggle to stop their hillsides eroding and creeks filling with sediment so that the beloved family swimming hole is no longer useable. Rather, farming in and of itself is subject to 'normal' ecological challenges, and furthermore the farm acts as the correct place for developing an appreciation of 'nature'. Finally, even more important than the selective view of ecology is the erasing of indigenous history. These are thoroughly Pākehā tales that very rarely connect with past or present Māori worlds.

This tendency towards ahistorical 'whiteness' runs across many history-making projects about the golden age of Pākehā pastoral farming.[12] These farm stories follow a pattern of historical erasure, sometimes even isolating themselves from wider contemporary social and political worlds.[13] As one such author lovingly characterizes the farms and farmers of the Canterbury high country: they are 'a race apart'.[14]

All of these narratives of what farmers, politicians and scientists considered the golden age of New Zealand farming reside within invisible worlds. They tell the story of the importance of pastoral family farming, but they tell it in the kinds of remarkably selective ways that we recognize as the hallmarks of modernity. Such worlds are segmented and their realities have boundaries and knowable limits. Human worlds are separated from 'nature'. The human world that resides inside the fence line of a farm is dominated by scientific legitimacies, technical competencies, rational decision-making by educated actors and clearly demarcated social roles, and its inhabitants are untroubled by complex indigenous histories or the obligations of wider ecologies and social worlds. Modernist farming has, in effect, the ontological character of a full and vivid life, lived inside a boundary that separates it from wider invisible worlds.

The idea that I want to pursue in this chapter is this: there is something about the power of modernist farms themselves that helps enact these walls of invisibility. Something happened inside farming worlds during this transition from colonial farms to modernist farms that enacted an ontology that had profound compartmentalizing and 'invisibilizing' effects. What follows is an alternative 'farm-centred' history of the golden age of farming, which deliberately places at its centre the creation and ontological powers of the modernist farm.[15] The chapter will describe how farms successfully transitioned from being colonial agents of annihilation into modernist agents of stabilization, compartmentalization and pacification.

The ontology of the modernist farm

The idea of ontology hasn't previously been used to elaborate the complex world of farms, but it does arrive into a field of scholarly enquiry where such worlds have been extensively discussed and critiqued. While Norman Borlaug saw what I'm calling 'machine-like' farm ontology as a pinnacle achievement of modernity – delivering abundant food to a hungry world – a host of critics have emerged who characterize the transition from complex to modern farming systems as having vexed consequences. Their accounts share some important characterizations of the 'shape' of the kinds of modernist farms that were increasingly replacing earlier peasant farming systems (or even family farms in the earlier stages of capitalist transitions) during the twentieth century. These farms are 'machine-like', with mechanistic, naturalistic causalities, a progressively more simplified and less ecologically complex set of relations, increasingly reliant on external inputs, and a simplified rationality directed solely towards production of food and fibre rather than a broad set of social, ecological and economic goals. They run in predictable ways towards knowable goals and are, in their various separate elements, amenable to scientific elaboration. This critique of modernist farming very much mirrors my earlier hypothetical debate between Norman Borlaug and Vandana Shiva: modernist farms enact both highly attractive (productivist) outcomes and highly negative (world-destroying) outcomes.

For example, Wendell Berry, possibly the most celebrated author of agrarian life in the United States, pondered long and hard as to the problems caused by modern agriculture.[16] He considered that modern farms were conceptualized as 'machines', with a constantly elaborating mismatch between the aspirations of modernist agricultural science and the ecological and social realities of farming worlds.[17] A similar metaphor is central to Charles Massy's popular recent book on regenerative farming in Australia. Massy contrasts the 'mechanical mind' of industrial agriculture with the 'organic mind' of both indigenous land-use and regenerative agriculture approaches.[18] In the same vein, historian Deborah Fitzgerald chronicles how, in the United States, a series of 'industrial logics' drove farms towards more simplified systems based around a narrowing group of species and activities.[19] Her account of the capture of US agriculture by industrial logics resulted in a de-humanized system of entirely instrumental relations: animal and crop production specialized into a single species; living creatures became productive units; farmers became managers; systems became totally subordinated to metrics and technical logics. Farms become factories, and all vestiges of a social or cultural life of the farm disappeared.[20] Put simply, in Fitzgerald's account, modernist farms become socially pathological and this is a logical consequence of their actual design and shape.[21]

The great ecological critic of modernist agriculture in Green Revolution settings, Miguel Altieri, suggested that this style of modern agriculture only existed because of its ability to (temporarily) rupture ecological realities. He argued that the internal composition of the modern farm, composed as it was using the mechanistic logics of agricultural science, was an exercise in ecological denial, and such denial was leading to an ultimately futile battle with 'ecological diseases'.[22] Attempting to implement 'command and control' systems of farming 'over the top of' landscape ecologies, he argued, created an escalating reliance on external subsidies and inputs which were effective in the short term, but in the long run were doomed to fail.[23] This is the second strand of critique of modernist farming systems: they increasingly become ecologically pathological.[24]

In part, the great transition from colonization to modernity is a story of simplification. This is the centrepiece of historical geographer Peter Holland's account of farming transitions in the New Zealand landscape after colonization. He focused on two paired dynamics: the transition towards a narrowing suite of plant and animal species/products, and an increased reliance – once the initial flush of fertility had receded – on external inputs like artificial fertilizers.[25] His overall assessment is that by the mid-twentieth century, lowland pastoral farms had converged on a series of simplifying systems relations.[26] Holland concluded that this transition was only a temporary fix for farming the New Zealand landscape, and that every one of the dynamics that had contributed to the productivity of modernist farming in mid-twentieth century was under some kind of stress or experiencing a reversing trajectory by the end of the twentieth century.[27]

All of these accounts signal that the 'farming system' inside the emerging boundaries of the modernist farm in the mid-twentieth century was becoming less complex, simplified around fewer species, simpler relations, higher levels of external inputs, more reliant on rationalized and instrumental forms of knowledge, and that these elements were both highly productive and increasingly generated problems in the long-term sustainability of farms as social and ecological systems.

In the following sections, I want to explore how this 'machine-like' ontology of the modernist farm was actually enacted in New Zealand. The following narrative breaks down the transition from colonial to modernist farm ontology around two sets of dynamics that enact a new shape and form to farming:

1. The formation of different kinds of ontological boundary around the modernist farm, which divided farms into interior and exterior worlds.
2. The populating of the interior of the bounded modernist farm with particular kinds of knowledge, objects, metrics and relations.[28]

These are the two defining characteristics of the ontology of modernist farming in New Zealand, and in combination they have very important social, ecological and economic effects. In Tim Mitchell's terms, they make it possible for the farm to act in both political and economic worlds.[29] The 'making' of the modernist farm is partly the making of a bounded entity, disciplined in a single reality of farming knowledge, with particular interior characteristics that allow it to act as capital, as a node in economic worlds, as a stabilizer of markets and exchanges, and consequently also as an entity that enacts the great modernist separation of economy, society and ecology.

Boundaries: Enacting the interior and exterior of the modernist farm

The hypothetical debate in Chapter 1 between Norman Borlaug and Vandana Shiva, about the different ontologies of peasant and modernist farming, revealed many differences between those ontologies, but the one that I continue to return to is the importance of particular kinds of ontological *boundary* around the modernist farm. In much of his writing, Jules Pretty makes a similar observation, calling for recognition of the social and ecological connectedness of peasant agriculture, qualities that appear to have been lost in the transition from peasant to modern farming.[30] This raises the interesting question of when and how the social and ecological 'connectedness' of farming disappeared and was replaced by something more 'bounded'.

The argument I am going to make in this section is that the modernist farm, in perhaps its most crucial point of ontological distinction, is 'made' by the enacting of a boundary between the interior and the exterior world of the farm.[31] Consequently, before we can examine what ends up inside the world of the modern farm, we need to ask how a boundary arrives and separates these interior and exterior worlds.

This boundary emerged in five important and overlapping ways:

- political demarcation of legal institutions of private title,
- enactment of 'socially and culturally bounded' ontology in farm practice,
- enactment of 'ecologically bounded' ontology in farm practice,
- separation of economic worlds between production and consumption, and
- the attempted assimilation of Māori farming worlds and exclusion of indigenous farm practice.

1. Private title

The significance of the transition from indigenous land-use to blocks of land under the private ownership of family farmers is familiar across colonized landscapes in the 'settler states'. Securing colonized territories through settlement by family farms was a politically successful strategy deployed in many colonized landscapes, such as the homesteading project in the American West.[32] The operation of such boundaries – around both towns and farms – in dividing off and compartmentalizing land as 'privately owned' lies at the core of Cronon's celebrated elaboration of the relations between European and indigenous peoples and ecologies in the New England colonies, in *Changes in the Land*.[33] In Cronon's account, boundaries of private property enact two core ecological contradictions from which many problematic consequences flow.[34]

Chapter 2 recounted how Māori were alienated from land by various means, but most importantly by the actions of the Native Land Court after the wars of the 1860s. This was the first and greatest rupture: moving from a kinship-based world of organization of land towards a British system of private title. A subsequent historical drama was the political struggle that occurred inside Pākehā land-use in the closing decade of the nineteenth century and resulted in the initiative to 'break up' the great estates that had been established by the first generation of wealthy Pākehā immigrants in the South Island.[35] The legislative framework around family farms that emerged in the late nineteenth and early twentieth centuries established clear parameters of legal control and protection for family farm owners. By the 1920s there was a normalized pattern of land ownership, in which family farms under private title were dominating the cultivatable landscape. The only 'problem' that keeps reoccurring in this new bounded world of privately owned farmland is the last remaining parcels of Māori land that are fragmented and held in multiple ownership. They remain a stubborn obstacle to full realization of 'normal' land ownership system in New Zealand. I'll return to this 'obstacle' later in this section.

2. Social and cultural boundedness

While the formal legal institutions that created private boundaries are very important, they are not the only way that boundaries are enacted. They are also enacted in cultural practice.[36] Daily practices reinforce the ontology of the family farm as 'bounded': as having a line that demarcates a zone of control, of possession, of rights, and which delimits both a sphere of practice and a limitation of its consequences. This cultural boundary line migrated to New Zealand with British immigrants who had faced a world that was increasingly fractured by the enclosure movement in seventeenth- and eighteenth-century Britain, eradicating a sense of land being held in common or having common-use rights.[37] Unlike their peasant ancestors, British immigrants came from a farm culture in which there was a boundary that separated your land from your neighbour's, which told you where you were and weren't allowed to engage in farming activities. This was, of course, strikingly different to indigenous cultures of land-use. As Australian scholar Bill Gammage described the contrasting cultures of land-use in Australia pre- and post-colonization, 'fences on the ground make fences in the mind'.[38]

Family farms were also sites for generating particular discourses of farm life valuing cultural and political qualities of autonomy and self-reliance.[39] Such ideas were reinforced by wider ideological narratives about the farm, which rural sociologists have identified as central to the identity-building project of rural New Zealand. Notions such as farming being the 'backbone of the nation' and foundational to the prosperity of the country, along with virtuous, 'tight-knit' rural communities as enacting an idyllic alternative to the woes of urban life, are common elements in New Zealand and Australian social history.[40] This kind of cultural activity reinforced a boundary around the family farm.[41]

A parallel social dynamic is the kinship-based character of family farming in its Western form, in which nuclear families contained inside single farms increasingly replaced wider kinship bonds and land-use organization in peasant farming systems. The family farm is defined by its kinship structure; by enacting kinship it enacts a social boundary around the farm/nuclear family.[42]

In this way, Pākehā family farms enacted a social world that formed social relations in strikingly different ways to the older kinship-based world of Māori land-use. While Māori enacted a world with boundaryless ontology, where the lineaments of social relations and obligations stretched to the farthest horizon, the social world of Pākehā family farming was enacted within, and helped to reinforce, a bounded social world of the farm.[43]

3. Ecological boundedness

At the heart of Cronon's classic study of colonization in New England is the claim that fenced off and privately owned farms had cumulative effects on the political control of land, the emergence of a colonial economy and the ecological transformation of the landscape. Fenced-off farms acted as key agents of ecological disruption. Their cultivated interiors – populated with grazing animals and ploughed to a depth beyond the normal rooting systems of native grasses – changed the interior ecology of farmed land and exhausted soils – thus necessitating further expansion of the frontier – and marginalized older indigenous relations with land. Fenced farms also became incubators of new species that then escaped to ecologically devastate wider ecosystems. The fenced-off bounded farm was Cronon's key agent of change in explaining the conquest of New England.[44]

The consequences of Cronon's 'entrapment of agricultural cycles inside the fixed boundaries of individual possession' began to accumulate during the transition to modernist farming worlds during the twentieth century. Rachel Carson's *Silent Spring* massively disrupted the excited certainties of 1960s modernist farming with her devastating revelations about the ecological effects of DDT.[45] In essence, her critique highlighted an ontological boundary that had been enacted around new technical developments in modernist agriculture, which focused entirely on technical dynamics *inside* the boundaries of the farm and ignored wider ecologies.[46] This wasn't only relevant to the practice of agricultural science. The new approach to farming in New Zealand after the 1920s effectively reinforced an 'ecological boundary' around the privately owned and bounded farm. It established a 'zone of control' inside a highly unstable wider ecosystem.[47] Fences created sites of management, interventions and contained spaces where new species were introduced. This new approach to farming suggested that ecological crises and instabilities could be managed *inside* the boundaries of each farm. It also emphasized the suitability of technical fixes for internal ecological problems.[48] In short, the science of good modernist farming (as practised by both scientists and farmers) enacted an ontological boundary around the farm that artificially divided farm ecologies into interior and exterior worlds and then tended to act as if the exterior world didn't exist.

Key farm practices (or erasures) also helped enact this boundary. The arrival of a suite of agrichemicals – particularly pesticides like DDT – in the 1950s seemed to break the tie between ecological processes inside and outside the farm boundary. Pesticides suggested that farmers now had the apparent ability to manage pests inside the farm boundary. Fence lines also acted to signify the surrendering of responsibility for consequences outside such boundaries. Waterways were understood as having a legitimate function of carrying waste out of the farm's zone of control,[49] and waste could be burned or dumped inside the farm boundary (or dumped or burned somewhere outside farmed spaces on, for example, a public riverbank).[50] The farm boundary acted as a magic curtain beyond which contaminated water, waste and other materials could pass and become inconsequential.[51]

While such demarcations were enacted in basic and mundane farming activities, this is an ontological boundary that operates through a series of grand deceits. Ecologically, there is no clear boundary around a farm or a farming system. Water flows through farms and farming systems. Beneficial and non-beneficial flora and fauna usually don't respect farming fence lines (although some more intensive systems like high-value fruit, grape or vegetable production may try to erect physical barriers, which usually only function at great cost). Energy flows through farming systems, air circulates, carbon cycles, and nitrogen is released and recaptured. While some farm practices like ploughing, pest management, distribution of fertilizer and the containment of foraging animals are influential on these, and are located inside the farm boundary, ultimately it is deceptive to ignore all wider ecological processes and flows and/or to assume that attempts to capture and control such processes will succeed.

The fact that this kind of bounded ecological ontology of modernist farming is both ecologically incoherent and epistemologically indefensible is testimony to the power of those other institutions, relations, objects and practices that continue to reproduce it in the face of reality.

4. Separating production from consumption

An important boundary is enacted by the strange ontological separation of production from consumption, which took shape in an extreme form in New Zealand.[52] An ontological boundary at the farm gate separated the intensive and knowledge-filled world of farm production from outside worlds of food consumption creating an important silence: the silence of markets.[53]

New Zealand was, from its earliest moments of pastoral hegemony, suffused with productivist rationalities and an accompanying lack of interest in how to 'add value' or make valuable market connections and value claims.[54] This is an important dynamic that will become considerably more significant as the narrative in this book unfolds. New Zealand's export industries seemed immovably locked into the provision of simple commodities – most potently symbolized by the almost total reliance on exporting of frozen entire meat carcasses that would be dis-assembled after they arrived in Britain, or simple durable dairy products like butter and cheese.[55]

The lack of vision for a more 'value-added' approach to marketing products was almost certainly partly conditioned by the long geographical distance between New Zealand and its markets, as well as by the lucrative nature of the ongoing retention of the privileged supply relationship to Britain.

This reproduced a familiar ontology for me. As farmers, our primary loyalty and emotional bonds were to a particular place – the farm. Our products disappeared down the road in trucks towards processors and markets that were a curiosity (and a site of union conflict) rather than an essential fact of our lives. We were not strongly connected to our product once it left the farm (other than its monetary value). In comparison, J.D. van der Ploeg, in his compelling evaluation of contemporary European farming in terms of 'peasant ontologies', describes a different set of relationships between farms, environments, cultures and, most importantly, foods themselves.[56] Peasant ontologies in Europe, as a fundamental construction of the world, involve an embodied, sensory relationship between producers and their products. They see themselves as both skilled producers *and* knowledgeable consumers. Throughout the golden age of modernist farming in New Zealand, the opposite tendency applied. Farmers were highly attuned to the look and health of stock, and attended agricultural shows and competitions specifically to fine-tune and evaluate the physical and aesthetic parameters of their animals as they were produced. They were much less familiar with the same product when it was being consumed.

This provides one of the strangest boundaries in modernist farming in New Zealand: the disinterested production of food that is destined for an abstract market. It is also a farming environment in which the only sensible rationale is to concentrate on producing as much as you can.

5. Separating Māori and Pākehā farming

A final boundary was the one that operated in powerful ways during longstanding attempts to assimilate Māori into Pākehā farming worlds. This was a boundary that sought to enclose and erase other ways of farming – bringing everyone inside a white modernist farming world. Assimilationism was the guiding rationale of political policy in a multitude of colonial settings around the British Empire, and this applied equally in New Zealand. While most histories concentrate on the drive to eradicate the Māori language as a core strategy of the policy of assimilation,[57] another great historical impediment to the expectation of assimilation was the legacy of the Native Land Court's actions, which still left a residuum of farmland under native title with multiple owners. This was an anomaly in a modernist world converging on privately owned family farms. Consequently, the positioning of Māori farming and the 'problem' of multiple land ownership tell an important story of how distinctive styles of Māori farming were progressively marginalized through the twentieth century.

Historians of nineteenth-century Māori land-use universally record that at the start of the colonial encounter, Māori agriculture was strong. It went into rapid decline after the wars, and became almost extinct as part of a wider crisis of Māori society between the 1860s and 1920s.[58] Keenan reports that while in 1862, 57 million acres of land was under Māori title, by 1898 this had reduced to only 4 million acres; by 1929 there were only around 1,500 Māori farms remaining and those were mainly on highly fragmented titles.[59] By the 1920s the last remnant of Māori farms was isolated at the edges of the colony, marginalized during a period of rapid expansion of Pākehā farms.[60] This was hugely influenced by a lack of access to credit for farm modernization, which was almost entirely directed by both the state and private creditors towards privately owned, single-owner (i.e. Pākehā) farms.[61]

Once again the 1920s proved pivotal and the focus of revival was the modernist farm itself. Sir Āpirana Ngata was the driving force behind a series of initiatives to realign the small remnant of Māori farmers with the kinds of modernist farming approaches that were consolidating among Pākehā during the same period.[62] His most significant political achievement in the cause of modernizing Māori farming was the 1923 Native Land Amendment and Native Land Claims Act, which created a legal basis to consolidate fragmented and multiple-owner Māori land holdings and create a pathway to private title owned by individual Māori farm families.[63] This move to assimilate Māori land ownership into the wider and increasingly hegemonic model of family farming in the 1920s was accompanied by a series of initiatives to increase the adoption of stock, management systems and technologies to bring Māori farms into alignment with the Pākehā/modernist farming world.[64]

Such assimilationist strategies embody strong ontological projects. To demonstrate this, Ngata's creation of the Ahuwhenua Trophy for Māori farming excellence is very instructive.[65] Keenan's history of the trophy narrates how Ngata, a devotee of competition and efficiency, devised a competition to encourage change among Māori farmers.[66] Through the subsequent decades, farms that won the Ahuwhenua Trophy were evaluated for their modernist character and lauded as being indistinguishable from their most successful Pākehā counterparts. What differences that remained were assumed by many to be eventually resolvable by the wider assimilation of Māori into Pākehā worlds.[67]

The Ahuwhenua Trophy provides, in microcosm, a portrait of how assimilation into modernist farming was elevating new styles of knowledge and erasing older ways of knowing and using land. It was one agent in enacting a boundary between old/bad/ Māori and modern/good/Pākehā ways of participating in farming worlds; the essence of the new way was that Māori farms and farmers should assimilate and cease to be distinguishable from Pākehā/modern farms.

Despite Sir Āpirana Ngata's intentions, Māori farming was never fully assimilated into modernist worlds of privately owned family farms, and this 'failure' was the subject of constant anxiety and/or derision until the 1970s. The most cogent moment in which these anxieties were formally expressed (about both farming and wider challenges for Māori) was the infamous Hunn Report of 1961.[68] This identified multiple-ownership of farmland as an enduring impediment to Māori economic development, and clearly suggested that if Māori couldn't be relied upon to correctly develop their land then the government should intervene to shift 'under-utilized' land into Pākehā ownership. Even more extreme examples can be found inside government departments forming policy in the years after the Hunn Report, where the last great push for land alienation was aligned with rank paternalism.[69] The message was clear: complete the process of assimilation or lose the opportunity to join modernity. A boundary line was drawn: real farming was (privately owned, modern) Pākehā farming, and the visible remnant of Māori farming should disappear as rapidly as possible through assimilation or through direct government appropriation of remaining Māori land.

Bringing all these boundary-making activities together – the politico-legal demarcation of property lines, the ecological and socio-political boundary, the boundary separating production from consumption of farm products and the assimilationist strategies excluding a specifically Māori approach to farming – the *bounded* ontology of the modernist farm emerges as one of its most significant characteristics.

Such boundaries have effects: they define their interior as a separate entity, a knowable thing, an item of capital with its own specific value that may be evaluated, exchanged and traded. By dividing up the world, a boundary creates an anchor and a node, and in doing so makes other networks and actions possible.

The interior ontology of the modernist farm

The interior ontology of the modernist farm has characteristic (and increasingly unified) ways of knowing the world and what constitutes legitimate expertise about farming. It is populated with an increasingly less complex array of species, technical objects and mechanistic relationships. It is a world of stabilizing measures of the technical and economic performance of farms. All these, in combination, enact farms as a stable form of capital and anchor economic worlds. And it is a world in which 'economies of affect' develop, which create deep and stable ties between the human participants in farm worlds and their farms. The combined effect is the enactment of productivist rationalities of farming life.

1. Knowledge, science and learning

At the heart of social theoretical discussions about modernity are debates about the way that the production and demarcation of what was considered to be legitimate knowledge have been significantly altered due to the rise of 'rationalism' and 'science' as elements of modernity. In some cases, this involves a close examination of the conjoined rise of scientific endeavour and the rationalities of the modernist nation state.[70] Consequently, the ways that scientific knowledge was legitimized and circulated, in both science institutions and the increasing homogenization of research and educational worlds, are of central importance to understanding the hegemony of modernist farming through most of the twentieth century.[71]

One of the celebratory narratives of New Zealand farm history is that a dedicated group of agricultural scientists in the early to mid-twentieth century saved New Zealand farming from ecological catastrophe and set it on the only pathway that could enrich the nation.[72] The great period of stabilization after the 1920s had, at its heart, a scientific project called the 'Grasslands Revolution'. It faced a particular crisis of ferality: New Zealand's newly denuded hills were collapsing, their soil was unstable, their slopes brittle and the high rainfall was becoming an enemy rather than a friend to grasslands farming.[73]

The Grasslands Revolution has been the subject of some extended and subtle consideration by environmental historians in New Zealand.[74] It is an important period in the farm history of New Zealand in two interesting ways. It reveals a moment when agricultural scientists did, undoubtedly, make a decisive intervention into stabilizing an unstable world. This success had political consequences. Agricultural science experienced the 'golden age' as a long period in which they were impervious to critique – which underscores how painful later critiques were going to feel. It also points towards a transition in the way farming was being understood. Farming was being 'rendered technical'.[75]

The contribution of useful technical knowledge to New Zealand farming started early in the life of the colony. Crucially, however, in the earliest stages of learning there was considerable interaction between Māori and Pākehā, and a widespread acceptance that generic scientific knowledge should be balanced against situated environmental knowledge. For the latter, Peter Holland identifies that Māori were recognized by Pākehā farmers as experts – particularly in relation to navigating a challenging landscape, weather forecasting, hazards and assisting early naturalists with finding plants and birds, and this expertise was drawn upon by early settlers.[76] This was not surprising given that successful Māori farming was providing the majority of the food to settlements like Auckland. It was not until after the 1870s and 1880s that local environmental knowledge and the technical skill of Māori as land-users and horticulturalists began to be slowly abandoned in favour of increasing convergence on technical knowledge to support the production of wool, sheepmeat, butter and cheese. Even then, Pākehā farmers became quickly attuned to the highly variable nature of the New Zealand environment and the necessity of multiple approaches and strategies for land management.[77] Good science, in this context, was highly contextualized ecologically and hard to generalize across such a variable and unstable landscape.[78]

But then key ecological frontiers began to be breached and chaos began to ensue. The catastrophic consequences of widespread forest burning and wetland drainage (along with an explosion of introduced species that became 'pests' in the new environment) began to overwhelm settler farmers; local ecological wisdom had no immediate insight into how to manage these disrupted frontier spaces.

The Grasslands Revolution[79] – credited to scientists like George Stapledon and William Davies and written into the folklore of agricultural science by its evangelistic advocate Bruce Levy – coalesced a range of technical insights into how to stabilize the collapsing soils of New Zealand and, after the acquisition of the phosphate-rich island of Nauru at the end of the First World War, focused on identifying which combination of introduced grass species could respond to artificial fertilizers to send deep roots into unstable hillsides. It enacted a different ontology of a 'farming system'. The bounded farm became the site for which external inputs could be sourced and internal processes technically arranged for maximum productivity. Exterior ecology could be ignored, interior ecological ruptures suppressed through subsidies and artificial inputs.[80]

Successful experimentation combining nitrogen-fixing clover with deep-rooting ryegrass and applications of phosphate fertilizers began to 'hold' some of the most dramatically collapsing hillsides.[81] The results of this new combination of actions and species were reduced erosion of hillsides and a partial stabilization of pastures, as an increasing flow of external inputs began to subsidize ecological losses.[82] The success of this technical fix then met another interesting agent – the post–Second World War fleet of small planes and trained pilots who combined to facilitate 'aerial topdressing' of high hill country in the 1950s.[83] Through the agency of small planes, the 'third frontier' of indigenous grasslands became even more accessible and exotic pastures were pushed up hillsides and deeper into mountain systems.[84] The Grasslands Revolution was a scientific triumph, with notable limitations. It reversed the trajectory of the crisis by stabilizing a grasslands-based model for the landscape, while entirely ignoring the potentially much more ecologically desirable (and stable) options of returning trees to hillsides and reversing the draining of wetland 'filters' in flood-prone landscapes.

In the face of the chaos of colonial ferality, it was a revolution insofar as it created a set of 'solutions' that could operate inside bounded, fenced territories of control. It gave farmers a 'toolkit' for managing the ongoing risk of ecological collapse and, while it failed to create a stable wider landscape, it made farms a zone of control, a kind of rocky outcrop inside a slow moving ecological avalanche.[85] At a more abstract level, it set an ontological template: no matter the scale of ecological challenge, technical, scientifically leveraged solutions could be found and applied inside the boundaries of the farm. Except in those notable cases of failure – like the plague of rabbits –the success of the Grasslands Revolution suggested that a solution was still achievable at some point in the future, and that everyone should keep their focus inside the boundary of the farm and keep emphasizing technical interventions.[86]

Out of a variety of scientific opinions, a remarkably consistent and homogeneous approach to the science of grasslands farming had taken shape. This was partly a political project as the state played a role in coalescing the broad and experimental approach of colonial farmers into narrow and more homogeneous institutions.[87] These included the Department of Agriculture, farm journals, two agriculturally focused colleges (later upgraded to universities), state-funded research institutions like the Department of Scientific and Industrial Research (DSIR) and specific funding of Grasslands Revolution research (especially in Bruce Levy's Grasslands Division of the DSIR).[88] These actions helped reproduce the core project of grasslands science and created a set of publications and institutions that standardized one particular approach to pastoral farming.[89] This would then set the pattern for agricultural science institutions for the remainder of the twentieth century. It would also set a pattern of agricultural policy-making in which the narrow goal of 'science-informed' production of a narrow suite of pastoral products became the core rationale of almost the entire edifice of rural policy.

The content of the new scientific approach to agriculture was not surprising, and aligned with similar patterns of emergence of modernist agriculture in Australia and North America. What was surprising was the narrowness of the scientific ontology that then took hold of New Zealand, and the intensity of the state-science relationship. The cross-cultural collaboration, diversity and experimentation that characterized the way that knowledge was produced and circulated in early colonial farming,[90] and any sense of the wider ecological consequences of new farming systems, evaporated almost entirely from formal institutions supporting the science of agriculture through the mid-twentieth century.[91]

This new, narrow and technically focused approach to farming was also predicated on day-to-day on-farm practices that enacted a knowable and predictable farming world. Farmers were not simply uncritical consumers of scientific expertise generated at agricultural colleges and the Department of Agriculture, and their farms were by no means passive tableaux for the reception of pure scientific knowledge. Rather, two domains of on-farm and off-farm expertise existed in a dynamic relationship to each other.

Growing up on a modernist farm in the last years of the golden age of agricultural science revealed, in my recall, a collaborative relationship between on-farm and off-farm expertise. On-farm, we accepted as a basic truth that the skills and practices that comprised everyday farming simply couldn't be learned from a book or from abstract learning. Farming was an applied, gendered, embodied skill in which tacit knowledges were essential for the successful operation of a farm.[92] Off-farm, however, there were some specific sites of legitimate expertise in agricultural science that were well acknowledged. For example, many important technical inputs and techniques – like pesticide regimes, pasture management and grazing strategies, and the elaboration of new breeds of stock and plants – were recognized as the province of scientifically informed expertise *outside* the farm. We negotiated and collaborated across these two domains through various activities like field days, extension events and in the critical consumption of brochures and manuals. This moment at the end of the golden age nevertheless reflects some of its origins as well. In the family farms narrated in the previous chapter, Glenn Rd became a site of elaboration of new scientific knowledge.

Te Rahui likewise was a site where the Roberts family promoted 'rationalism' and held discussions on 'scientific farming' in the 1920s. Those family farms were sites of dialogue between farm-based knowledge and a new and elaborating wider world of agricultural science.

One important site where on-farm practitioners and off-farm scientific and technical experts (both groups comprised almost exclusively of men) met in their most direct interaction was in the education system. In New Zealand, this tended to happen at two agricultural colleges (later universities). Lincoln College/University was established in Canterbury in 1880 and Massey Agricultural College (later Massey University) was established in the 1920s, at around the same time as the DSIR. These two colleges introduced a specific configuration of agriculturally related specialist disciplines, which were then consolidated in the 1930s and 1940s around the specific disciplinary categories being elaborated at the Grasslands Division of the DSIR. Both the DSIR and the colleges organized subjects through disciplines that (in modernist style) segmented elements of the farm and reinforced a strong technical focus for agricultural learning. This was often articulated – in accordance with modernist epistemologies – in terms of the acceptability of hard scientific methodologies and the necessity of removing 'external distortions' specifically to improve the accuracy of those methodologies.[93]

Seen through this lens, the defence of farm-based applied learning by farm men, the elevation of embodied and not abstract knowledge, and the defence of complicated 'hard' science methods against distorting external influences help enact a modernist world of segmentation and hard causal boundaries.[94] Such practices sit at the heart of 'rendering technical' the elements of farming systems and result in a de-politicization of decisions about land-use. Farming and its consequences become, in effect, a matter of technical, scientific decision-making. Values, wider social claims and political contests have no purchase in a farming world that is 'rendered technical'. The containment of these discussions inside shared male worlds of farms, colleges, field days and machinery demonstrations created a self-reinforcing but ontologically demarcated zone of legitimate knowledge about the modernist farm.[95] It was a world in which some things were becoming powerfully centred as scientifically legitimate, while many other worlds were being rendered invisible.

2. Species, objects and measures: Stabilizing farms as capital and affect

Having identified the creation of boundaries and the circulation and legitimation of particular kinds of knowledge as important elements of the ontology of the modernist farm, we can now turn towards some of the other important dynamics of the interior of farming worlds. Two things are worth noting that bear upon both how farms act in economic worlds, and also how they act to cohere emotional worlds for their participants. By examining the relationships between key species, objects and measures, we can see both how these relations stabilized (in collaboration with boundaries and predictable knowledge) to form: (1) 'farms as capital' that allowed farms to act as anchors of economic worlds, as well as (2) how 'economies of affect' emotionally anchored the attachment of farm families to their farms.

Farms have long acted as an important form of capital in the establishment and stabilization of capitalist economic networks in colonial settings.[96] But there is often a tendency to consider capital to be pre-existing and fixed in its shape and fungibility (although clearly not its monetary value).[97] In the New Zealand context, however, farms operated as capital in very different ways for Pākehā compared to Māori. For one, farms became anchors of prosperity; for the other, an anomaly for which various extreme fixes and interventions were proposed. The difference between Māori and Pākehā experiences of how farms operated as capital is intriguing and points towards interesting differences in how farms are formed, take particular stable shapes and are evaluated in capitalist economies.[98] In my account, the farm must be understood as more than just a particular combination of fixed categories of land, labour and capital. Paraphrasing Tania Li, to 'render farms investible' they need to be demarcated by legal (and other) boundaries, contain knowledge that aligns in predictable ways, and also have an interior filled with the right kinds of species, objects, measures and relations. All these are necessary for the farm to participate in (and, in the case of New Zealand, anchor) capitalist economic worlds.[99]

Commencing with what, in an orthodox account, would be the interior labour dynamics of farms, farm household members and other labourers on farms participated in making family farms into good capital in very specific ways. New Zealand took shape after the abolition of slavery in the British Empire, and labour availability was always challenging in a colony where most of the new arrivals wanted to be farmers rather than farm workers (a dynamic that confounded the planned evolution of the colony by Wakefield). The most reliable way in which the labour requirements of farms could be met was through family farming with the enhanced capacity of family farms to self-exploit to meet labour needs.[100]

But farms are the site of powers other than that of human labour. Farms were taking their shape in damaged ecosystems, but also with other material vitalities and non-human agencies. Much of the history of modernization of agriculture centres new agrichemicals as agents of great power. This was the case in New Zealand with dynamic contributions from phosphates obtained from Nauru after the 1920s, along with the increasing elaboration of synthetic pesticides like DDT after the Second World War.[101] But alongside these agrichemical agents and their spectacular powers were other, natural agencies. Brooking and Pawson's 'empire of grass' centres grass seed as the great agent of stabilization in damaged farming ecosystems. In de-forested farmlands, the presence of fallen timber and extensive hardwood root systems meant that ploughing could not easily be undertaken – a major setback in a wider food regime that was highly oriented towards wheat production. Grass seed, however, was the ecological pioneer that could be sown, and could penetrate rooty soils and eventually overgrow and incorporate nutrients from felled timber. So, alongside human labour, the power of grass was another vital ingredient in making land into farms. Based on this grasslands system (which was narrowed into ryegrass and clover mixes by the Grasslands Revolution), the two species of domesticated animal suited to both grazing on 'rough' pasture and tamping down regrowth of woody vegetation were sheep and cattle.[102] They were also more friendly for a labour-starved farming system, as they could look after themselves for much of the time and then be shorn or slaughtered at specific times or locations where labour could be gathered to do the task. The simplification of farming worlds around a couple of grass and stock species was partly driven by the requirements of this particular combination of human and non-human powers.[103]

Sown grass pastures, cattle and sheep needed to be managed inside demarcated areas and, as discussed above, the physical imposition of a boundary had effects on both farming systems and farming cultures.[104] In the New Zealand colonial context, erecting fences was a fundamental activity in early farming and was used to transition away from open grazing of cattle and sheep, on leases of Māori land, into management within contained spaces and pastures. Fences are the objects that make boundedness visible and give a spatial fixity to the farm as capital.

As family farms, the bounded space of the farm needed other key objects to render them liveable by families. New Zealand had an abundant supply of timber which provided the basic material for building in the colony, later supplemented by corrugated iron for roofing and walling sheds.

There are other key items that make farms productive. Shearing shed design was set in place in the second half of the nineteenth century and hasn't changed much since then. In the early 1900s, however, a series of technical developments in the evolution of dairy milking sheds changed the composition of buildings on farms. These were subject to evolving design and experimentation until the 'herringbone' shed stabilized as the industry norm in the 1950s and doubled the size of a dairy herd that could be milked by family labour.

One of the most familiar narratives of agricultural modernization is the transition from animal power to machine power and the increasing centrality of machines at the heart of agricultural systems. These formed the first wave of technological substitution by exchanging somatic power for steam followed by fossil fuel and electric power.[105] This is evident in New Zealand in the adoption of tractors and, to a lesser extent, Caterpillar bulldozers for land clearance, along with automated shearing tools and milking machines.

Stories of the accumulation of these species, materials and objects are central to the histories of my family farms narrated in the previous chapter. While the farms existed on paper as legally demarcated properties, their existence as lived environments happened through the construction of houses – like Ashburn – the erection of fences or drystone walls, the replacement of forests and wetlands with grass pastures (using heavy machinery like the D2 Caterpillar at Glenn Rd), and the population of these with sheep or, in my case, with the bull Hatter and his prize-winning bovine progeny. The narrative of farm history in my family is not simply focused on the capital value of the legally bounded property, although that had its moments and was the focus of the short life of Archie Campbell. It is the story of this whole ensemble of humans and non-humans that made farms productive. For these farms to work as capital, over the longer term, they needed all these ingredients to assemble their collective powers.

It is hard to understate the importance of metrological dynamics that helped enact modernist farming by making it predictable and orderly.[106] This is particularly true of metrics of productivity. From the early establishment of private title over farms, measures of estimated productivity of farmland were fundamental to financial valuations in the transaction of land. While such measures were often unstable,[107] they did eventually participate in the stabilization of modernist farming and the generation of productivist rationalities. Carrying capacity of 'stock units', productivity per acre (later per hectare) and land value for resale per acre/hectare became the foundational pillars of the 'knowability' of the performance of the modern farm.

These central metrics of land value and productivity interact with other measures. Farm accountancy involves a set of practices that enact farms as knowable and predictable economic worlds.[108] Profits flow and are contained inside the boundary of the accounts of the farm enterprise. Measures like debt to equity ratios, cash flow, depreciation of assets and various measures of earnings act to render the farm knowable as a business entity.[109] In modernist farming systems, they also have a direct and crucial influence on the central species/products in the system – evaluating their worth in narrow monetary terms and the success or failure of the farm on indices of productivity of these species.[110] They also tend to lock in short-term planning around production targets, monthly accounts and annual reporting. Longer-term trajectories and strategies are less measurable and thus become less actionable.

In sum, all these forms of labour (both human and non-human), land and other materials and objects, along with stable forms of knowledge and standardized measures, play their own roles in enacting the farm as a demarcated, stable and knowable form of capital. In a colonial world characterized by ferality and chaos, this ensemble stabilized and organized the farm in a way that was bounded and predictable enough so that – in the eyes of those who allocated credit (both government and private) – they could be considered a secure economic entity.

Two historical dynamics confirm that such an assemblage was not automatically achieved as a 'natural' outcome of economic laws (and had profoundly racialized consequences). First, the colonial state had to continually intervene to make land available to Pākehā farmers and secure its legal boundaries – as witnessed in the invasion of the Waikato that destroyed the anomalous Heather's Homestead/ Marotahei. This was followed by government actions to place credit into the hands of Pākehā farmers, standardize scientific knowledge and deploy strategies to make farming 'cohere' as the dominant form of land-use. Such interventions were needed up until the 1920s, when private investment in farmland and a more orderly transfer of farms in private markets finally became the norm. Seen in this light, the golden age represents the period when farms finally became normalized as 'freestanding' items of capital and anchors of economic worlds.[111] Even more revealing is that as the modern (Pākehā) farming world stabilized, the very judgements that normalized and stabilized Pākehā family farming were being used to penalize and exclude Māori land-owners. Pākehā farms became stable capital, while Māori land became a fragmented modernist anomaly.

This account of how farms became capital tells part of the story of the importance of the increasing coherence and alignment of the internal ontology of the modernist farm. The other important dynamic is the psychological interior to the farm, which became the subject of powerful affective relations for farm families and which also did important work in stabilizing the modernist farm.[112] As the popular autobiographies of farm life had narrated, Pākehā learned to love their farms and all they contained.

In the colonial economy, the Māori economic world was saturated with affective relations – particularly aligned with ties of kinship and anchored to a belief that the land was a living entity.[113] Land-use was organized around kinship, and the wider landscape was also organized by kinship ties and existed in a complex but unbounded world of obligations and consequences between humans and the land.[114] In the Pākehā family farm, autobiographical and fictional accounts of the golden age of family farming tell a strikingly different story of the affective world of family farms. Kinship ties are important but they are specifically bounded *inside* the interior of the family farm. Families dwell inside the boundaries of the farm and, in fact, the affective ties of the immediate family play a part in actually reinforcing the social ontology of the bounded family farm.

At the same time, specific items like houses, gardens, new plantings of exotic ornamental trees, the establishment of 'farm vistas' whereby the farm is a platform for viewing 'wider nature', and even a world of barns, stables, milking sheds, tractors and cars have affective ties and become emotionally 'centred' in farming worlds.[115]

Finally, there are complex affective relations between humans and animals. Domesticated companion species like horses, ponies and dogs are central to the affective world of family farms, but animals involved in farm production have a more instrumental life.[116] Historically, differences have emerged between sheep/beef and dairy farming: dairy farm families developed stronger affective ties to their cows, giving them names and following their lives over many years, compared to the opposite affective strategy with sheep and beef cattle, which were destined to be slaughtered and thus needed to be kept at an emotional distance from farm family members.[117]

Affect builds in multiple ways, whether it be the familiarity of using machines; the enhanced ability to undertake tasks using tractors and bulldozers; the efficiency of milking sheds; or the less utilitarian affective ties of gardens, families, vistas and companion species. All create an internal coherence to a farm system that emphasizes these elements and renders less important those things that, ontologically, are external to the system. Furthermore, many key items on a modernist farm, such as machinery, key production species, the infrastructure of the property like fence lines, buildings and the actual land itself, generate affective ties through both financial ownership and the important social transactions that enable purchase and ownership (both legal and affective).[118] Accordingly, modernist farms have an 'economy of affect' that is centred inside the farm and involves a bounded world of connected objects. Compared to what went before, such farms are dramatically less affectively exposed to wider ecological, social and kinship obligations.

Such farming worlds assemble in ways that enact and reproduce a particular rationality: they are farms that are, at heart, *productive* and are legitimized by their productivity. The final great affective tie in these modernist farming systems is their beautiful simplicity of function. The entire ensemble of bounded technical objects aligned in mechanistic relationships increasingly converges on a single operating logic: production. The increasingly important metrics that I learned from my grandfather in the 1970s, and which have only grown more important on farms like #370 Five-Mile Rd, told us that we were good farmers because we were continually increasing our productivity. Productivism emerges from complex practices, grounded in relations, objects and measures, that aren't simply the end-product of human attitudes.[119] Modernist farming is characterized by productivist rationalities not because its human inhabitants have productivist attitudes, but because the modernist *farm* is productivist as an ensemble effect of all its human and non-human elements.

The great stabilization and its inevitable disruption

The transition from colonial to modernist farming systems narrated in this chapter represents the culmination of the 'great stabilization' of farming in New Zealand. It examined the many ways in which different elements of the ensemble of the family farm participated in enacting this great stabilization. The result was that family farms became anchors of economic worlds, enabling the kinds of economic ontology that Timothy Mitchell identified as crucial in stabilizing colonial capitalism. Modernity's farms have a remarkably powerful stabilizing ontology: the farm has knowable boundaries and its interior is populated with an increasingly standardized world of knowledge and convergence on agreed 'realities' of farm production. It is populated by a mechanistic world of objects, measures and relations, all of which align with and help enact a rationality centred on a homogenizing landscape of solely pastoral family farming and a narrowing rationale of productivism.

The golden age of pastoral family farming is not merely an effect created by the wider powers of modernity. Instead, it must be understood as one of the great sites of creation of modernity in countries like New Zealand. Farms helped make science more credible and authoritative. The great project of modernist farming created a coherent national economic and political project, and its cultural expression became a cipher for the normative character of a 'good society' in New Zealand. The bounded ontology of the modernist farm became a relentlessly reproduceable agent of separation and division, carving up the landscape into isolated private spaces, and enacting a great social and ecological separation between interior and exterior farm worlds. In sum, farms help enact the great modernist separation of social, ecological and economic worlds.

The next question is: how did this particular ontology act in political ways inside farming worlds? If the colonial farm acted to silence and render invisible *other* indigenous worlds, the modernist farm had important political effects *inside* the new bounded world of the farm. These effects can be described as the politics of pacification. In Callon's terms, farming worlds become 'cooled' in a particular shape.[120] Others use ideas like 'de-politicization'.

This chapter has shown how modernist farms enacted these effects. Farms had boundaries that contained the interior world of the farm, yet also did important work keeping the exterior out of view – whether it was an ecological exterior of invisible consequences of our actions; an economic exterior in which 'externalities' and markets inhabited some other mysterious space; or a social exterior by which other social groups, cultural claims or alternative historical narratives were given no standing to speak to the social interior of the farming world. The work of this boundary de-politicized our world and had the practical effect of rendering farms immune to a great deal of critique.[121]

Similarly, farms were 'rendered technical': the growing elaboration of legitimate knowledge of farming systems in strictly scientific and technical terms increasingly narrowed the space into which value claims, ethics, wider cultural claims and connections could find a foothold in the technical workings of a modern farm.[122]

This had important consequences for the 'culture' and gendering of farming. Farming worlds became white, and in doing so culture effectively became invisible. Farming worlds that were based around a narrowing set of embodied technical skills, and the enshrining of these as the sole legitimate way to 'know' farming, increasingly made this a masculine world, learned by men and with men as its knowledgeable gatekeepers. Finally, in a world that became increasingly affectively centred around a narrowing set of often financially important objects, the internal focus of such affects diminished wider claims of kinship, ecology, society, politics or history.

These are the politics of a pacified world. As Tania Li argues, it is a world that is not so much characterized by the political as by the 'anti-political'. It works by continually shutting down the places, tensions and contests that create political tensions and options. And it stayed that way for nearly half a century. As long as everything stayed in place, our little farm-shaped vessels would bob along the surface of what seemed to be an eternally placid ocean. I could grow up inside that world knowing it as my only reality, without contest or critique, and with no alternatives in sight. The miracle of New Zealand farming in the golden age was that the icebergs floating in the invisible exteriors of our farming worlds stayed out of sight for so many decades. It couldn't last. In Callon's terms, worlds are always unstable, materialities are never inert, exteriors exist even when they are unthinkable and so things inevitably 'overflow'.[123]

There is a parallel scene to my imagined moment standing in a serene paddock under the tutelage of my grandfather sometime in the late 1960s and early 1970s. One day in 1972, I biked home from school and encountered an alarming scene. My mother was crying in the kitchen, watching her small black-and-white television. The news had just broken that Britain had agreed to enter the European Common Market. The price for their entry was the 'betrayal' of New Zealand's loyal farmers. My mother understood the extent of the disaster. We had lost not only our privileged entry for goods to the 'home market', we had also lost several of the key economic and political pillars of our farming world. Things were falling apart and the centre couldn't hold. Mere anarchy was loosed upon our farming world.

The last vestiges of colonial ties had been severed and a neoliberal revolution was about to sweep away institutional certainties and old alliances in political and economic worlds. Environmental concerns were slowly mounting and about to overflow into full view around a series of farming controversies. The inviolable authority of agricultural science was about to be subjected to vigorous political contestation. The conformity and discipline of modernist farming were fracturing and experiments in new styles of farming were emerging. Finally, indigenous voices were starting to be heard. Worlds that had, in Callon's terms, been cold for over fifty years were starting to get hotter, things were starting to overflow, and new disruptive fields of politics were about to become uncontainable.

Notes

1   While there wasn't universal support in literature and the creative arts for the greatness of the colonial project in New Zealand (see Calder 2011), the general tone was very much in line with the patriotic boosters. The twentieth-century narrative usually included mythologies of how New Zealand had 'the most enlightened race relations in the world', an 'egalitarian society', and was the most loyal and successful of Britain's colonies (themes all reviewed in King (2003)).

2   The importance of pastoral farming products in contributing to New Zealand's national prosperity cannot be overstated, peaking during the Korean War, when supply contracts with the US Army resulted in the value of wool reaching 'a pound a pound', resulting in New Zealand having a standard of living that ranked 'between third and fifth' in the world (King 2003: 438).

3   Belich's (2001) history of twentieth-century New Zealand – *Paradise Reforged* – describes the rise of farmers as a highly politically influential class, with the idea that farmers were the 'backbone of the nation' emerging early in the twentieth century, and farmers providing an inordinately large number of political leaders as well as export revenue.

4   Culminating in the 'grasslands revolution' that forms a centrepiece of serious historical scholarship on New Zealand farming (see Brooking et al. 2002; Brooking and Pawson 2011; Star and Brooking 2011) and will be discussed at length in this chapter.

5   This table covers the period up until when New Zealand adopted decimal currency (1967). This was the first step in a progressive conversion of New Zealand from imperial to metric measures, which concluded (in law, if not in common practice) in 1976. Accordingly, the discussion of currency and other measures like land area will be reported in this and the following chapter according to either imperial or metric measures depending on where the narrative falls around this period of transition.

6   These non-fictional histories are supplemented by highly popular fictionalized versions of family farm life like the novels of Mary Scott (her most famous novel *Breakfast at Six*, which told the tale of a young couple taking up a farm in rural New Zealand, was published in 1953 and went through six reprints); or the Mills & Boon stories written by Essie Summers after 1956, which often featured New Zealand farmers as the male protagonists (and sold over 100 million copies).

7   Loveridge (2004, 2009).

8   This theme resonates across more than just the autobiographical literature on family farming. Deriving part of its historical resonance from the key Lockean discourse of the virtue of productive land and undesirability of 'waste' land that were circulated in colonial worlds, this idea aligned during the twentieth century with the great modernist justification of activities and practices due to their productivity.

9   This was a theme that was explored in more depth in Morris (2014) – in particular the way that the cultural role of 'stewards of the land' was being increasingly fractured and contested by the end of the twentieth century.

10   This is more than just a literary theme. The discursive production of what, elsewhere, we termed 'pastoral hegemony' (Campbell et al. 2009a: 94) is a central theme of many of the histories and ethnographies of rural New Zealand through the twentieth century. For example, Elvin Hatch's ethnography of Fairlie in South Canterbury describes the rising social status of family farms in the 1920s and 1930s and an increasing social acceptance of pastoral family farms in the eyes of the diminishing

class of larger runholders (Hatch 1992: 33). This strongly contrasts with the kind of 'range wars' that characterized conflict between farmer classes in the United States.

11 Morris (2014).

12 The need for Pākehā to narrate themselves ahistorically is a key theme raised by Turner (1999: 21): 'The new country is the site of contradictory demands: the need, ultimately, to forget the old country, and the need to ignore people who already inhabit the new country.'

13 As Calder (2011) recounts, this isn't true of the more serious end of the creative arts in New Zealand, with the complex consequences of colonization being the subject of dark brooding by the emerging literati of the twentieth century. Prominent among the dark brooders was poet Alan Curnow who, in 1941, penned the oft-repeated lines: 'Awareness of what great gloom/Stands in a land of settlers/With never a soul at home.' There was also, as Craig (2005) recounts, a vivid sub-genre of 'rural gothic' ranging from Frank Anthony's 'Gus and Me' stories, of hapless unskilled farming, to Ronald Hugh Morrieson's dark tales of rural horror.

14 Ansley (2012: 20).

15 As a narrative of an important period in New Zealand history, this one will deliberately seek out other agencies than those that usually populate the important state-centric, political and/or economic accounts of the New Zealand of that time. This is not to deny the importance of state, politics or economy, but they have been written about elsewhere (and will return to the narrative in the next chapter).

16 Particularly in his much-loved book *The Unsettling of America* (Berry 1977).

17 Berry's understanding of the pathology of modernist farming marks a path that my own narrative follows in many respects, identifying both a mechanical quality of the 'ideal modern farm' and a 'boundary' around its knowability (Berry 1977: 78–80).

18 Massy (2017). Massy's mechanical mind arrives in Australia with white colonists and is a central metaphor in his powerful diagnosis of the ecological and social pathologies caused by mainstream farming approaches. Massy's popularity has seen this metaphor circulated widely around alternative farming discussions in Australasia. While the effect of his 'mechanical mind' very much aligns with the characterization of modernist farming that I undertake this chapter, it grounds its explanation in what is a fundamentally psychological model. This contrasts in subtle but important ways with an ontologies approach – whereby settlers and farms, humans and non-humans assemble machine-like outcomes on their farms through the agency of laws, practices, objects, processes and multiple species as well as 'mindsets'. I do, however, think that the story that Massy actually tells of transformative farms, ecologies and practices could easily be reframed into an ontologies approach that would make such diverse agencies more visible.

19 Fitzgerald (2003). This follows closely from Ruth Harrison's (1964) seminal critique of the creation of 'animal machines' in 'factory farming'.

20 Bell (2004) characterizes this as 'monologic' agriculture in a world that needs agricultural dialogue.

21 The socially pathological outcomes of farming under capitalism are a core element of all critical rural sociology. Fitzgerald's point of difference is that she indicates there is something about the industrial design of farming systems themselves which results in some of these social pathologies. Other scholars contemplating farming under modernity, such as DuPuis (2002), argue for a less irreversible trajectory towards a modernist industrial dystopia, a theme that I will return to in Chapter 5.

22 Altieri's ecological diseases come in two forms: 'First, there are problems directly associated with the basic resources of soil and water, which include soil erosion, loss of inherent soil productivity, and the depletion of nutrient reserves, salinization and alkanization, pollution of surface and ground water, and loss of croplands to urban development. Second are problems directly related to crops, animals, and pests: loss of crop, wild plant, and animal genetic resources, elimination of natural enemies of pests, pest resurgence and genetic resistance to pesticides, chemical contamination, and destruction of natural control mechanisms. Each "ecological disease" is usually viewed as an independent problem, rather than what it really is – a symptom of a poorly designed and poorly functioning system' (Altieri 2002a: 198).

23 Like Vandana Shiva, Altieri's critique was founded on his observations of the failures of the Green Revolution and that modern, scientific farming was not the solution but rather one cause of this failure (Altieri 2002b: 1). His alternative approach was, in my terms, an entirely different ontology – recognizing ecological processes in farming systems as well as their articulation in indigenous knowledge about farming in specific environments (Altieri and Nicholls 2017: 231–2).

24 The ecological critique is not simply reserved for Green Revolution systems. In the United States, Bell (2004) describes a similar trajectory for Iowa with its convergence on corn, soybeans and hogs. Donald Worster (1990) similarly laments the loss of ecological complexity of all modern farming as the result of its Faustian bargain with capitalism.

25 Elaborating his argument in more detail: 'The dynamic environmental system of a New Zealand pastoral farm went through an important transformation as it stabilized around a particular suite of animal and plant products. After the initial surge of fertility released from the cutting down of forests and draining of wetlands (and initial cultivation of pasture), the biomass flows through farm systems began to differ greatly from the natural systems they were replacing (or the light ecological footprint of Māori resource gathering). Put simply, a large quantity of biomass is flowing out of the farm system in the form of plant and animal products and heading overseas to distant markets ... Trade in primary products was not environmentally neutral, but carried a cost in the currencies of the ecological resources of energy, water and nutrient ions. By the final decade of the nineteenth century, most lowland farms in southern New Zealand were dependent on supplements from external sources of nitrogen, phosphorus, potassium, calcium and other essential plant nutrients to remain economically viable' (Holland 2013: 194–5).

26 Positive feedback loops inside farm systems had become stronger and negative feedbacks were weakening as external inputs and subsidies compensated for ecological costs. Buffering in the system was weak and homogeneity of elements was strengthening, compared to the more experimental and diverse land-use styles of earlier Pākehā settlers and their Māori predecessors. Farming systems were consequently becoming highly responsive to changes in input regimes rather than internal ecological drivers. The landscape mosaic was becoming much more homogeneous (but compared to parts of the United States or Australia was still taking shape on top of a much more diverse landscape). Finally, primary nutrient input sources were now largely external, with the need to elaborate reliable supplies of phosphatic and nitrogenous fertilizers becoming essential for the wellbeing of the new farming model (Holland 2013: 210).

27 Holland (2013: 210).

28 A disclaimer is needed here for social scientific readers of this chapter. In seeking to reveal the agencies and effects of non-human actors in enacting farm ontologies – or in this case, an ensemble of humans and non-humans assembled in a family farm – this chapter is not going to provide a review of the broad social and cultural practices of Pākehā family farming in the twentieth century, which have been the subject of prior work by geographers, anthropologists and sociologists. Important ethnographies of family farming like Hatch (1992), Dominy (2001) and Morris (2002) elaborate many important social dynamics of gender, farm family succession, household practices like mealtimes, community events, and wider community status and standing as important aspects of the culture of Pākehā family farming in New Zealand. They stand alongside studies of the representation of family farming in popular culture (Bell 1996), the media (Carter and Perry 1987), literature (Craig 2005) and the arts (Morris 2012). All of these contribute to a complex and detailed understanding of the cultural world of the Pākehā family farm in New Zealand.

29 Mitchell's book *Rule of Experts* is a foundational text for new ways to understand 'economy' as enacted from both human intentionality and materialities like metrics and calculations. His understanding of economic worlds is strongly grounded in how such worlds enact and are shaped by ontologies: 'The economy, I have already suggested, can be understood as a set of practices that puts in place a new politics of calculation. The practices that form the economy operate, in part, to establish equivalences, contain circulations, identify social actors or agents, make quantities and performances measurable, and designate relations of control and command. The economy must, as Michel Callon has argued, operate as a series of boundaries, distinctions, exceptions, and exclusions. For example, the economy depends upon, and helps establish, boundaries between the monetary and the nonmonetary, national and foreign, consumption and investment, public and private, nature and technology, tangible and intangible, owner and non-owner, and many more. How are these boundaries and exceptions made? What calculations do they make possible? What problems and costs are incurred?' (Mitchell 2002: 8–9). If Mitchell's intention was to understand the enacting of the twinned entities of 'economy' and 'nation state', his 'boundaries, distinctions, exceptions and exclusions' that ontologically demarcate the world of economy in the modern nation state can equally be applied to the farm in New Zealand and how it anchored the transition from a colonial to a modern world.

30 Pretty (2013). The same argument resonates through Berry (1977) and Scott (1998).

31 The issue of boundaries – and their ability to generate divided ontologies – is central to this argument. Thomas Gieryn (1983) brought attention to the idea of 'boundary work' in his widely cited study of the ontological division of scientific worlds. Gieryn argued that the way in which social practices created boundaries dividing social worlds was fundamental to understanding social life. Social anthropologist Peter Wilson considered the issue of boundaries in the study of lived spaces like homes, pondering the significance of the evolution of domesticated spaces – with walls – that enacted public and private life as ontologically separated interiors and exteriors (Wilson 1991). Linklater (2013: 10–11) makes an even more specific claim about the effect on the social life of English peasants, of the transition from single-room dwellings for extended peasant households into privately owned farm houses with separate rooms for members of nuclear families in the sixteenth century. Cronon (2003: 156) extends this into an important analysis of the division of the colonial landscape in New England into a world of 'fields and fences' with important consequences. This analysis is strongly mirrored by Scott's (1998) account of the ways

in which the modernist state divided, mapped and created boundaries in landscapes thus having the ontological effect of 'bracketing off' social and economic worlds into different realities. My argument follows all these accounts: just as many consequences flowed from the arrival of walls into social life and maps and boundaries in statecraft, so too there are many consequences that flow from the enacting of boundaries around farms. From the moment of the creation of a boundary, an ontological effect is created separating farming worlds into interiors and exteriors.

32 This is a key element of Linklater's (2013) claims about the significance of 'fee simple' or 'real estate' systems as a key innovation in the annexation of land and creation of entire new societies – transitioning Britain from collective peasant land-use to privately owned capitalist farms as well as creating a potent mechanism of appropriation that changed the economic and political calculus around the potential economic value of colonies.

33 Cronon ([1983] 2003).

34 First, that European and Native American land-use practices and ecologies would never be commensurable and that one would eventually be destroyed by the other. Second, the intensification of land inside the private property boundaries of new European farms triggered a cascade of ecological changes that within two centuries had undermined the very venture of farming in New England (Cronon 2003: 169).

35 A subject that has received extensive historical attention from Brooking (1996) along with Fairweather (1985).

36 Even in contemporary rural worlds, legal boundaries and ontological boundaries have a messy and imprecise correspondence. Most farms have 'paper roads' and stream reserves owned by the state, which are ignored and absorbed into the operating farm, and many farms utilize space that isn't legally incorporated into the legal shape of the farm – like riverbanks and roadside margins. Accordingly, legal boundaries and social practice are mutually reinforcing, but not identical.

37 While the influence of the recent enclosures on British migrants to New Zealand directly reflects this cultural desire to fence, contain and own, Schama (1995: 526–38) pursues the power of walls and fences much deeper within European cultural history, arguing that the very idea of the garden (deriving from the Old English word for fence – *geard*) is premised on its dividing fence or wall between the wild and the tamed, at one level, and different groups of people and kinds of society at another. Linklater (2013) argues that the sixteenth century, and the lead-up to formal enclosures, saw the greatest transition from peasant collectivity to fenced and privately owned farmland in Britain.

38 Gammage (2012).

39 Stock and Forney (2014).

40 These ideas are encapsulated by rural sociologists in the terms 'rural fundamentalism', 'countrymindedness' or 'agrarianism', and form a key theme of analyses of rural change by Australasian rural sociologists (see Lawrence 1987, Gray and Lawrence 2001).

41 While it isn't the focus of this book, it also enacted a wider rural–urban boundary around farm-based rural communities.

42 This points towards the rich vein of debate and theorization in rural sociology due to the family farm's 'in between' status – needing to be understood as both an economic and a social unit.

43 There are parallels here to Miles Fairburn's wider critique of the 'atomized' nature of social and cultural life in colonial New Zealand (Fairburn 1989).

44 Cronon (2003: 156): 'The colonial interaction of forests, furbearers, hunters, axes, grazing animals, plows, crops, weeds – and the rival ways of owning and selling these things – all contributed to a redrawn map of New England. It was a map that, over the course of European settlement, more and more traced, not the earlier world of movement between hunt and harvest, but the new world of cropland and pasture, of agricultural cycles entrapped within the fixed boundaries of individual possession. In the hands of the colonists, New England had become a world of fields and fences.'

45 Carson (1962).

46 The existence of an unrealistic and distorting conceptual boundary that magically separates the internal reality – and proper zone of study of agricultural science – and external realities outside the boundaries of the farm system is a theme common to both Wendell Berry (1977) and James Scott (1998). As Scott characterizes the relationship between modernist agricultural failure and inward-focused gaze of scientific endeavour: 'The third element, however, operates at a deeper level: it is the systematic, cyclopean shortsightedness of high-modernist agriculture that courts certain forms of failure. Its rigorous attention to productionist goals casts into relative obscurity all the outcomes lying outside the immediate relationship between farm inputs and yields. This means that both long-term outcomes (soil structure, water quality, land-tenure relations) and third-party effects, or what welfare economists call "externalities", receive very little attention until they begin to affect production … ' (1998: 264). Thomas Gieryn's influential analysis (Gieryn 1983) sees such 'boundary work' as the automatic outcome of the daily professional practice of science. Scientists do their work well, and advance professional and political agendas, by drawing a strong boundary between 'science' and 'non science'. In Gieryn's rendering, the practice of science automatically generates a divided ontology of science and non-science, thus dividing the world of knowledge on either side of that boundary. Similarly, Karin Knorr-Cetina, in her book *Epistemic Cultures* (1999) used the term 'negative knowledge' to characterize the practice of disciplinary cultures in the sciences. Negative knowledge is the knowledge that exists outside the boundaries of a discipline's epistemic reach and is usually ignored. Negative knowledge may contain the kinds of knowledge needed for a scientific discipline to avoid or resolve 'wicked problems', but it serves a more useful purpose by existing to define the limits of a discipline's view and also, therefore, the limits of a discipline's responsibility.

47 The opposite can also be true. Cronon's (2003) description of the New England colonies described fenced-off farms as the incubators of agents of wider ecological chaos and destruction. In the New Zealand setting, the wider chaos is already well underway by the 1920s, triggered by fire, flood and drainage.

48 Star and Brooking (2011: 166) identify only isolated voices describing a connected world of farming and environmental impacts arising from the establishment of grasslands farming at the start of the twentieth century, with only a few – like botanist Leonard Cockayne – speaking to what would now be understood as an ecological framing of farming and its consequences.

49 Much in the same way that the abattoirs and papermills dotting rural New Zealand used rivers to carry away their waste.

50 These were also characteristic practices of both industry and households in urban New Zealand.

51 Michael Bell describes this dynamic in an anecdote from his own family life of camping on an island in the middle of the St Lawrence River and dumping the resultant rubbish during the boat journey home across the river, an action justified

(then) by his grandmother saying: 'the river is big enough for us all'. He then describes the conditions under which his family realized that the capacity of wider environments to absorb harms was not limitless (Bell 2009: 183–4).

52   Anthony Giddens describes 'distanciation' as a fundamental quality of modernity – the increasing separation of worlds of production and consumption and the separation of lived worlds connected by globalizing capitalism – across increasingly vast distances of space and time (Giddens 1980).

53   This silence is a key theme in Pawson et al. (2018), where we argue that, by the 1920s, there was a: 'national focus on what might be called "productivism". Eminent British agricultural scientist Sir John Russell identified this during a visit in the 1920s, recalling that "the producers were not at all concerned with marketing problems but always asked me how much more could be got out of the land". Although an interest in consumer tastes– for example in the meat industry – has by no means been absent historically, productivism has meant primarily an emphasis on how to produce more' (2018: 5).

54   Subsequent academic use of the term 'productivism' to describe a particular orientation of contemporary farming systems tends to cluster around the identification of strategies to increase the volume, velocity and efficiency of farm production. As a discourse, 'productivism' has subsequently been the focus of many sophisticated social analyses (including in New Zealand). Rob Burton's key work on how 'good farming' is understood through measures of productivity has been rightly influential in focusing social scientific attention on the cultural centrality of production in farming worlds (Burton 2004a, 2004b; Burton and Wilson 2006, 2012). Similarly, Chris Rosin has identified discourses of productivism as legitimizing all sorts of political positions in farming worlds in New Zealand (Rosin 2013, 2014).

55   The extended period of near total reliance on commodities runs from the 1920s to the 1970s: New Zealand earned 90 per cent of its export value from four (grass-based) products – wool, meat, butter and cheese – between 1890 and 1930, and this had only dropped to 60 per cent by 1970 (Pawson et al. 2018: 4). Matt Henry notes that the 'cross-over' point for the export volume of 'carcasses' (a low-value commodity) dipping below 'cuts' (higher-value, semi-processed meat products) was only reached in the early 1990s (Henry and Roche 2018).

56   van der Ploeg (2008). See also Pretty (2013).

57   King (2003: 234) identifies the 1867 Native Schools Act as the foundation point of a division between spoken Māori at home and the increasing use of English for education – with exclusive use of English language becoming the key pathway to assimilation.

58   For example, Best (1941).

59   Keenan (2013).

60   The differential access to credit is a key element in Belich's (1996) account of the entrenching of Māori disadvantage.

61   As Stokes (2002) argues, Māori were stuck between two worlds of action: facing fragmentation under multiple ownership while being unable to access the benefits of private ownership through access to credit under the Government Advances to Settlers Act (1894).

62   Ngata is an immense figure in early twentieth-century politics, recognized in both Māori and Pākehā worlds (Salmond 2017: 344–6). Most of the history written of this period in Māori farming is focused on Ngata's attempts to modernize Māori land-use (e.g. Keenan 2013). Lambert (2011) treads through the delicate ground of both recognizing Ngata's huge mana and vision, while also acknowledging that

the rationale of his programme was to ensure Māori survival through rapid and successful assimilation into Pākehā modernity.

63   This targeted what was seen as the key impediment to modernization – the lack of 'correct' private title for farms.

64   As Lambert (2011) argues, the mission to modernize the remnant of Māori farms – under the leadership of Ngata – was widely supported in both Māori and Pākehā worlds (Lambert 2011: 4).

65   Keenan (2013) and Lambert (2011).

66   This was by no means the only aspect of Ngata's campaign of modernization. Lambert (2011: 3) recounts that Ngata strongly promoted agricultural education of scientific farming principles and even sent his own son to Hawkesbury agricultural college in Australia.

67   A close ally of Ngata, Charles Goldsmith, lamented the slowness of Māori to emulate Pākehā farming and characterized this as a racial deficiency that could only be remedied by more rapid inter-marriage: 'There are many quite successful Maori farmers ... and it is significant that most are of mixed extraction. It is that bit of [P] akeha blood in him that prods the Maori ... His farming ability must evolve with his character, his education, his appreciation of the finer things of life, and of values. He is by nature happy-go-lucky. He needs ambition to spur him on, and that generally comes with an injection of [P]akeha blood. It is a foregone conclusion that the Maori will in the dim future be absorbed into the white race. By that time the solution to his land problems may come to light' (Speech to the Dept of Agriculture on the East Coast by Charles Goldsmith, late 1950s. Archived: www.grassland.org.nz/publications/nzgrassland_publication_1831.pdf).

68   The report by Jack Hunn to the Department of Māori Affairs in 1961 is a subject of considerable historical commentary. At one level it punctured the complacent assumption that Māori were happily on a pathway to full assimilation as befitting a country with 'the best race relations in the world', arguing instead that Māori were actually experiencing massive social and economic challenges. But Hunn's 'solutions' were simply further strategies for finally forcing Māori into modernity. In Rosenberg's critical summation of the recommendations specifically regarding Māori farming: 'The attitude of the Government is expressed clearly ... "Everybody's land is nobody's land. That in short is the story of Maori land today. Multiple ownership obstructs utilization, so Maori land quite commonly lies in the rough or grazes a few animals apathetically while a multitude of owners rest happily on their proprietary rights, small as they are." ... If Maoris are unwilling or unable to achieve these results under present conditions of ownership, the conditions of ownership should be changed, and transfer into European hands should be made easier, if necessary, to achieve full land utilization in farming terms' (Rosenberg 1966: 213).

69   Butterworth (1974) reproduces one singularly derogatory example of this, in quoting an official brochure of the Department of Māori Affairs in 1965: 'They (Pakehas) always seemed to assume that the Maori really knew perfectly well how to plan his farm ahead; that he refused to plan purely out of naughtiness. But any teacher of Maoris, whether children or adults, will know that his ability to make long-range plans and carry them out is especially difficult to develop. Maoris will work for a long-range objective only if they are carefully trained to do so. Only among a minority is this ability aimed at as part of the parental training of children, nor do many teachers succeed in inculcating it in their pupils' (Butterworth 1974: 55).

70 Scott (1998) is by far the most explicit exponent of an approach to the history of
    modernity that looks directly at science and the creation of divided, rationalized,
    metrologized worlds with the governing intentions and strategies of the modern
    state. He specifically uses agricultural science (alongside forestry science) as an
    exemplar of the creation of science projects in close relationship with modernist
    nation-building projects.

71 This is a recent project of geographer Matt Henry, who deploys the idea of 'thinking
    infrastructures' to elaborate the emergence of a modernist world of agricultural
    education, research and policy in New Zealand during the twentieth century
    (Henry 2019).

72 The national debt to farming is a constant refrain in mid-twentieth-century New
    Zealand. In the words of booster-in-chief Bruce Levy, describing the debt of urban
    New Zealand to the excellence and intelligence of rural New Zealand: 'However
    we regard agriculture in New Zealand … the truth is that we in New Zealand have
    depended in the past, and must continue to depend in the foreseeable future, on
    the export income derived from the soil through the animals that the soil supports.
    Unless we keep this fact constantly and prominently in mind our economy will
    collapse' (Levy 1955: 7).

73 The moment of realization of the scope of the unfolding ecological catastrophe
    is most eloquently rendered in the immortal prose of Herbert Guthrie Smith. He
    recounts how he took over his pastoral farm in 1882 just as it was moving past its
    first flush of fertility released by forest clearance. For the next forty years, he lived
    an unsolvable paradox. He needed to clear re-growth of bracken fern to keep space
    for grass, but the more that he cleared the more his hillsides 'melted' and choked his
    waterways, silting up his beloved Lake Tutira. In the Preface to the third edition of
    Tutira, his life-long narrative of science and progress gave way to a lament for the
    possible loss and destruction of all he'd tried to achieve, along with a reflection on
    the unexpected consequences of his farming actions, questioning: 'my contribution
    towards more quickly melting New Zealand through erosion into the Pacific … Have
    I then for sixty years desecrated God's earth and dubbed it improvement?' (Guthrie
    Smith, 1999: xxiii).

74 Summarized in the collection by Brooking and Pawson (2011).

75 By being, in Tania Li's terms, 'rendered technical', farms become less amenable to
    political discussion and dispute (Li 2007b). The link between 'rendering technical'
    and a de-politicization of worlds is not immediately obvious. This and the following
    sections will argue that the practice of science, and its demarcation of technical/real
    and political/abstract knowledge, acts to shift worlds of knowledge from potentially
    contested to uncontested.

76 Holland (2013: 16–34). Holland et al. (2011a) also refer to items like a handbook for
    settlers that strongly encouraged seeking out advice from local Māori about their
    local environments. This differs significantly from the parallel historical moment in
    Australia, where the existence of Aboriginal farming systems and knowledges was
    continually denied or erased outright (Pascoe 2018).

77 Holland (2013: 198) argues that New Zealand farmers had to adjust to a 'fine grained
    mosaic of ecological patches': 'The one-size-fits-all model of land development did
    not work during the colonial period.'

78 One farm journal, quoted by Holland (2013: 208), urged in 1907: 'every farmer
    should experiment for himself. He need not do it in a lavish or extravagant way, but
    on such a scale that he can prove for himself what answers on his farm.'

79   Reviewed in both its technical componentry and the contribution of its leading
     scientists by Brooking and Star (2011).

80   This was eventually highly contested within the disciplinary world of agricultural
     science – but not until nearer the end of the twentieth century – with the emergence
     of 'farming systems' approaches. In high-profile works like McConnell and Dillon
     (1997), the 'farm systems' approach is premised on a critique of the narrow technical
     focus of bounded, modernist agricultural science and the obscuring of ecological and
     social dynamics in farming systems.

81   It is notable that this wasn't an entire substitution of mechanistic for ecological
     processes. The natural nitrogen-fixing property of clover was central to the
     effectiveness of this package.

82   An interesting feature in New Zealand was the speed of adoption of external inputs.
     Star and Brooking (2011) note that British systems of managing fertility – manuring
     and rotation – were simply overwhelmed by the collapse of soil structure, and New
     Zealand's transition from reliance on internal farm processes to boost fertility to
     external inputs of fertilizer was comparatively rapid compared to other countries
     using British farming systems.

83   While the impact of aerial topdressing was spectacular, it built on another more
     familiar agent – fire. The burning of tussock in the high country to facilitate grazing for
     sheep became a major tool for farmers throughout the twentieth century (Mark 1994).

84   The great drama of this other ecological frontier is narrated in Holland et al.
     (2002) with the ecological dynamics of this breached indigenous grassland frontier
     discussed in Mark (1994), Mark et al. (2003), and Mark and McLennan (2005).

85   There was a range of opinion among scientists as to the desirable pathway forward.
     Levy (1955) pushed for even more expansion of the intensified grasslands model up
     hillsides and into currently 'unproductive' lands (his characterization of Māori land).
     Some dissidents (recounted in Brooking and Pawson 2011) counselled caution, with
     Cumberland in the 1940s joined by others like Kevin O'Connor in arguing that the
     gains of the Grasslands Revolution were temporary and/or geographically limited in
     scope.

86   If the erosion crisis was, in Kenneth Cumberland's reckoning, 'nature's revenge', then
     the ongoing rabbit crisis might be understood as 'nature's fool' in a performance
     of Bruce Levy's *King Lear*. The rapid transition from abject crisis to unilateral
     declaration of the Promethean power of agricultural science by the conclusion of the
     Grasslands Revolution needed its constant, furry reminder that kings who believe
     their powers to be unlimited can tend to go mad. The never-ending 'war on rabbits'
     will return in Chapter 4.

87   See Holland (2013: 111–23).

88   Wood and Pawson (2011).

89   As Wood and Pawson (2011: 158) describe it: 'The growing influence of the state
     nevertheless marked a major change to the architecture of agricultural networks,
     as for the first time since the days of word-of-mouth it vertically integrated the
     production and distribution of information … [and] had the potential to become a
     force for conformity.'

90   This high level of in situ experimentation by Pākehā farmers – particularly about
     pasture strategies – was a key feature of early Pākehā farming, as recounted in
     Holland (2013) and Holland et al. (2011b).

91   Looking forward to some of the conflicts that would emerge later in the twentieth
     century: this forms the basis of a significant divide between agricultural scientists

providing technical and mechanistic solutions within the interior of the bounded modernist farm, and ecological scientists examining ecological 'exteriors'.

92 Carolyn Morris elegantly elaborates these dynamics in 'A Dog of One's Own' (Morris 2007).

93 This is an important point. Practising good science in these contexts requires using methodologies that exclude external interference by values, politics and social dynamics. They also tend to be conceived within mechanistic ontologies rather than broad systems ontologies. Consequently, the rising importance of 'hard science' methodologies in agricultural science, and translation of these into farm learning, enacted and reinforced both an ontological boundary around the farm and the mechanistic (not systems) relations of its interior.

94 This narrowing of the content and pathway to legitimate farming knowledge has consequences. First, farming is narrated as a hard occupation to learn – a life-long process – with dense technical skills for both farmers and researchers, and anyone who doesn't have a deep background in farming, or strong academic skills in a technical science, is automatically considered at best a second-tier expert. Second, for scientists, any defence of these kinds of boundary could be strongly justified as part of a wider defence of 'science'. The critique of the ontological consequences of 'Cartesian reductionism' in some scientific epistemologies is a standard theme in science and technology studies. (For a good review in relation to agricultural science specifically, see Kloppenburg (1991) and Flora (1992).) To use a legal analogy, experts seeking to bring knowledge and understanding from outside the twin sites of expertise on the modernist farm – technically skilled farming men and scientifically trained agricultural scientists (also usually men) – were seen as having a legitimate right to speak to other fields of enquiry, but simply didn't have the 'standing' to speak to issues in agriculture. Some useful social scientific work in New Zealand and Australia was undertaken on exactly how this kind of dynamic has made it so difficult for women to attain leadership positions in agriculture-related businesses and farming organizations, or required the creation of parallel 'women's' organizations for women to participate in (see Liepins 1998, 2000; Pini 2005). It is interesting that these 'alternative organizations' for women later became the prime movers behind breaking some modernist boundaries around farming worlds through the promotion of social scientific research into rural New Zealand and a (short-lived) commitment by the Ministry of Agriculture to expand their focus from strictly farming (and fishing and/or forestry) to include 'rural affairs'. This ontologically disruptive political role for rural women's groups is reviewed in Loveridge (2016).

95 At a more abstract level, Bruno Latour describes these kinds of knowledge-creating practices and objects as 'immutable mobiles' (discussed in relation to agricultural science and alternative agricultural knowledge by Kloppenburg [1991]). They are able to be transported around the world and applied in multiple settings (mobile), but are impervious to the specific influence of place or situation (immutable). In this sense, immutable mobile knowledge worlds are ontologically bounded and serve to enact such boundaries.

96 This argument has already partly been made in Cronon's (2003) account of the New England colonies, in which the lack of labour and the difficulty of moving commodities to transportation hubs to reach markets rendered land as having the most immediate potential to act as capital – thus prompting many and various strategies and practices to secure its ability to act as capital in colonial economies.

97   For agrifood theorists reading this account, my rendition of 'capital' is intended to
      provide a bridge between orthodox political economies of agriculture, which tend to
      see categories like 'land', 'labour' and 'capital' as central, but with a tendency towards
      having a pre-existing fixity when deployed in social theoretical accounts, in contrast
      to the kind of projects of stabilization and pacification described by Callon and
      Mitchell in the Actor Network account of how economic worlds become fixed and
      workable. My account uses farms to show how they operate as capital in the ways that
      orthodox political economy accounts anticipate, but also that this status has a pre-
      history: farms are *enacted* as capital and there are multiple elements needed to render
      them fungible and valuable in order for them to anchor economic worlds. Capital, in
      other words, needs a stable ontology.

98   There are clear parallels in my account to contemporary agrifood discussions about
      the dynamics of financialization, which I'll consider in Chapter 5.

99   See Li (2014, 2017).

100   One of the core insights of rural sociology's 'survivalist' school of family farming
      under capitalism.

101   Hunt (2004).

102   Writing in the Australian colonial context, environmental historian Tom Griffiths
      described sheep and cattle as the 'shock troops of empire' – particularly due to the
      material effect of their hard, cloven hooves on soft outback soils and groundcover
      plants (Griffiths 2002: 228). In New Zealand, the same shock troops had the ability to
      graze on grass while stamping down regrowing bush seedlings and breaking through
      bracken and mānuka thickets to make pathways for (fire-bearing) farmers to follow.

103   There is also a disruptive contribution made by pests to this process of stabilization.
      Isern (2002: 234–40) recounts how the hugely destabilizing effect of rabbits was
      factored into economic evaluations of the worthiness of farms. Successful farms had
      to face down ferality and establish demarcated zones of ecological (semi)control.

104   In other colonizing contexts, the power of fences is even more apparent. The
      introduction of barbed wire in the American West both established title over land
      and enabled the containment of cattle in specific pastures. The 'range wars' in the
      United States, in part, were enacted by the erecting and cutting of barbed wire fences
      (McCullum and McCullum 1965).

105   A summary of the orthodox account of mechanization can be found in McNeill
      (2000: 212–26).

106   The recent academic interest in metrology is reviewed in Legun and Henry (2017).

107   Part of Guthrie Smith's narrative concerns the overly inflated production measures
      that influenced the purchase price of Tutira in 1882, and the long struggle to satisfy
      creditors that productivity was eventually going to return to those levels.

108   This has strong parallels with the work of Timothy Mitchell in colonial Egypt and Tania
      Li in Indonesia, where the role of 'experts' as independent generators of powerful and
      legitimate knowledge became a source of authority operating in the modern state and
      economy. In the same way, farm accountants (and bank finance officers) became these
      kinds of external experts reproducing key metrics about the farm in New Zealand.

109   This is a simplification of a fascinating historical evolution of accountancy measures
      for farms (for an Australasian example, see Carnegie et al. 2006). Accounting
      historians like Lisa Jack have documented how the enacting of particular measures
      around farms during the twentieth century was often highly contested but then
      stabilized to represent uncontested 'objects' of accounting practice that have
      unintended consequences for subsequent farm practice (Jack 2005).

110 Outside the farm, metrological projects that standardized and stabilized trade in key commodities also began to be assembled after the 1920s. The most important of these were the actions of the newly formed Meat Producers Board, which created the first metrics to standardize the meat supply chain to the UK (Henry and Roche 2018: 46).

111 Even then, the state had to intervene again during the Great Depression to prevent the assemblage falling apart.

112 The power of emotional affect in economic worlds has been the subject of long discussion in social theory. Marx's idea of 'commodity fetishism' was taken up by subsequent theorists from Lukacs to Adorno, who used it to explore the way in which affective relations became attached to consumption objects. More recently, theorists like Sarah Ahmed (2004) have delved into the way that emotions/affects are an under-recognized element of the shaping of social worlds.

113 A key theme in Salmond (2017).

114 Salmond (2017: 316–26).

115 Curtis (2002) hints towards this in his insightful ANT-inflected analysis of a colonial farm photograph from New Zealand. The emotional centre of the photograph is the ensemble of objects and kinfolk that anchor the domestic interior of the farm.

116 Buller and Morris (2003) and Holloway (2007).

117 Morris (2007).

118 The emotional effects of ownership of different kinds of farming capital are revealed in the changing institution of 'sharemilking' in dairy farming. Stock and Peoples (2012: 273) make this point in a sophisticated consideration of the subtle, but crucial, differences that emerge in the way in which farmers think and act when we compare 'land-owning' farmers and 'cow-owning' farmers in New Zealand. Both are affectively anchored in their farming systems through the objects they own (either land+cows or only cows).

119 For example, Mairi Jay's account of productivism on New Zealand dairy farms identifies the importance of a particular metric of productivity – the daily measure of milk delivered to the processor – as a key driver of farmer efforts to increase their productivity (Jay 2007). The 'productivist' effect on their farms is a co-production of both cultural effects and the material world of the modernist metrologized farming world itself.

120 Callon describes 'hot' and 'cold' moments in economic networks: 'In "hot" situations, everything becomes controversial: the identification of intermediaries and overflows, the distribution of source and target agents, the way effects are measured. These controversies, which indicate the absence of a stabilized knowledge base, usually involve a wide variety of actors … In "cold" situations, on the other hand, agreement regarding ongoing overflows is swiftly achieved. Actors are identified, interests are stabilized, preferences can be expressed, responsibilities are acknowledged and accepted. The possible world states are already known or easy to identify: calculated decisions can be taken' (Callon 1998: 260–1).

121 De-politicization is an idea with currency outside ANT circles and has been used to describe deliberate strategies to diminish the responsibility of the state towards its citizens (see Flinders and Wood 2014; Reynolds 2016).

122 This is an important idea introduced by Tania Li in her essay on the management of Indonesian forests. Her example reveals multiple practices that stabilize a potentially politically, ecologically and culturally contested (and thus unstable) relationship between humans and forests (Li 2007b). 'Rendering technical' is one such practice

and involves the translation of all knowledge into narrowing worlds of technical, scientifically demarcated knowledge, and the establishment of such knowledge as the only legitimate way to understand a complex area of action (discussed in Tall and Campbell 2018).

123 Callon (1998: 255). For assemblage theorists, the provisos outlined in Chapter 1 need to be reiterated to remind that all such 'big trajectory' narratives oversimplify historical change. What my account of big trajectories of change in modernity potentially disguises is that things are never ordered in such simple and complete ways. As described in Forney et al. (2018), assemblages are never entirely stable, they are 'almost complete, but always in the making of completeness' while also being 'unmade continually and resisting such unmaking'. In Deleuzian terms, they are always 'territorializing', 'de-territorializing' and 're-territorializing'.

4

The crisis of modernist farming

The overarching theme of the past two chapters has been a characterization of the rising trajectory of a modernist farming world. In part, this rising trajectory was built on a continual process of rendering invisible and erasing other ontologies of land and land-use. Emerging out of its role in the colonization of New Zealand, the pastoral family farm stabilized and became the hegemonic form of land-use. This chapter turns towards the second half of that trajectory, as disruption and disarray begin to erode the great citadel of modernist farming. When faced with monolithic worlds, in which all negotiations of powers, inequity and even reality have cooled into a seemingly immovable mass, how can things change? What happens that makes the invisible visible again, renders unthinkable things thinkable and opens up the possibility of alternatives?

The long and stable regime of modernist agriculture remained a firm fixture in New Zealand's political, economic and cultural life for over half a century, but seemingly entered a period of crisis and destabilization in the space of just one day. On 1 January 1973 Britain entered the European Common Market. This moment signalled the termination of long-term trading relationships with ex-colonies like New Zealand and ended a system of external trade networks that had been operating since the mid-1800s (particularly since 1882). Trouble had lurked below the surface for a while.

As the previous chapter described, the golden age of stability, prosperity and cultural hegemony in pastoral family farming was built on immense ecological contradictions, rendering indigenous worlds invisible, a reliance on one major market, a small suite of products, an uncurious approach to marketing of food exports in favour of productivist rationalities, a mechanistic and technical approach to farming systems, and a level of cultural consent for pastoral family farming that was homogeneous on the surface but had deeper undercurrents of unease. The first day of January 1973 is a single date that made visible many transitions that were either already underway or about to unfold in multiple aspects of farming worlds.

Orthodox accounts of the subsequent trauma for New Zealand farming identify 1973 as the commencement of a period of political crisis that rolled through the 1970s, eventually escalating into an economic crisis that was then intensified through the implementation of radical neoliberal reforms after 1984. For the farming community, this period became known as the 'rural downturn', a distinct end-point to the golden age of New Zealand farming.

This chapter will traverse this important period of disruption and crisis for New Zealand farming, then consider both the fractures and disruptions that became evident after the crisis, along with one important area where some farming worlds have continued to elaborate a distinctly modernist ontological character. I will briefly review accounts of the crisis which, grounded in radical political economy, saw the crisis as symptomatic of wider crises of late capitalism and a changing relationship between the state, the economy and the agriculture sector. While radical political economy opened up new lines of critique – especially compared to the framings of orthodox economics – it was an approach that also enacted its own ontological limits on how to understand what had happened. Such approaches have always had a core focus on the relationship between the state and the agricultural elements of the economy. Consequently, much of the rest of this chapter will be devoted to other ways of understanding the crisis that unfolded after 1973, and will argue that much of what happened could also be understood as the manifestation of wider crises in key elements of modernist farming.

The chapter examines four important fracture points: (1) the feral powers of the non-human world, (2) a crisis in science, (3) the emergence of 'greening' dynamics in food export industries and (4) the re-emergence of indigenous ontologies of land-use. The importance of these four lines of fracture becomes increasingly clear in one of the central dramas of twenty-first-century farming in New Zealand – a crisis in the ecological and social legitimacy of intensive dairying. This drama has deep historical echoes. It takes shape around a new effort by modernist farming systems to breach an ecological frontier – this time a breach enacted by irrigation in the quest to turn dry lands wet. This has unleashed chaos, in much the same way that earlier breaches did, but this time the consequences have played out in a country where the cultural, political and economic hegemony of pastoral farming is no longer secure.

This is a different world for modernist farming (and its alternatives). All these fractures and conflicts reveal spaces that allow new alternatives to emerge – where different kinds of farming can take hold and homogeneity can be fractured into greater multiplicity, and where greater opportunities open up for the vital powers of farms and farming ecosystems to express themselves. Yet all this still takes place in conflict with the many ongoing powers of modernist farming that continue to suppress and deny the possibility of other worlds.

The crisis of 1973 and its neoliberal aftermath: Accounts from radical political economy

The crises that commenced in 1973 and intensified after 1984 provided the pivot around which an entire generation of radical scholarship in sociology and geography emerged in New Zealand.

Economic geographers in New Zealand have generally argued that the crisis of 1973 was a key symptom of the slow deconstruction of British colonial economic arrangements.[1] Drawing on the traditions of radical political economy to describe the broad contours of collapse in New Zealand's pastoral economy and trade relationships, the period from 1973 to 1984 was notable primarily for a rupture in the relationship between the state and the agricultural economy.[2] In Richard Le Heron's account (along with those of a host of other geographers and sociologists) New Zealand had held its position as the last major contributor to imperial food relations, at which point the entry of Britain into new economic arrangements with Europe cast New Zealand adrift and into crisis. Political responses to the crisis included a brief period of subsidization of sheep farming by the Muldoon National Government, the diversification and expansion of roles of large monopoly-exporting State Producer Boards,[3] and extensive borrowing by the state to fund large-scale industrial projects (including new industrial facilities to produce agricultural inputs like urea).[4] These state interventions failed to restabilize either the agricultural sector or the wider New Zealand economy, and by the early 1980s the country was moving into profound economic crisis, which created the conditions for advocacy and then adoption of radical neoliberal reforms after 1984.[5]

New Zealand undertook what was, by comparison with other countries, a rapid and highly doctrinaire approach to neoliberalizing agriculture and became, as a result, something of a test case of either the outcomes of 'pure' liberalization (for orthodox economists) or a cautionary tale of the negative consequence of neoliberalization in agriculture (for critical scholars, particularly those working in the traditions of radical political economy).[6]

In the years after 1984, the solid state-agriculture relationship that had been an important feature of the golden age of farming went into a period of crisis and reconfiguration, and a crisis unfolded in both the economic and social life of farming. After the liberalization of agricultural policy in 1984–85, farm incomes fell, debt levels escalated alarmingly, farm families experienced significant stress, farms were foreclosed due to unsustainable debt and the size of viable farms increased in the face of declining incomes.[7] Some social dynamics in the previously stable ensemble of the modernist family farm started to disintegrate. Social relations inside farm households could be seen changing during the crisis: families began to 'self exploit' to survive the crisis,[8] the gendered division of labour shifted as women took on more roles on the farm and often took over farm bookkeeping and accounting,[9] notions of farm succession were disrupted with a changed relationship between farm generations,[10] and the level of paid labour dropped significantly as tasks were reallocated to family members.[11] There was a general sense of dismay at the seemingly declining political influence of farmers as a constituency, along with rising concern that its representatives had actually encouraged this crisis to happen.[12]

The New Rural Sociology along with its fellow travellers in geography (and its successor movement – critical agrifood studies) generated an important alternative to the narrowness and inhumaneness of what were then the ascendant ontologies of neo-classical economic modelling and policy. In the radical narrative, questions about the relationship between farming and capitalism created very specific ways of narrating change, suggesting a range of causalities and relationships situated within the state-economy-agriculture relationship that were simply not able to be captured by econometric models of the natural functioning of the agricultural economy. Farm foreclosures and suicides, failure to transfer farms that had been held in families for generations, disintegration of community networks and trust, and dramatic changes in the nature of work in farm households are all important consequences of liberalization. There was a sense of betrayal and cultural collapse taking place that simply could not be captured in the narrow ontologies of the new economic orthodoxy.

There are, however, some important limitations in the radical narrative. First, while the crisis was real, radical accounts honed in on a set of meta-causes that continually referred back to the dynamics of late-capitalism through its proxies – the state and national economy – sometimes in dynamic relations with wider global trade regimes in an era of globalization. This had two effects. It narrowed the range of potentially important influences and drivers of the crisis while at the same time creating structural accounts that tended to decrease the opportunity to consider how alternatives might arise.[13]

The radical political economy moment also seemed to significantly underplay three critical elements that appear, in the longer historical narrative presented in this book, to be of central importance. What was the relationship between this crisis in farming and new dynamics around science, ecology and post-colonial indigeneity?

While all three of these silences will be reviewed in the rest of this chapter, the post-colonial lapse was particularly significant. In focusing on one profound crisis, those of us writing in the radical political economy tradition had failed to notice a parallel set of dramatic transitions and struggles about land in New Zealand. Having seen off the grim machinations of assimilation, Māori were now starting to assert new political initiatives around farming, land and food.

In early 1975, the highly esteemed leader of Northern Māori and founding president of the Maori Women's Welfare League, Dame Whina Cooper, held a hui (gathering) to determine how to stop further land alienation from Māori.[14] From there, the most famous hīkoi (march) in New Zealand's contemporary history took shape with 79-year-old Cooper leading what eventually became a march of 30,000 people on a 1,000-km trek through the key Māori settlements of the North Island, establishing collective strategies for resistance to land alienation and new tactics of land reclamation. The hīkoi arrived at Parliament on 13 October 1975 proclaiming the slogan: 'Not One More Acre of Land!'[15] It was by no means the first protest, the first act of resistance or the first hīkoi. But it became a moment in the national consciousness that symbolically demonstrated that the tacitly accepted state strategy of assimilation was at an end. A 'Māori renaissance' was emerging.[16] A new moment in the politics of land was taking shape and would have important consequences. It seems that there was much more happening in the great struggle of de-colonization in New Zealand than simply what happened when farmers lost trade access to the UK in 1973. That such a dramatic moment in New Zealand's politics of land seemed to have been almost entirely invisible to us as radical scholars studying Pākehā family farming and the wider farm economy has been cause for significant reflection on my part.

To mark the significance of this ontological shift in the politics of land for both scholars and the actual participants in struggles for de-colonization, I will now use a new name for this country, born out of the new post-colonial politics. We now inhabit Aotearoa New Zealand.

While these tectonic shifts were happening in the post-colonial politics of land in Aotearoa New Zealand, other crises were emerging that would bear directly on the hegemony of modernist farming. In line with developments around the world, a crisis in trust in modernist science was emerging, along with a host of new alternatives to mainstream food and farming that were 'greening' food industries. How, then, do we understand the disruption of modernist farming, and how do we evaluate the effects of such disruptions? What happens to render visible things that were previously invisible, and under what conditions do alternatives become thinkable?[17]

The new politics of farming: Disruption and alternatives

In the rest of this chapter, I want to consider four key vectors of disruption that serve to highlight four places where land-use was transitioning (often in spectacular eruptions) from hegemony to contestation, from homogeneity to multiplicity, and thus, the many sites where alternatives to modernist farming began to take shape and have varying effects:

- Ferality
- Science and trust
- Greening
- Indigeneity

These four areas involve some key milestones that trace an interesting diverging movement of relations and powers in modernist farming. The extent to which these kinds of disruptions signify a new political environment for modernist farming is revealed in stark terms in the escalating contemporary conflict over the breaching of a new ecological frontier by intensive dairy systems. By using irrigation to turn dry lands wet, dairy intensification has unleashed a new round of chaos and destabilization. But this time, unlike its colonial predecessors, the social and political environment around farming is radically different.

1. Ferality: Cyclone Bola and rabbit calicivirus disease

Colonized countries, especially ones with the rapid level of ecological disruption experienced in Aotearoa New Zealand, live in the constant presence of ferality.[18] The unruly vitality of climate and disrupted ecosystems is the long-term bane of modernist, industrial farming logics that operate on the principle of creating the maximum possible amount of homogeneity and predictability in farming systems.[19]

After the long period of relative success of the Grasslands Revolution in stabilizing hillsides under specific pasture strategies, and a long period of relatively low incidence of major flooding events on Aotearoa New Zealand's highly fragile East Coast, the fundamental ferality of Aotearoa New Zealand's ecosystems was re-asserted in the second week of March 1988 when Cyclone Bola, the most destructive storm in the country's recorded history, was unleashed (see Figure 6).[20] Bola originated near Fiji, but as it tracked southwards towards Aotearoa New Zealand it developed an ill-timed 'asymmetry' of rain-bearing cloud that slammed into the pastoral farming areas of

Figure 6 Cyclone Bola soil erosion, 1988
Artist attribution: Marion Familton

the East Coast region of the North Island. In the area around Gisborne and East Cape (including the site of my ancestors' family farm Te Rahui as well as Herbert Guthrie Smith's Tutira), the storm rapidly deposited astonishing levels of rain across the region. Most of the area received nearly 500 mm of rain in seventy-two hours. The peak rainfall recorded was 917 mm in the remote settlement of Tolaga Bay.[21]

The damage inflicted by the storm was not just caused by the high level of rain (something that modellers now predict will happen more frequently under even moderate climate change scenarios for Aotearoa New Zealand). The true damage was due to the effect of extreme rain on the steep hillsides that had been deforested and converted to pasture over the previous sixty to eighty years.[22] The pasture cap on fragile soils was rent open and hillsides collapsed with the twin effect of leaving slopes scoured and denuded of cover (some lost as much as 70 per cent of their pastured area), and waterways and lakes inundated with sediment.[23] Over 1,700 farms were eventually classed as having experienced major adverse effects and a government relief scheme provided NZ$110 million of support.[24]

Cyclone Bola was a shocking event for the farming community as families experienced their farms disintegrating beneath their feet. What was even more significant was the rapidly emerging consensus that large parts of this region were no longer suitable for pastoral farming and should be converted permanently back into forest.[25] This was, in effect, the feral rebuke to the overreach of Bruce Levy's ambition – that the maximum possible extent of Aotearoa New Zealand's forest, indigenous grass and wetland landscape could and should be converted into grasslands-based pastoral farming.[26] It reminded anyone pondering such matters that the Grasslands Revolution was a 'solution' that was neither permanent nor universally applicable in the face of the destabilized quality of Aotearoa New Zealand's farming ecosystems. It was a significant moment of retreat in the ecological frontier of pastoral farming.[27]

Alongside the deluge came a plague. In Chapter 3 of this book, the ontological enacting of an ecological boundary around the farm, and its ecological incoherence, was argued to be one of the defining characteristics of the modernist farm. One dynamic that pitilessly exposed the fallacy of this ecological boundary was the 'war on rabbits'.[28] Part of the declining pattern of pastoral success in the run-up to the Grasslands Revolution was the desperate and often losing battle to control rabbits. The state intervened with massive investment in control through the introduction of stoats and ferrets; the erection of 'rabbit-proof' fences; the employment of 'rabbiters' to shoot, gas, poison and dig out dense populations; and the widespread deployment of poisoned baits. By the 1960s, however, the state began to undertake a slow surrender and ceded responsibility for rabbit management to regional government agencies.[29] This may seem like a small shift, but it set the stage for a political and ecological crisis that demonstrated the degree to which farm–state relations and old political alliances were being disrupted.

The reduction of government funding for rabbit control and a series of government reviews in the 1970s and 1980 shifted policy from total eradication to simply managing areas of high infestation.[30] Rabbits are a feral power that the state simply had to admit it couldn't eradicate. This ran counter to the desires of many farmers who were passionately committed to the idea that the government (and its scientists) should pursue total control through complete eradication. Tensions came to a head when the government, following advice from more ecologically minded scientists, decided in two separate reviews not to introduce the rabbit-killing disease myxomatosis – decisions that were condemned by many farmers and their representatives. Government and scientific attention then turned to a new biological control agent, rabbit calicivirus disease (RCD), which at that time was being evaluated in Australia.

Among some farmers, there was a feeling of betrayal of the state's commitment to the ideal of 'command and control' in farming systems. Feral powers erupted in August 1997 when farmers illegally obtained a sample of RCD from Australia, and then pursued a series of simple measures (putting the livers of dead rabbits through a kitchen blender and distributing the results to other farmers) to propagate the virus around Aotearoa New Zealand.[31] It was an action carrying breathtaking political and ecological risks and was both condemned and celebrated in different communities.[32] Seen through the long lens of colonial ecological disruption, this was a latter-day repetition of actions that had dangerously destabilized Aotearoa New Zealand ecosystems. Seen through the lens of modernist farming and its quest for homogeneity, control and technical solutions, however, such a strategy made perfect sense.

Taken together, Cyclone Bola in 1988 and the illegal introduction of RCD in 1997 straddle a period of dramatic change in the state relationship with environmental management. The introduction of a new environmental management framework, the Resource Management Act (1991), indicated a shift (but not a complete overturn) of the modernist project of state intervention to homogenize environments and attempt to control ferality, which had characterized the previous century and in particular the period through pastoral farming's golden age. It introduced a complex new regime of environmental management, predominantly devolved to regional councils and including management of environmental impacts of farming. In its most significant omission, however, lobbying from farmer groups during the formation of the legislation won a blanket exemption for every farming activity up to 1991. It was a free pass for the environmental impacts of everything that had happened, to date, inside the boundaries of the farm. The ecological consequences of modernist farming during its golden age would never experience retrospective examination by the state.

On reflection, the crises of ferality during the period from 1988 to 1997 demonstrated some profound disruptions: pastoral family farming was no longer the predominant industry driving national policy formation (while still being very important), the wider public had a much-reduced level of cultural consent for the actions of farming, and a shift in the key political relations shaping environmental management had occurred. From being composed in a state–farmer alliance to pursue total control of any ecological threats to farming, the environment now required 'managing', and part of the responsibility for this management was being shifted from national to regional governance and was introducing external scrutiny inside the boundaries of farms. At the same time, the frontier ecologies of farming were shifting and the furthest aspirations of modernist control were shrinking as pasture began to retreat out of the highest slopes and steepest gullies of hill country farms. This new configuration of relations and responsibilities would only be reinforced as subsequent biosecurity incursions disrupted landscapes and primary production systems.[33]

The management of these crises also revealed a fracturing of the unified modernist project of science. There were now new divisions of knowledge production often producing contradictory outcomes relative to ecologies, technologies and intervention strategies as well as a retreat from the universal embrace of 'progress' leveraged through technological expertise. As RCD showed, this fracturing of the project of modernist science wasn't something that was welcomed by a large proportion of the farming sector. A further rupture in public acceptance of a close relationship between modernist farming and modernist science then became the central focus in the controversy that erupted around genetically modified organisms (GMOs).

2. Science, trust and new social movements: Mad cow disease and GMOs

If wider public concerns about environmental management in farming revealed an increasing level of contestation of farming worlds by wider groups, the other element in the emerging contestation of modernist farming was an erosion of trust in particular kinds of scientific expertise. This was signalled (at a comfortable distance from Aotearoa New Zealand) by the crisis of mad cow disease or bovine spongiform encephalopathy (BSE). The first signs of BSE were evident in the UK from the mid-1980s, but a full-blown crisis of trust in British beef (and scientists) accelerated during the early 1990s, culminating in a crisis for the government and an economically damaging EU ban on British beef in 1996.[34]

Mad cow disease represented a breaching point in public perceptions of risk in agriculture and food systems. This peaked in 1996 when the UK government, for the first time, advised that BSE in cattle was causing Creutzfeldt-Jakob disease in humans. In response to this an immense public, political and media storm called the role of the British government's agricultural scientists into question, with many commentators claiming that scientists had put the economic needs of farmers ahead of the safety of beef consumers.[35] The crisis became an intense object of academic interest, demonstrating emerging chaos in previously settled relations of scientific expertise and food consumption[36] as well as a disruptive destabilization of settled ways of knowing, measuring and evaluating risk and safety.[37]

If mad cow disease was a food scare echoing from the other side of the world, the debate over the potential introduction of GMOs into agriculture struck much closer to home. As the controversy over adoption of GMOs in agriculture began to accelerate around the world,[38] Aotearoa New Zealand was in a position to politically and legally consider a 'first release' scenario for GMOs in agriculture, and the Royal Commission of Enquiry into Genetically Modified Organisms (RCGM) was established as part of the governing agreement of a new coalition government in 1999. GMOs are interesting partly because they have vital materialities that either can or can't be controlled, depending on your ontology of the farm.

The Royal Commission became a complex vehicle with deeply fraught political contests and crises, where many constituencies mobilized and aligned around the decision to release or not to release; its twists and turns, political dynamics and contested science claims have been extensively examined across many academic fields.[39] One important political fight that emerged was extremely mismatched: the tiny new organic agriculture sector, which saw GMOs as undermining the potential of a unified 'clean green' strategy for agricultural exports, was pitted against the established order of agricultural science, which was excited about the revolutionary potential of GMOs as a transformative technology that could change outcomes for agriculture while buttressing the increasingly beleaguered project of modernist science.[40] I'll return to this other new entrant shortly.

The provision of scientific and expert advice revealed important new fractures.[41] There was a distinct majority-minority split in the science community between agricultural scientists and academics working in genetics on the one hand, and social scientists, ecological scientists and those seeking to engage Māori-inflected approaches to epistemology and scientific knowledge production (giving more space to traditional ecological knowledge and holistic methods and ontologies) on the other.[42]

In hindsight, the Royal Commission on GMOs was a major milestone in the elaboration of new political dynamics and contests in Aotearoa New Zealand agriculture. It represented the first time that significant constituencies of liberal, urban citizens had taken a political stance on the character of agricultural systems in Aotearoa New Zealand. It also revealed the growing power of wider green political discourse in Aotearoa New Zealand (as was the case around the world). It created a brighter spotlight on alternative visions for agricultural futures for agriculture,[43] and it created a space for Māori critique of land-use practices and approaches.[44] Collectively, it made sustainability, environmental risks and food safety major political themes in Aotearoa New Zealand agriculture for the foreseeable future. It showed, in Callon's sense, that a previously 'cold' relationship between science and the production of food in Aotearoa New Zealand was now becoming considerably more 'hot'.[45]

The Royal Commission made visible a new terrain of conflict between scientists, science institutions and farmer politicians whose view of future change in Aotearoa New Zealand agriculture was entirely ontologically contained inside modernist farming approaches, and a range of critiques that lurched into view in a sudden and quite startling way from other academics, wider publics, social movements and political alliances. Disruptive forces were at play in previously settled worlds of modernist science that were making alternatives much more thinkable. This disruption included farmers, who in survey responses now started to reveal a growing minority who were interested in environmental practices and the potential for 'greening' farming systems.[46]

3. Alternatives: Organics, eco-label audits and farmers' markets

The crises of ferality and increasing evidence of a loss of trust in scientific expertise took shape alongside the parallel development of alternative 'green' products in Aotearoa New Zealand, through the adoption of certified organic production or the use of audits deploying measures of sustainability and environmental qualities like that used by the GlobalGAP alliance. The late 1980s and early 1990s were characterized in New Zealand as a period when previously homogeneous export organizations like the NZ Kiwifruit Marketing Board began to experiment with a niche of certified organic export products and subsequently initiated a wholesale move towards 'eco-labelling' of export products.[47]

The academic narrative of the 'greening' transition in Aotearoa New Zealand revolves around some quite specific events and some unusual materials and technologies – in particular, the arrival and enactive power of new forms of environmental certification, protocols and their systems of audit.[48]

If there is a 'genesis moment' for the creation of an entire new vector of connectivity and information flows in Aotearoa New Zealand agriculture, it might be found, in a mythological sense, in a paddock near the village of Dunsandel. In this paddock, two parties met in 1991. One was Wattie's Frozen Foods Ltd.,[49] and the other was an experienced, conventional cropping farmer who had previously met onerous production and quality targets for producing peas under contract for Wattie's. Our farmer is not culturally 'alternative', has mainstream views about farming, doesn't care much about the concerns of urban environmentalists and, in 1991, is working very hard to keep his farm viable during the latter stages of the rural downturn.

When these two parties met, there was a third 'party' present at the negotiations. Wattie's field contract staff arrive with a small sheaf of A4 paper upon which are printed the words 'BIO-GRO Standards for Organic Production'. As far as milestones go, this one is a massively under-recognized inflection point.[50] After an entire colonial history of 'silent markets' based on the separation of production and consumption and the filtering of information via formal state intermediaries (like producer boards), a new form of governance technology had arrived that created an entirely new vector of information and connectivity. It established a new way for retail entities to communicate and discipline production and it operated, in some cases, as a new site of political engagement between producers, consumers, business intermediaries and new social movements (like the organic farming movement, Fair Trade or animal welfare organizations). While technologies of audit are a selective and limited vector of connection, they were also, in effect, starting to sketch in some of the lineaments of a previously invisible world.

From its 'genesis moment' in 1991, within fifteen years certified organic production had grown in interesting ways: highly lopsided towards exporting over domestic markets (it was taking place, after all, in a country that exported over 90 per cent of its food production),[51] it had a significant series of conflicts and negotiations with the local organic social movement (including whether the state should act as an arbiter of organic standards or whether the neoliberalized state in Aotearoa New Zealand could actually be trusted in such a role),[52] but eventually became a solid niche in many export industries.[53]

Starting with the creation of the first formal BIO-GRO standards for organics, the kiwifruit industry then became the site of elaboration of wider environmental standards for kiwifruit production by participating in the new European alliance of retailers, consumer groups, farmer groups and scientists elaborating the EUREP-GAP (later GlobalGAP) standards across fruit and vegetable supply chains into Europe.[54] By 2004, almost the entirety of Aotearoa New Zealand's major horticultural export sectors, in particular apples and kiwifruit along with the viticulture sector, were using some form of protocol that either aligned with GlobalGAP or administered a parallel system.[55] Moves towards auditing sustainability and environmental performance were more sporadic in the heartland of pastoral farming, but did take shape around the actions of some smaller, boutique meat export companies as well as dairy giant Fonterra, which experimented with organic milk production on around 200 dairy farms.

The enactive powers of these new systems of environmental auditing in export industries have been the subject of significant academic reflection. In sum, these new technologies of audit are not simply the bearers of other institutional powers (i.e. passively carrying the requirements of a social movement, an audit alliance of retailers or an export industry body).[56] They also have their own enactive powers and should be recognized as such. They enact new ontologies of food and farming.

The arrival of the 'greening' audits into Aotearoa New Zealand export sectors had three important effects in respect to the arguments being elaborated in this book. First, environmental audits link producers to consumers in interesting new ways. They breach the ontological barrier between production and consumption and create new vectors of discipline on farm practice that emanate from a very different range of groups and institutions than those that conditioned farm practice under the golden age of modernist farming. In some cases, they also create new networks of connection with environmentally concerned new social movements, like those interested in organic farming, animal welfare, health consequences of farming technologies like pesticides, or wider planetary environmental concerns like climate change, energy use or water conservation.

A second quality is that audits enact ontological binaries in ways that discomfort and disrupt the hegemonic certainties of modernist food production. One repeated experience during research interviews with conventional export organizations in the 1990s was their concern that by adopting an organic product, they would raise unwanted questions about their conventional products in the same markets. Certified organic had this ontological quality – it separated foods into good and bad sides of an audited binary. The whole ensemble of new labelled foods being retailed around the world is premised on the idea that these alternatives act in opposition to something less desirable.[57] In all these settings, 'alternative' food audits are enacting two things simultaneously: they are proclaiming their own overt qualities (assumed to be good, but open to political contestation as to whether they actually deliver these qualities), while also generating some kind of binary relationship with an undesirable other (the existence of which is usually only implied). In other words, they are enacting disruptive *binary* food ontologies.

The final quality of new environment audits like organic or GlobalGAP is that they have interesting effects on the practice of farming and the subjectivities of farmers. For many kiwifruit orchardists, the requirements of their new Integrated Pest Management-based audit system hinged around the monitoring of pests on their vines. This had unexpected effects. It forced kiwifruit growers out of their offices and into their orchards to physically inspect their vines. Growers reported that this was unexpectedly transformative – especially after a couple of years of massively reduced pesticide use when native birds like fantails began following them down the rows of vines catching insects. Seeing the return of native birds to their orchards was a transformative moment.[58]

But these audits were interacting with important things happening to the human participants in the systems as well. Native birds arriving back in orchards opened up wider ecological networks and connections that breached the ontology of the ecological boundaries around properties. Demands for particular qualities and values in the production of kiwifruit signalled the existence of discriminating consumers in far-off markets, or brought contact with certification agencies and/or the social movements that generate them. Distant places became closer, and social consequences and networks became more visible. For social researchers in the ARGOS project, we noticed that this quality stretched across realms of farm practice. We called it 'breadth of view'.[59] Looking back now, this was an important insight. It was an idea that exposed the difference between social practice and discourse trapped inside the ontological boundaries of farms and orchards, and a changed body of practice that recognized exterior social, economic and ecological worlds.[60]

If new audit technologies have disrupted and changed elements of agrifood worlds and opened up new meanings for food, a further dynamic that has emerged in the last fifteen years and which has changed production–consumption ontologies is the 'turn to the local'.[61]

The local food phenomenon was slow to reach Aotearoa New Zealand, which may not be entirely surprising in a country that is exporting over 90 per cent of the food it produces. Farmers' markets are the most obvious manifestation of a wider food trend: the turn towards valuing local foods. This has been extensively studied as a new political and environmental praxis in the context of regions like Europe.[62] For Aotearoa New Zealand, however, the farmers' market phenomenon has a slightly different political character.[63] Farmers' markets bring food consumers right to the farm gate.[64] They perform a curiously benign politics of re-connection.[65] Having farming and boutique food consumption placed in such proximity to one another is profoundly different for Aotearoa New Zealand. While not being as confrontational as direct protests over things like GMOs, the farmers' market movement in Aotearoa New Zealand uses a 'politics of proximity' to puncture the ontological boundary separating farmers from their traditional markets.

Seen through this lens, the farmers' market phenomenon (and the turn to the local more generally) represents a small but specific new style of production–consumption linkage for food production in Aotearoa New Zealand. It is the boutique and user-friendly version of a wider set of ontologically breaching ruptures that were erupting elsewhere between farmers and consumers. In combination, both the arrival of new environmental audits and the emergence of short food chain linkages like farmers' markets demonstrate the kind of new production–consumption relations emerging around new technologies, objects and institutions within the disrupted space that opened up during the neoliberalization process and collapse of stable long-term trading relations.[66]

4. Māori farming, food and the politics of de-colonization

All these many and various disruptions, confrontations and sometimes quite congenial sites of revolution around the edges of modernist farming started to take their most concrete form in the 1990s and early 2000s. They all did particular kinds of work in making alternative futures more visible and thinkable. It is important, however, to remember that ontological politics is also founded in the politics of invisibilization and silencing. Consequently, when listing all that was once invisible and now started to become more visible, it is also important to reflect on that which remained invisible.[67] The political and ontological centre of modernist farming still existed and continued to exert its ontological powers in various ways. This became evident in Māori contests over multiple aspects of land and food.

The event recounted at the start of this chapter – the great hīkoi that brought Māori ownership of their land back into political contest – formed part of a wider upwelling of activism and political engagement by Māori. Something new and important was happening in the state–Māori relationship. Sir Ranginui Walker is the most prominent academic narrator of the long struggle by Māori to confront the logic of assimilationist policies and there are key moments in the Māori relationship with the state that are important markers in this journey. Of particular significance was the creation, in 1975, of the Waitangi Tribunal as a mechanism to address any conflicts that emerged from that date onwards relating to commitments by the Crown made under the Treaty of Waitangi in 1840. This took shape on the eve of two historically significant land protests that had emerged after the hīkoi and eventually provided a new framework for politically responding to those protests over land loss after 1975.[68] The Waitangi Tribunal underwent a dramatic revolution in 1985; however, when the High Court ruled that its purview should be retrospectively extended all the way back to 1840, thus establishing the Tribunal as a legal avenue for redress for major historical grievances between Māori and the Crown.[69]

As Sir Ranginui Walker argues, the political initiatives and struggles that created the Waitangi Tribunal resulted in a policy forum that enacted the opposite of the two key discourses that underpinned the assimilationist project: 'New Zealand has the best race relations in the world', and 'progress is served by the ultimate assimilation of Māori into the Pākehā world' – by making visible the extent of Māori disadvantage and historical inequities stemming from acts that took place since colonization.[70]

A second pillar of the new politics of indigeneity in Aotearoa New Zealand came through a surge in radical scholarship and activism by a new generation of Māori scholars. The most internationally celebrated manifesto of a new Māori approach to scholarship is the book *Decolonising Methodologies* written by Linda Tuhiwai Smith in 1999, which gathers the insights of multiple Māori scholars and activists to establish a new political ontology of scholarship for Māori in Aotearoa New Zealand. This intervention has been taken forward under the project of enacting Matauranga Māori in scholarship and research. Smith's classic work enacted a potent attack on the hidden ontological framing of modernist epistemologies and argued for acts of academic de-colonization to make space for indigenous methodologies to flourish.

These two moments – the emergence of a political site of negotiation between Māori and the Crown at the Waitangi Tribunal and the flourishing of a new decolonizing ontology in Māori scholarship – sit among a host of other sites and practices that were starting to demarcate spaces for alternatives to be thinkable and new potentials recognized. They also, however, demarcate a significant boundary around (as yet) inviolable terrain at the heart of the modernist farming project in Aotearoa New Zealand.

Much of the previous chapter established the centrality of key practices and relations in enacting an ontological boundary around the modernist farm and its key science relationships. These had both explicit and implicit intentions and positioned Māori knowledge and farming practices as highly inferior and/or an undesirable remnant of pre-modern thinking that required assimilation. With the increasing resistance to assimilationism, and the emergence of open political contests around Māori and land from the 1970s, the politics of invisibilization have, at times, given way to an overt and visible politics of state institutional and political resistance to meeting Māori claims over land and farming. When invisibilization starts to fail and multiple claims to land emerge, the state is forced into choices about whose rights take precedence. To date, in Aotearoa New Zealand, the state has solidly defended the private-property owning farmer.

There are two key processes in which this state response has become evident. First, there are concrete political decisions by the state that have acted to protect private farmland from exposure to new styles of governance and partnership. The Waitangi Tribunal, in exerting its post-1985 powers, had the potential to recommend the government re-purchase of private farmland to settle claims. I clearly recall my grandparents' fears that distant historical claims might threaten their farm.[71] This came to a head in 1992 with a Tribunal recommendation that one parcel of a privately owned farm be repurchased by the government and returned to Māori.[72] The government reacted immediately and passed an amendment to the Treaty of Waitangi Act that specifically forbade the Tribunal from making any recommendation that involved private land – which effectively took privately owned farms off the table as an object available to the state to use for compensation or redress.[73]

A second element of Crown actions to restrict the scope of new Treaty partnership requirements is evident in the establishment of the RMA (1991), which required that new resource consents be subject to processes of consultation with multiple stakeholders – including local iwi (tribes) – to create a site of policy dialogue that suggested a greater level of co-governance of resource decision-making.[74] However, in the passing of that new Act, and under extreme pressure from the farming lobby, the government agreed to the exemption of all existing farm activities to 1991 from the need to be compliant with RMA requirements and processes. This effectively meant that farmers were not required to enter partnership processes under the new Act. While the RMA would trigger a new era of consultation with iwi, almost all of (voluntary) local Māori capacity was drawn into non-farm-related resource consent discussions for the subsequent decades. Farms have effectively remained outside of that process. As will be discussed later in this chapter, current tensions around water governance are not yet aligning with any stable coalitions of stakeholders who might act to influence and guide RMA processes. In the absence of such coalitions, the Act is still not gaining much purchase over farming activities.[75] The 1990s firewall around private farms is holding.

Alongside these two government strategies is a less specific, but potentially even more influential, set of policy changes in relation to the neoliberalization of Aotearoa New Zealand in the 1980s and 1990s. Rationalities of 'market-led' governance and increased competition moved a range of policy frameworks into narrower sets of actions and intentions – which sometimes undermined or sought to disestablish those sites where the actual enacting of new Treaty partnerships was being attempted.[76]

A final action by the state to create firewalls around the 'centre' of the great modernist farm project involves one of the key sets of practices traversed in this book: the ontology of agricultural science. State R&D policy is one key realm where science ontologies are enacted. The neoliberal project included major changes to the funding of agricultural R&D through the creation of new competitive systems of allocation of funding for agricultural science.[77] This came with a constantly elaborating framework for consideration of Treaty obligations, with the current system requiring research bids to make some contribution to a set of broad goals described as Vision Matauranga (VM). The inclusion of VM (and its various prior incarnations) into agricultural science funding processes has been highly contentious. It resulted in open protest by some senior research professors at universities, and various administrative manipulations to ensure that VM is 'present' but not 'influential' in the operation of 'good science'. Consequently, science programmes tend to compartmentalize VM elements into the 'social', 'values' or 'applied outcomes' sections – anywhere except those aspects that determine core research ontologies. Again, the firewall holds around the centre of modernist farming worlds.

In summary, the state has maintained its basic framework of protection for private property (including privately owned farms) and shown no inclination to meaningfully dismantle the firewall around a key institution of modernist farming – its scientific ontology. When the state has shifted towards partnership in processes around agricultural science funding, the ongoing project – at the level of the lab-bench and research institutions – of erecting silos and firewalls has made sure that any required incorporation of Treaty partnership processes is 'present but not influential' where matters of agricultural science are concerned.

As a result, a renewed sense of vitality and experimentation in Māori food and farming worlds has, until recently, taken shape mainly outside the ongoing relationship between the state, private farming and agricultural science.[78] There are exciting things currently happening with Māori farming, but they are taking place outside the core political relationships of modernist farming. In reviewing these defensive actions by the state to maintain the modernist farming firewall, it is important to recognize that outside that battle for the central ground of modernist farming, there are many important and performative things happening that are renewing Māori relations with food and farming. There are hopeful actions such as in communities where Māori women have re-established marae gardens sites to rebuild local food and community relationships.[79] Other areas of significant activity include the restoration of wild-food gathering – in particular the way in which Māori communities are emerging to take governance and management roles over traditional food sources and environments;[80] there is a small certification service that is attempting to develop and operate a certification standard for 'Māori organic' food;[81] and particular food items like heritage potatoes are being bred and elaborated to simultaneously retrieve older environmental knowledge and create new niche products.[82] Internationally, one of the significant vectors of indigenous food renewal has been through chefs and 'high cuisine' adopting and elaborating indigenous foodways. In Aotearoa New Zealand there have been several attempts to create restaurants selling Māori cuisine, but these have generally not succeeded.[83]

While this new activity is partially frustrated by the ongoing defensive actions of the state in relation to modernist farming – even when new Treaty partnership requirements open up potential spaces for dialogue – one place where new activities and experiments in Māori land-use come into closest contact with vital ecologies and new ontologies is in new initiatives in Māori farming. In a book about farming and colonization, the role of Māori farms in de-colonizing landscapes is of critical importance. In the next chapter, I will consider at some length the ways that Māori farms, and other new experiments in land-use, are enacting new ontologies and making alternative worlds possible.

Breaching another ecological frontier: Turning the dry lands wet

The fact that all these contests, alternatives and responses have happened points towards a disruption of the hegemonic status for modernist farming in Aotearoa New Zealand. But threatened hegemonies still involve centres of power that exist and act in various ways – even if the political terms of engagement have changed in a world of declining social and political consent and rising critique. Before considering the status and scope of the many disruptions detailed in this chapter as they are being enacted at the level of farms, however, it is vital to also assess the state of health of the modernist farm project. To do so, a key rift in land-use in Aotearoa New Zealand looms into view. Just as it lurked in the background in the discussion of the two case study farms in Chapter 1, the water crisis of provinces like Canterbury has become a compelling concern and source of conflict.

In effect, yet another ecological frontier has been breached, and like its predecessors, the consequences have been chaotic.

The first three frontiers of ecological colonization took shape around important indigenous ecosystems: the removal of forest cover, the draining of wetlands and the replacement of indigenous tussocks to create exotic grasslands. The next ecological frontier follows a similar trajectory but uses a subtly different array of objects and relations.[84] The two great frontier movements narrated thus far were the way that farms turned forests into grasslands and made wetlands dry. This next great breach is to make dry lands wet. It has been the underpinning dynamic enabling an expansion of intensive pastoral systems for dairying in previously dry provinces like Canterbury and North Otago through irrigation (and has also been deployed as a 'homogenizing' factor making dairy systems more predictable in other provinces, like Southland).

The post-neoliberal story of New Zealand farming revolves around the rise and rise of dairying. It is a style of farming that was always present, yet generally culturally and politically subordinated to sheep farming during the golden age. Since the 1980s, the rising power and scope of dairy farming have produced enough drama and conflict to fill an entire book.[85] In brief, a period of intense restructuring resulted in the formation of the mega-cooperative Fonterra in 2001.[86] This consolidated the rise of new pastoral systems for dairying based around use of ryegrass and nitrate/urea fertilizers. At the time of Fonterra's formation, the cooperative contributed nearly one-third of cross-border trade in dairy products in the world, and was the world's largest dairy export organization. It almost totally controlled New Zealand's largest industry and vied with tourism to provide the nation's highest level of foreign exchange income.[87] This new consolidated configuration of the dairy industry was ideally poised to take advantage of a second highly significant development – the signing of a Free Trade Agreement with China, the first achieved by any Western country.[88] This gave Aotearoa New Zealand 'first mover' advantage into the Chinese market, and the resulting 'white gold rush' triggered a boom in investment into dairy farms.[89] Here the historical echoes ring loud and clear. Once again, conditions were ripe for an expansionary surge of farms, but such pressures faced a simple barrier in that all the immediately available land in 'wet' provinces had generally already come into dairy systems by the time of the China boom. An ecological frontier had been reached and a new conquest loomed. This new frontier was the dryland farming regions of New Zealand's southern East Coast. The object and new relations that would break through the problem of 'wet land' scarcity were a specific set of irrigation technologies.[90] The centre pivot irrigator would take its place alongside the axe, flame and farm drain as a key agent in breaching a new ecological frontier.

This new ensemble of modernist dairy farming has taken shape behind familiar ontological boundaries but uses a new set of objects and measures. First, there was an important adjustment to the balance of internal and external inputs into farming systems. The clover is gone in favour of high-producing ryegrass, and the external reliance on technical inputs has ratcheted up to a new level with extensive reliance of heavy use of nitrogenous fertilizers, and an eventual reliance on imported palm kernel expeller (PKE) from Indonesia as a cheap supplementary source of stock food.

As the key technical object that sits at the heart of intensive dairy systems, the centre pivot irrigator has vital powers. It is the magic device that moves your farm much further down the track to adopting factory logics. With a consistent supply of fertilizer, and a stable soil base to hold water and ryegrass, irrigators make one of the most unpredictable elements of the farming system – available water – into a predictable constant. With an irrigator, much becomes more predictable, and a new ensemble of measures, values and potentials can then become the basis for valuing farmland. It is much easier to value a farm when it is simplified to the point where it becomes a 'machine for producing grass'.[91] From that point on, the two key variables in the survival of your farming system are the payout from Fonterra (or one of its small group of competitor dairy processors) and the interest rate on the mortgage that you secured to buy your land and/or to convert from sheep to dairy on-farm infrastructure.

The place where this ensemble can be most effectively used to generate economic capital is by breaching the ecological frontier of dryland regions. With the arrival of every new irrigation company/cooperative – and the centre pivots they used to distribute water – land valuations soared, which anchored the 'white gold rush'. While many dairy farmers in traditional provinces like Taranaki and Waikato look at the new dairy world created by irrigators and disapprove of the unsubtle powers being unleashed, this is indeed a new frontier. And like its predecessors, it has both an impeccable internal logic and unleashed ecological chaos.

Writing in 2004, Aotearoa New Zealand's Parliamentary Commissioner for the Environment Dr Morgan Williams argued that these new dairy systems were a 'ticking time bomb' in Aotearoa New Zealand farming.[92] In stark statistical terms, the ten years to 2004 had seen a 19 per cent rise in stocking intensity, a 34 per cent rise in milk production per hectare, but an astonishing 162 per cent rise in use of nitrogenous fertilizers per hectare in dairy systems.[93] The ability of the new ensemble of irrigators, ryegrass, urea, cows and, after 2008, cheap credit[94] to massively intensify pastoral systems was happening, however, within fragile dryland freshwater ecosystems. Downstream from these farms were important streams, rivers and lakes, and deep below lay major aquifers. The sudden rise in nitrogenous fertilizers, sediment and pathogens running off intensive dairy units was not breaching frontiers in a sudden explosion of fire or the dramatic opening of drainage systems. Rather, they created a slow-moving and diffuse tsunami of nutrients that entered freshwater systems, and these became progressively overwhelmed.[95]

This new breach in an ecological frontier in Aotearoa New Zealand has taken place within a dramatically different context to its colonial precursors. Previous frontier breaches had unleashed destruction and chaos that were not only tolerated but celebrated by many as a sign of progress. But this time, things are very different. Williams's 'ticking time bomb' warned of what more recently would be described as a loss of the 'social licence to operate' for farmers.[96] He sounded this warning in the aftermath of two events that demonstrated the character of the new and fractured level of consent for farming among the wider public. One was the Royal Commission on GMOs, but the other was a political protest that erupted in 2002 and became known as the 'Dirty Dairying' campaign.

Shortly after the formation of Fonterra, the previously docile lobby group for recreational freshwater fishers and hunters, Fish and Game New Zealand, in collaboration with the urban-based Royal Forest and Bird Protection Society, launched a media campaign called 'Dirty Dairying', targeting the dairy industry for its impacts on the quality of freshwater sites of fishing and duck hunting in Aotearoa New Zealand.[97] The campaign received wide media coverage and united sympathies across amenity users of rural freshwater resources (often rural folk themselves) and the insurgent forces of urban environmentalism. The campaign was remarkably successful.[98] Fonterra was sensitized to the potential market impact of negative environmental stories, and entered into negotiation with the Ministry of Agriculture and Forestry (MAF) and the Ministry for the Environment to create a voluntary industry accord that would (temporarily) ease the pressure from outside groups. To implement the 'Dairying and Clean Streams Accord' (usually referred to as the 'Clean Streams Accord' (CSA)), MAF agreed to act as the impartial arbiter of a series of targets for improved mitigation measures for streams, rivers and lakes.

As a political action, the Dirty Dairying campaign was highly successful in provoking a response. As an actual measure for mitigation of dairy impacts on freshwater systems, however, the CSA has been much more contentious.[99] New policy alliances were formed to manage the crisis – particularly a grouping of government agencies, industry groups, iwi and NGOs called the Land and Water Forum – and key farm practices became core artefacts in establishing a response by industry.[100] The effect of these practices was to create boundaries between cows and water, thus re-inscribing the ontological boundary around farm systems, even if such measures were, in reality, porous and had imprecise effects. As I've argued in this book, ontological boundaries around farms are highly effective, except ecologically. This lack of ability to deliver knowable outcomes was 'rendered technical' through the application of a software package called Overseer, which provides a 'nutrient budget' for farmers to use.[101]

Much of this crisis over the consequences of freshwater impacts of dairying systems did get absorbed inside the ontological boundaries of the modernist farm. However, this crisis was unprecedented in two important ways.

First, it revealed an important new alliance between amenity users of farming landscapes, many of whom were traditional rural folk, with an urban constituency of environmentalists directly critiquing farming practices.[102] The level of concern expressed in 2002 would only grow with the boom in dairy activities and a sudden increase in the scope and intensity of dairy farming in Aotearoa New Zealand, which escalated after the opening up of the Chinese market in 2008.

Second, for urban environmentalists, farming had never been a traditional target. Protest actions had been directed towards hydro dams, species preservation and a nuclear-free status for Aotearoa New Zealand. Even in the recent GMO mobilization, the fact that no GMOs were under commercial cultivation meant that farmers were only an indirect target of concerns in that conflict compared to agricultural scientists. The Dirty Dairying campaign made farming itself an environmental issue, and directly targeted existing farm practices and waste streams. This was unprecedented, and startling for farmers in Aotearoa New Zealand.[103]

If the RCGM had introduced an alliance of liberal urban environmentalists, Māori, scientists and consumer advocacy organizations into the contested terrain of what is a good or safe agricultural technology, this new campaign would raise direct questions about the farming landscape itself. One of the deepest ontological assumptions about our family farms as bounded spaces was under attack: the idea that farmers are autonomous and have control over environmental outcomes within the boundaries of their farms. Now, from a broad coalition outside the world of farming, voices from exterior worlds were directly contesting what farmers did and challenging their 'social licence to farm'. For the first time since the coalescing of cultural hegemony around the golden age of pastoral family farming in the early twentieth century, it was now politically legitimate to link farming systems to wider environmental harms.

Seen through the long lens of Aotearoa New Zealand's history of colonization of landscapes, this new ecological frontier is a familiar moment of conquest in pursuit of new assemblages of 'grasslands as capital', but unlike its predecessors, it has become a bitter and contested site of struggle among Pākehā citizens.[104] As with all the prior breaching moments of ecological frontiers in earlier colonial history in Aotearoa New Zealand, this breach has unleashed chaos and destabilization. But unlike the previous times such breaches were made, the Pākehā political and cultural hegemony around pastoral family farming is no longer securely in place. A strong relationship remains between the state and modernist pastoral farming, and both have staunchly defended ongoing elaboration of narrow, modernist approaches to agricultural science pursuing technical fixes within the boundaries of modernist farming systems. However, the limits to the power of this relationship are now being exposed, wider materials and politics are overflowing, and there is profound disruption to any attempts to engage in strategies and practices of post-breach stabilization. This space simply will not become pacified.

The great disruption

In this chapter, a chronology of dents and fractures in the hegemonic edifice of this modernist farming world has been narrated. Partly this stemmed from a substantial break in the relationship between the state and farming worlds during neoliberalization, but this only tells part of the story. Material worlds – particularly ecological ones – are intrinsically unstable. Things overflow, containment fails and thresholds are breached, and these globally recognized verities are doubly true in the feral ecologies of Aotearoa New Zealand where colonization had broken existing patterns and the speed of landscape change outpaced any comparative transitions in the United States or Europe. These disruptions came in many forms and challenged various parts of the great assemblage of modernist agriculture. The great unifying project of scientific knowledge was increasingly challenged and the unquestioned public acceptance of scientific expertise began to decline. Inside worlds of science, disciplinary differences opened up between scientists working inside a tightly bounded ontology and those who sought to understand effects that socially and ecologically crossed such boundaries.

A further world of disruption began to emerge from the rising power of consumption aligned with the expectations of new social movements. The opening up of 'green' market niches, and alternative production–consumption linkages, challenged modernist farming worlds in a variety of ways. In commercial settings, 'greening' markets created open discussion of alternatives. The disruptive ontological work of these new niches was amplified and aligned in unexpected ways through the agency of new technologies of audit and certification – particularly in their automatic enacting of binary of good/bad qualities for food products. Finally, a series of landmark judicial decisions in Aotearoa New Zealand, along with the rise of political protest and resistance by Māori, brought an end to the era of tacitly assumed 'full assimilation' of Māori into Pākehā worlds, and new spaces and sites of political action began to take shape. There were some important reactionary movements by the state to protect core elements of the modernist farming world, but around the edges, new indigenous ways of thinking about and acting with a living land began to emerge – many of which intrinsically enacted different ontologies of land-use to the closed and bounded world of the modernist farm.

The culminating effect of these new disruptions is most vividly displayed in the emergence of controversy and political challenge in the very heart of the modernist farm project. Having successfully prospered by breaching ecological frontiers in colonial worlds, the breaching of another ecological frontier through the irrigation of dryland farming regions in the twenty-first century has unleashed ecological and social chaos that has proved difficult to contain and stabilize.

The story of this chapter has been of the moments, practices and conflicts that revealed previously invisible worlds and brought ontologically exterior realities back inside increasingly disturbed and turbulent interior worlds of farming. Declining certainties about modernist, techno-scientific and mechanistic worlds are disrupting and eroding the solid centre of modernist farming. Things overflow. Cool worlds become hot. Cyclones roar, freshwater systems are eutrophied, indigenous worlds loom back into view, social licences are revoked and new worlds start to appear. Such differences prompt a question: how are *farms* acting in new ways to enact different worlds? Do outcomes change when we start farming inside visible worlds?

Notes

1   The views of a collective of economic geographers were summarized by Britton et al. (1992) and then reworked in Le Heron and Pawson (1996).

2   For example, Richard Le Heron's work was central to a particular style of economic geography interested in the 'restructuring' of economic spaces under late capitalism (Le Heron 1988). His work on the restructuring of the pastoral industry in New Zealand (Le Heron 1989a, 1989b) formed the basis for a later book (Le Heron 1993) positioning New Zealand's agricultural crisis in comparison to similar crises and transitions in farm–state–economy relations in other countries.

3   Sandrey and Reynolds (1990: 65).

4   Dalziel and Lattimore (1991).

5   Britton et al. (1992), Le Heron (1993).

6   A summary of both New Zealand and Australia as exemplars of neoliberalization is found in Campbell and Lawrence (2003) and then reviewed ten years later in Lawrence and Campbell (2013).

7   Campbell and Lawrence (2003), Fairweather (1989, 1992).

8   One of the key aspects of my own PhD work (Campbell 1995).

9   Keating and Little (1994), Taylor and McCrostie Little (1995).

10   Keating and Little (1991).

11   Coombes and Campbell (1996).

12   Campbell and Moore (1991), Campbell and Wards (1992), Liepins and Bradshaw (1999).

13   This is the core critique of political economy made by Gibson-Graham (2006). A series of debates in the radical political economy of agrarian change in the early to mid-1990s aligned around exactly this problem: to what extent could radical approaches rely on a structural critique of capitalism to effect change? These

were central theoretical moments in the transition from radical agrarian political economy – with its focus on farms and agricultural economies within nation states – to 'agrifood' approaches, which sought to link sites of production to sites of consumption at a global (or local) scale and consequently opened up multiple sites of specific political action and alternatives.

14 Historian Michael King was the biographer of two remarkable Māori women who played pivotal roles through the mid-twentieth century. Both Te Puea Herangi – through the Kīngitanga – and Dame Whina Cooper – through the Maori Women's Welfare League – were central to the formation of pan-Māori rather than tribal strategies for state engagement. Both were also deeply involved in efforts to maintain spoken te reo Māori and other cultural knowledge, with Cooper turning her full focus towards land as a last great cause near the end of her life (King 2003: 478–80).

15 Walker (2004), Salmond (2017: 46).

16 There is a rich vein of scholarship and consideration of the roots and complex pathways of the 'Māori renaissance', land protests and new politics of the Treaty of Waitangi, written by significant scholars like Dame Evelyn Stokes (see Stokes 1987, 1992, 2002) and Sir Ranginui Walker (Walker 2004).

17 In a book that is specifically directed at understanding situated powers and vitalities that prompt change (particularly at the level of the farm), the transition from settled golden age to dire crisis does rely a great deal on powers residing at other levels, particularly the state and its role in political and economic life. Both Dame Whina Cooper's hīkoi and the disintegrating status of farmers as an economic and political class can be understood primarily as dramas of relations with the state. The 'state-centric' narrative of these crises and transitions is not the focus of this book – although it is important enough to appear at multiple points in the upcoming narrative – but it can't be entirely ignored. That narrative is better told in major histories like King (2003) and Belich (2001).

18 While this section focuses on ecological feralities like weather and pests, there are other feralities that plague the simple mechanistic worlds of modernist farming and agrifood chains. An excellent example is the wild consequences of a dead mouse that unravelled vast networks of dairy export infrastructure in 2013 (a crisis so complex that this single mouse has become the focus of recent academic reflection in Lewis et al. (2017)).

19 Or, put the other way around, homogeneous modernist systems operating on one-size-fits-all logics will inevitably either eradicate all local ecological variation (through industrialization and external subsidies) or be constantly disrupted by the feralities of local ecological powers.

20 Trotter (1988).

21 Trotter (1988) and Phillips and Marden (2005).

22 The threshold for rainfall causing landslip damage in Aotearoa New Zealand's deforested hill country is estimated to be 200 mm in one rain event, a figure that was vastly exceeded by Cyclone Bola (Phillips and Marden 2005).

23 As part of the scientific evaluation of what happened during this cyclone, Phillips and Marden (2005: 531) report that across Aotearoa New Zealand, pastoral hill slopes were between four and sixteen times more susceptible to landslides during storm events than slopes covered in mature forest.

24 Phillips and Marden (2005: 532).

25 Hicks (1991) and Phillips and Marden (2005).

26 Geographers Chris Cocklin and Melanie Walls went further than this by positioning the crisis in the context of what had then been a massive removal of state support

for forestry under neoliberalization. Cyclone Bola, in combination with ecologically unstable pastured hillsides in the East Coast, created a catastrophe so compelling that it forced the then avowedly neoliberal government to invest in the extensive East Coast Forestry Scheme to move land from pastoral use to forestry (Cocklin and Wall 1997).

27 McLeod and Moller (2006) identify the pivotal years when land-use indicators reveal the maximum extent of 'developed pasture' in the landscape – at the end of the 1970s and early 1980s – before a retreat commenced with around 2 million hectares of developed pasture returned to native vegetation, converted to forestry or moved into other uses by 2006.

28 A key theme in Isern (2002), Holland et al. (2002) and Holland (2013).

29 Gibb and Williams (1994) provide an intriguing history of rabbit control in Aotearoa New Zealand with discussion of key debates in the 1940s and 1950s, contrasting the duelling goals of 'commercial control' through encouragement of a rabbit skin export industry as against a more modernist desire for 'total eradication'.

30 Gibb and Williams (1994) suggest that this followed a fracturing of scientific opinion between those seeking technologies and biological interventions in search of maximum rabbit deaths, and those taking more ecological (and evidence-based) approaches.

31 Dann (2002).

32 Nigel Clark (1999: 145) recounted the sense of farmer triumph over dangerous ferality, reporting one farmer who was quoted in the media: 'I hope it is very virulent and spreads like hell. I can't remember when I last felt this excited.' Dann (2002), writing three years later, pondered how it could be possible that no-one had been prosecuted and that farmer groups didn't see this event as a significant blow to their claimed credibility as environmental managers.

33 Since RCD, numerous subsequent crises of ferality have vexed the capacity and/or desire of the state to intervene, including: the discovery of Painted Apple Moth (and a controversial aerial spray campaign) in 1999, a biosecurity crisis in the honey industry with the arrival of varroa mite (2000), a significant invasion of freshwater systems in the South Island by the weed *Didymosphenia geminata* (2005), a crisis in the kiwifruit industry with the arrival of *Pseudomonas syringae pv. actinidiae* (PSA) (2010), and a crisis in pastoral farming systems with the arrival of the cattle disease *Mycoplasma bovis* (2017). These are all specific incursion events that are, collectively, only problematic for farming on a small scale compared to the larger destabilizing feralities that were starting to become visible in freshwater systems – and will be considered at length later in this chapter.

34 Murcott (2019: 162).

35 Murcott (2019: 162).

36 For the following decades a variety of 'trust in food' research projects took place around Europe which sought to understand the extent and depth of the shifting sense of risk and decreasing trust in expertise being exhibited around the consumption of food. Many such projects indicated the mad cow disease food scare as the sea-change moment within this long cultural transition (see Murcott 2019: 162).

37 Michel Callon considered this a significant breaching point in the certainties of modernist science causing a spiral of incomprehensibility: 'The crisis relating to mad cow disease is a classic example: here, the turmoil has reached its apogee, foreshadowing situations which will probably become very common in the near future. This hybrid forum is overflowing continuously, with an ever-growing, ever-more-varied cast of characters ... The controversy lurches first one way, then the other – because nothing is certain, neither the knowledge base nor the methods of measurement' (1998: 260–61).

38   This period was characterized by an increasing volume of media articles on GMOs
     and increasingly politically positioned characterization of GMOs within media
     narratives (Fitzgerald et al. 2002).
39   Within the critical social sciences, two notable Australasian collections were
     Hindmarsh and Lawrence (2004) and Hindmarsh et al. (2008).
40   Campbell (2004).
41   Political scientist Joanna Goven has been particularly interested in the way the
     RCGM and other science controversies have been characterized by the emergence of
     political hierarchies and contests between science approaches, including strategies
     of silencing some scientific (and other) voices rather than collaborative knowledge
     production (Goven and Wuthnow 2004; Goven 2006).
42   The RCGM undertook consultation with Māori groups in a parallel process to the
     main hearings of the Commission (see Rogers-Hayden and Hindmarsh 2002).
43   Campbell (2004).
44   A space that, around this debate, began to be increasingly filled by a new body of
     work from Māori scholars (e.g. Cram et al. 2000; Pihama et al. 2002).
45   A theme he returned to (with Caliskan) in directly considering the disruptive
     cultural and political potential of GMOs: 'The question of commodification has
     taken on a new salience due to the proliferation of "living" entities that have become
     candidates for marketization. Things such as genes, proteins, embryonic cells, GMOs
     and so on, currently being produced in laboratories through biomedical practices,
     raise difficult problems in terms of economic framing. By nature, novel entities
     tend to behave in ways that can be astoundingly difficult to predict or control. The
     domestication of novelty takes time, and not infrequently stabilization can prove to
     be impossible. The question of controlling biological entities is nothing new, as the
     history of livestock shows. Yet the expanding industrialization of the life sciences
     contributes powerfully to the proliferation of such entities and to their dissemination.
     Hence the emergence of haunting questions about the possibility of their being
     subject to marketization' (Caliskan and Callon 2010: 6).
46   John Fairweather and his research group conducted extensive surveys among farmers
     during this period and found a minority supporting a highly modernist, techno-
     centric pathway like GMOs, another minority supporting a 'greener' pathway, and a
     mixed, ambivalent, plurality around them (Fairweather et al. 2003).
47   Campbell (2018).
48   For a review of this development at a global scale – and its complex relationship to
     neoliberal governance – see Campbell (2013). Most international literature credits
     the emergence of new social movements concerned with the environment and the
     formalization of Green political parties as being indicative of rising cultural concerns
     about environmental issues – thus creating potential market opportunities for 'green'
     products. While not discounting the importance of this wider cultural shift, the
     Aotearoa New Zealand case is remarkable for the peculiar and enactive powers of
     technologies of audit in making particular 'greening' outcomes happen.
49   An iconic Aotearoa New Zealand food processing company. The following year,
     Wattie's Frozen Foods would be purchased by the large multinational HJ Heinz and
     Co. to become Heinz Wattie's Ltd.
50   There was a prequel to this encounter. The first farmers who met with Wattie's
     were organic pea producers who provided a small amount of product but had not
     produced enough peas to fill one shipping container. Wattie's then turned to its
     supplier base of highly skilled conventional growers to produce the volumes they

needed (the full story is told in Campbell 1996). In this specific moment, there were two non-human agents – the audit standard and the standardized shipping container!

51 Although, as argued in Coombes and Campbell (1998), the relations between export and domestic sectors were not antagonistic.

52 Campbell and Liepins (2001).

53 A situation that did cause discomfort among some members of the global organic social movement. At the world congress of the International Federation of Organic Agriculture Movements (IFOAM) – which was held in Aotearoa New Zealand in 1994 – the rise of cross-border trade in certified organic products was hotly debated as to the sustainability of such long transportation chains – a debate that then resurfaced with even more vigour when 'food miles' became a significant concern for UK supermarkets in the mid-2000s (Saunders et al. 2006).

54 Campbell (2005).

55 Wharfe and Manhire (2004), Campbell (2018).

56 Rosin et al. (2016, 2017).

57 Campbell (2009).

58 All these specific points of change in orchard practice and changes in grower subjectivities added up to what Chris Rosin has characterized, using convention theory, as a 'new spirit of farming' (Rosin 2008). The wider shifts in grower subjectivities under audit disciplines were summarized in Campbell et al. (2012).

59 See Hunt et al. (2011).

60 In this narrative, the disruptive potential of audits is emphasized. In Chapter 1, the slight ambivalence of Mike and Violet on Rendell Stream Farm to organic certification indicates that this is a technology that both disrupts and then re-orders and has the potential to re-homogenize 'alternative' in ways that preclude experimentation. Such is the nature of assemblages. One such effect has been the 'metrologization' of audit systems, which involves audits converging on 'that which can be measured', as against 'softer' criteria like social dynamics on farms and orchards which are seen as desirable in Triple Bottom Line audit systems but are just much harder to stabilize and act upon. The result is a 'measuring sustainability' problem: acting on those things that can be measured with wider values, systems and dynamics that are important for achieving more sustainable production increasingly becoming marginal in audit systems (see Bell and Morse 2008; Rosin et al. 2016, 2017; Sautier et al. 2018; Hale et al. 2019).

61 A comprehensive review of the 'local turn' in food systems theorizing and practice can be found in Goodman et al. (2011).

62 For useful examples, see Kirwan (2004) and Goodman et al. (2011).

63 Farmers' markets do not appear in voids and without consequences. In an intelligent engagement with the arrival of the Dunedin farmers' market, Dwiartama and Piatti (2016) situate it as part of a wider assemblage of local food initiatives that combine to create the ontological space of alternative food in Dunedin.

64 Putting it in embodied terms, Carolan (2011, 2015, 2016) describes the particular ontological politics of embodied, affective, food consumption.

65 For some scholars, just too benign. Guthman et al. (2006) question the ability of farmers markets to actually reach vulnerable populations experiencing food deficits.

66 The transformative power of such new producer-consumer linkages is a major theme in Goodman et al. (2011), building on the earlier insights of Goodman and DuPuis (2002), particularly in relation to the generative power of new practices and relations to overcome the cognitive and material distancing that is central to modernist, industrial, food systems.

67   This is the contradiction animating a new generation of post-colonial scholarship in the critical study of food politics. Chris Mayes asks this question of new styles of food politics in Australia which have both exposed the inequities, unsustainability and ethically compromised nature of much of contemporary worlds of food, yet: 'A common solution proposed to address these various problems is a return to environmentally sustainable and socially responsible smallholder agrarian farming. Such proposals are attractive, yet they tend to romanticize past hardships. Furthermore, they often elide the historical role of agriculture in systems of unfree labour, restrictive gender roles and settler colonialism.' (Mayes 2018: 6). He goes on in his book to elaborate a core problem with food sovereignty movements and their relationship to other inequalities, concluding with the challenging insight: 'The power of land and land cultivation can be a source of flourishing and companionship, but, as has been argued, it is deeply entangled with dispossession and violence' (Mayes 2018: 221–2).

68   There were two prolonged land occupations at the Raglan Golf Course and at Bastion Point in Auckland in 1977–8 (King 2003: 485; Walker 2004: 212–19).

69   Walker (2004: 253–5).

70   Walker (2004).

71   An epic argument about this new development – which took place between my grandparents, me and my siblings over the dinner table – comes to mind. My grandmother became increasingly frustrated by our liberal protestations until she finally shocked us all when she declared: 'Who won the Land Wars?' Which at least established that despite our farm's history being invisible, it could be retrieved *in extremis* and put to dubious use.

72   The Te Roroa Report of 1992 (https://forms.justice.govt.nz/search/WT/reports/ reportSummary.html?reportId=wt_DOC_68462675) (accessed 29 May 2018). Of key importance in the recommendation, the government was not actually requested to directly purchase land from farmers. Rather, it was suggested that the government purchase specific plots of farm land if and when they came onto the market voluntarily from private owners.

73   Treaty of Waitangi Amendment Act 1993, No 92.

74   Following Agrawal (2005), the way that citizens are drawn into RMA processes is elaborated in Haggerty (2007).

75   The complexities and challenges of Māori involvement in resource decisions are a key theme in Kawharu (2002).

76   A useful collaboration describing the wider impacts of neoliberalization on Māori was compiled by Bargh (2007). A reminder that critiques of neoliberalism/capitalism can be blind to deeper injustices of colonization was argued in Bargh and Otter (2009). Bargh (2014: 144) also argues that neoliberalization poses a new form of 'assimilation by stealth' through collapsing everything into corporatist, neoliberal logics that exclude Māori difference.

77   Commencing in 1992, but going through seemingly continual new iterations as the state attempted to square off achieving science excellence within competitive funding models – with constantly underwhelming results (as discussed in Campbell 2011).

78   Despite some excellent attempts to open up chinks in the firewall inside science institutions, like Roskruge (2007), Lambert (2008) and Reid (2011).

79   The power of these new movements for restoration of cultural, ecological and social bonds via community gardens on marae is being extolled in an emerging body of research (e.g. Piatti 2015).

80 One important initiative, and which has strong community links to wider academic communities as well, is the long-term programme of research into harvesting of *tītī* (the muttonbird or sooty shearwater) in the southern coastal marine environment. This is a widely cited example of indigenous co-management of a treasured wild-food resource (see Moller et al. 2004; Stevens 2009).

81 Early engagement between Māori and the emerging commercial organic farming movement in the 1990s is reviewed in Barr (2000). A position statement on principles for Māori organic production called 'Hua Parakore' was released by Hutchings et al. (2012) and is discussed as an emerging element of an indigenous economy in Bargh (2014) and McKerchar et al. (2015). Other initiatives that consider how mātauranga (knowledge, education) might inform wider sustainability indicators in farming have been considered in Reid et al. (2013).

82 Lambert (2008).

83 Morris (2010) provides an interesting discussion on why, in the post-colonial political and consumption space of Aotearoa New Zealand, these initiatives are continually thwarted.

84 Describing ecological frontiers and their breaching in historical succession has been useful for structuring the narrative of this book. In reality, however, these may be important frontiers but they are not the only places where this concept can be applied. Alongside the colonization of indigenous grasslands in the uplands of the South Island – which has only been hinted at in this book – there were also a broad annexation and appropriation of the phosphate resources of Nauru after the 1920s to anchor the Grasslands Revolution that could be understood as the historical shifting of an ecological frontier.

85 The contents of which could likely be structured around the multiple dynamics and conflicts summarized in Le Heron (2018).

86 The story of the creation of Fonterra and its significant moves at a global scale is told in Gray et al. (2007) and Gray and Le Heron (2010), with its implications for intensified productivist approaches at the farm-level discussed in Burton and Wilson (2012).

87 Le Heron (2018).

88 Campbell and Reynolds (2020).

89 A second major initiative in 2008 was the launching, by Fonterra, of the Global Dairy Trade auction system to act as a centralized market mechanism for world dairy trading (Le Heron 2018).

90 An alternative focus for technical sites of transformation would be the controversial Lincoln University Dairy Farm, which was established in 2001 and became the site of testing and refinement of the huge productivity gains made possible through irrigation of dry Canterbury soils. The results were both impressive and vexing. That farm, by current accounts, is now frantically trying to see if the N genie can be stuck back into the bottle and what level of dramatic adjustment to farming systems will be required to do so.

91 For international readers, there is an important point to make about why intensification is happening via pasture systems. There simply aren't any easily available supplies of cheap subsidized grains and pulses to provide industrial stock food (hence the sourcing of PKE all the way from Indonesia). Increasing pastoral productivity requires increasing the rate of grass growth through the use of water and fertilizer.

92 Parliamentary Commissioner for the Environment (2004). The report unsubtly placed an aerial photograph of the Lincoln University Dairy Farm on its cover.

93 Since 2004, and post-the China boom, this has only intensified. Joy (2015) reports a more than 400 per cent increase in use of nitrogenous fertilizers.

94 The Reserve Bank of New Zealand maintains an index of average mortgage rates for residential home loans. This shows a dramatic fall in mortgage rates after 2008 – with rates falling by around 4–5 per cent as intervention measures were introduced to combat the effects of the Global Financial Crisis – leading to the (then) most favourable borrowing conditions in modern New Zealand history (see www.rbnz. govt.nz/statistics/key-graphs/key-graph-mortgage-rates).

95 A useful review of the freshwater/dairying crisis is provided in Warne (2017) and more detailed analysis of the technical components of the freshwater crisis in Joy (2015). Of particular concern is that the deep aquifers under the new frontier region of drylands Canterbury have already taken on a 'load to come' of nitrogen that has entered freshwater systems, but will take decades to slowly seep through deep groundwater systems and arrive in unwelcome destinations.

96 Social licence to operate has become an important recent discourse in policy circles in Aotearoa New Zealand (summarized in Edwards and Trafford 2016). It signals the extent which ontological boundaries separating farming practices either from wider ecological dynamics or from the claims of wider social worlds are disintegrating (a key point made by Tall and Campbell 2018).

97 The emergence of the Dirty Dairying controversy is described in Tall and Campbell (2018).

98 For a detailed account, see Holland (2015) and Tall and Campbell (2018).

99 Jay (2007) lists some of these concerns at the farm and industry level as: the inequitable impacts on farmers relative to the numbers of waterways they are expected to manage, the trustworthiness of Fonterra to implement the accords, and some tricky definitional questions as to what is a 'stream' needing management and what is a farm 'drain' that is exempt (see also Blackett and Le Heron 2008). A more directly environmental critique was compiled by the Fish and Game and Forest and Bird societies in Deans and Hackwell (2008).

100 As we argued in Tall and Campbell (2018: 172), if the crisis was caused by the political connection of what had been ontologically separated worlds of on-farm dairy practices and external environmental effects, then the core strategy was to re-establish this ontological boundary: 'keep the cows out of the water!' This involved: fencing of waterways, creation of designated stock crossings using culverts, compliance with regional council rules on dairy shed effluent discharges, adoption of nutrient budgeting using technologies like the software system Overseer, and designation/fencing of significant wetlands.

101 Tall and Campbell (2018: 171–2).

102 In their position statement, Fish and Game NZ (2002) stated: 'Fish & Game is NOT anti-farming, we are pro-environmentally sustainable farming.' The point of interest here, however, is not just that they were taking sides in supporting some styles of farming, but that they were critiquing farming at all.

103 As we argued in Tall and Campbell (2018: 161), 'the politics of rendering the connections between farms and farmed environments more visible has also made them more able to be politicized and responded to'.

104 Prior struggles on breached frontiers were, of course, the key site of conflict between Pākehā and Māori. While Māori are important critics of freshwater degradation, what is new about this situation is that they have been joined (finally) by a substantial constituency of Pākehā voices.

5

Farming inside visible worlds

Windsor Lodge and its legacies

I haven't set foot on the land at Windsor Lodge for over two decades, but during the writing of this book I have been able to re-visit my old family farm via the magic of virtual reality. An online database of aerial photographs provided a sequence of overhead images of Windsor Lodge from the 1970s to the late 1990s,[1] and Google Earth provides a more recent snapshot of the last ten years of major transitions in land-use. In looking at these aerial images of the familiar landscape, an interesting and contradictory set of transitions becomes visible.

By the time my grandfather died in 1999, for over a decade the farm had been an object of desire for the surrounding dairy farms. The neighbouring farmer who realized that desire and purchased Windsor Lodge incorporated it into his dairy unit. He opened up one boundary line and pushed raceways for dairy cows through the centre of the farm. A usefully elevated rise out the back of our farm became the site of a large new milking shed. My grandfather had an aversion to removing trees, something he had developed in his struggles on his first farm, Longridge, in the erosion-prone hill country of Hawke's Bay. Our first Waikato farm advisor was sacked when his opening piece of advice was to remove all the trees on Windsor Lodge in order to expand the area for pasture.[2] Now, Google Earth reveals the powers of homogenization in dairy landscapes. Nearly all the shelterbelts and shade trees (visible in Figure 1 on page 3 of this book) are gone. Apart from the shelterbelts around the main house, the entire farm – with one important exception – has only two large trees that stand in an otherwise unbroken sea of grass. Two wetlands at the back of the farm have been massively altered. One is now fully drained and incorporated into pasture, and no trace of it remains. The other – which was larger – has had its frontier shrunk: around ten hectares of mānuka have been cleared and the land drained into pasture, leaving a small ring of vegetation around the little lake where I caught eels as a child. The three or four hill slopes that my grandfather had left in mānuka were now 'clear' and holding grass. While it was sad to see what had been a varied farm landscape move towards a single kind of land-use, none of this is surprising given the cost per hectare of potential dairy land in Waikato and the wider drive towards homogenization of dairy landscapes.

There was, however, one important exception – my mother's wetland. The wetland had been a source of conflict in our lives in the mid-1980s, and now this little reserved space was the last remnant of non-pasture on the farm, thriving in the middle of what we'd previously called the house paddock. When viewed for the first time in decades, it was much larger than I expected. It had clearly expressed some impressive vitality, and had changed from a fenced-off area of boggy ground with straggly new planting into a flourishing body of mature native trees.[3]

The 'wetland battle' took shape in the 1980s one summer after I had left home. My mother chose her ground tactically to cause maximum discomfort to my grandfather. The house paddock, which stretched from the house down to the main highway between Ngaruawahia and Taupiri, was a long, sloping sward of grass that my grandfather treated with special care. It was highly visible from the road (and thus the farming gaze), and framed the view from the road up to the farmhouse.[4] In the middle of that slope rose a little spring, out of which grew a few sparse trees (visible front and centre of Figure 1). A constant rivulet ran down a shallow indentation in the hillside and stock walked through it continually, muddying up the surrounding pasture. It also needed a special diversion drain at the bottom of the hill to stop it turning part of the roadside flats back into a wetland. It was the kind of small irritant that was endemic to running an expansive amount of 'effective' pasture over a wet landscape.

One day my mother announced that she thought we should make a wetland reserve: put a little weir in to replace the drain below the spring, allow the wetland to partly refill, fence off around half a hectare of pasture and start establishing native plants (see Figure 7).

This was not a welcome suggestion for my grandfather. Fencing off an area of potential pasture involved two very different ideas of what it meant to be a 'good farmer', but after a considerable period of persistent, low-level, inter-generational 'dialogue', my mother prevailed. The new generation (and gender) of land-users made a small ascendant step and another future became possible. Fences went in, some moisture-loving flaxes, shrubs and trees were planted, and my grandfather had to sit in his living room pondering the ontology of his farm while a slow indigenous recapture of the centre of his house paddock took shape right in the middle of his view. His comfortable sense of where the acceptable frontier lay between pasture, wetlands, mānuka-covered gully slopes and big sheltering trees was retreating. I can sense his consternation: trees were good, and remnant wetlands were useful for a bit of sport for

Figure 7 Shifting the wetland frontier: Windsor Lodge, c. 1984
Artist attribution: Marion Familton

Figure 8 The Windsor Lodge wetland, 2019
Artist attribution: Marion Familton

his grandchildren, but they were not a substitute for pasture. If the pasture-to-wetland frontier was allowed to retreat, where would it stop?

Ecological powers and vitalities can be slow to manifest themselves. At the time I thought this was a mildly diverting but insignificant episode of conflict between two generations and styles of farming that were contesting the management of Windsor Lodge. It wasn't until I saw the Google Earth image thirty years later that I realized the potency of the small powers my mother had unleashed (see Figure 8). Three decades later, new plantings had flourished; dormant seeds had germinated; roosting native birds had added their own seed deposits; and a whole thicket of new trees, low shrubs, water reeds and mosses had been regenerating. These had presented enough of a barrier to the new dairy farming owner that he let them be, safe behind their fence. They maintain a living and dynamic reservoir of indigeneity in an otherwise homogenizing landscape and in doing so keep the option of other futures alive. I showed this image to my mother in the year before she died. It was a satisfying moment. A tiny cordon of the ecological frontier of the wetlands had been re-established and a small part of the invisible world of Windsor Lodge had become visible again.

New farms in old frontiers

The image on the cover of this book is from a painting by artist Jenna Packer. It is part of a wider series in which she explores the colonization of Aotearoa New Zealand,

Figure 9 Big Time.
Artist Attribution: Jenna Packer.

the recent politics of water use in farming and the looming threat of climate change. Her image captures the sense in which settlers in colonial worlds seem to gaze into an abstract future called 'progress' while apparently remaining oblivious to the chaos mounting around them. Modern farming worlds teeter, indigeneities re-emerge and wild feralities swirl, posing the question of how much higher the waters must rise before the settler farming couple finally notices, or is toppled into oblivion (See Figure 9).

As a colonized world, what happened and what is about to happen in Aotearoa New Zealand tell us something about how farms participate in the making and unmaking of modernist agriculture. This has relevance for similar transitions on a global scale, but it also reveals particular dynamics and challenges that are specific to the circumstances of colonization and post-colonial politics. Unlike the much earlier transition to modernist farming in Old World societies, or the direct conflict of old and new in the Green Revolution, the colonial transition in the settler states tells its own story. It is a story based around frontiers, both political and ecological.

My own forebears' family farms, which I described in detail in Chapter 2, reveal this kind of agency and its ontological politics. Leaving Heather's Homestead/Marotahei to one side for the moment, the first tranche of farms did significant work on both political and ecological frontiers. First, the Fencible's Gift acted to build a boundary between Auckland and the Waikato (just as Heather's Homestead/Marotahei was doing the opposite), and established the infrastructure to support new farms, encourage the arrival of more Pākehā farmers and eventually provide the launching point for the invasion of the Waikato – an act that was driven by the desire of Pākehā settlers for highly fertile Māori farmlands.

Ashburn Estate describes a particular moment prior to 1882 in which many colonial farms weren't particularly productive as farms, but did all sorts of other useful cultural work in rendering old personal histories invisible and creating new narratives and a sense of ownership of the land – what Belich calls 'settling' in its broadest sense. Prior to the opening of the refrigerated meat and dairy trade to the UK, farms were varied and experimental. They often failed or struggled to establish any pattern or coherence. After 1882, however, with the emergence of refrigerated transport things began to assemble in ways that, by the 1920s, would become a new and homogenizing pattern of pastoral family farming.

This transition from colonial to modern pastoral farming is demonstrated by the second generation of family farms. From Ashburn Estate came Glenn Rd in the Taranaki. From The Fencible's Gift (and the farm it protected – Clovernook) came Te Rahui in Gisborne. This new generation of farms made many things happen.

Glenn Rd pushed back the forest frontier. Its successors took possession in the aftermath of the great fires of the 1880s and then pushed further by draining the Ngaere Wetlands. Te Rahui took ownership of established Māori farmland near Gisborne and modernized it. This second generation of family farms were all increasingly segmenting and dividing the land into privately owned, culturally separated parcels and bounded spaces, replacing the connected ontology of a living land with a segmented ontology of owned spaces and investible units.

Having destabilized and disrupted indigenous worlds, these farms then acted as the agents of stabilization and pacification of those broken frontier worlds. The world of the farm was pacified inside an ontological boundary and its interior was filled with mechanistic, technical relations understood through increasingly unified measures and realities. They stabilized as a particular kind of capital – and my forebears and their successive generations became prosperous citizens.[5]

This stability had important consequences. For the Campbells' farms in the Taranaki along with the Roberts' farm Te Rahui near Gisborne, the farms become filled with scientific technical knowledge and began to join the unified reality of modernist farming. The owners of Te Rahui – Ned and Reine Roberts – were involved in the development of Rationalism as a social movement in Aotearoa New Zealand.[6] Glenn Rd prospered and produced five more similar farms in the Taranaki for the next generation of Campbells to inhabit. Both Glenn Rd and Te Rahui were also launching points for new farming infrastructure – such as cooperative dairy ventures, a box factory and local government initiatives to create transport infrastructure in the regions. And other species played their part. Campbell family fame was partly earned through the efforts of Hatter the bull and his many prize-winning progeny.

This is the real history of modernist farms in colonized worlds. Modernist agriculture was made from these transitions, and in making modernist agriculture, farms also helped make modernity itself. And part of that process was the enacting of a particular ontology that resulted in us farming inside invisible worlds.

However, farms act in multiple ways. They are not simply servants of a modernist impulse to homogenize and obey industrial logics. They have their own powers. Sometimes these powers close down options and make some futures impossible, but they may also operate the other way around. The one farm in my family whakapapa (lineage) that sits in a startlingly different place to the others is Heather's Homestead/ Marotahei. It participated in enacting a more collaborative world between Pākehā and Māori. It briefly made possible one of the many potential futures that ended up not happening in colonial Aotearoa New Zealand. It was an agent of multiplicity, connection and experimentation and disrupted the colonial frontier contest in the 1860s in important ways. When it was destroyed, a small materialization of the alternative future it was enacting died with it.

The question now remains as to how new farms have become echoes of Heather's Homestead/Marotahei in the twenty-first century. How, in this new historical moment, have they become agents of disruption and sites of experimentation enacting alternatives to modernist farm ontologies?

The previous chapter focused on large fractures in relationships between the state, agriculture, science institutions, social movements, political groups, pressures of de-colonization and a host of feralities. In this chapter I want to focus on how these have been enacted at the farm level, and how they enable farms themselves to be agents of experimentation and new potentials. Even small actions have large consequences: although Windsor Lodge disappeared as it was absorbed into the wider homogenizing world of Waikato dairy farming in the twenty-first century, that one small wetland remained and flourished, restoring part of the old wetland and forest frontier. This came about because of just one summer of conflict between my mother and grandfather. What, then, might happen on other farms around Aotearoa New Zealand (the vast number that aren't actually owned by my kin!) if humans and their non-human partners were to take concerted steps to experiment and change their entire farming world?

Farms that enact alternatives to modernist agriculture

I want briefly to walk inside the gates of four clusters of farms that are enacting different disruptions and alternatives to modernist food and farming worlds.[7] They are situated at the interface of complex frontiers of wetlands, forests and drylands, and some traverse the cultural frontier between modernist and earlier Māori ontologies of land-use.

The wetland frontier: Manuka Mire in Southland

The Waituna Lagoon is situated in one of the great frontier collision zones of farming in Aotearoa New Zealand. It is bordered on one side by a lowland forest stretching from the Catlins coast into the lowland river valleys of Southland. On the other side is the highly fertile and moist province of Southland, where pastures are situated on the sites of extensively cleared forests and drained wetlands. Southland used to be a centre of the colonial flax industry, but with the pushing back of wetland and forest frontiers it became a major sheep-producing region and then, in the 1990s and 2000s, a major site of conversion to dairy farms. Waituna Lagoon has long been an important place for food-gathering and recreation by both Māori and Pākehā. But its fragile ecosystem is stressed by the intensification of surrounding lowland pastoral farming systems and threatens to go the way of the ecologically dead Lake Ellesmere/Te Waihora in Canterbury. The lagoon was recognized as a Ramsar Wetland of Ecological Significance in 1976.[8]

The farm I will discuss is currently occupied by Gay and Ron Munro, and is inside the catchment of Waituna Lagoon. It sits at the centre of discussions of new farm strategies at the wetland frontier. The Munros host numerous researchers examining new farm–ecological interactions, they make submissions on policy matters, and they have been key members of the Waituna Landcare Group, which coordinates volunteer actions undertaking restoration projects or proactive modification of landscape interfaces between pastures and waterways.

At the centre of the Munros' networks, and the anchor of their claims to being regenerative stewards of their land, is their farm called Manuka Mire and its covenanted wetland. It is photographed, written about, walked on, admired and studied.[9]

As the Munros tell it, Manuka Mire was, by agronomic standards, a 'wet' Southland sheep farm with characteristics typical of a farm that has been drained out of wetlands. It had problems of 'sourness' due to the residual vegetation and wood left underground in the process of felling trees that grew in wet ground and the subsequent drainage work. In 1989 (within the period of the 'rural downturn') the Munros expanded their farm by taking over a piece of land with intriguing potentials. The new land was a boggy mire inhabited by stands of mānuka and surrounded by unsuccessful attempts to stabilize pasture at the wetland fringe. It was a farm with a modernist ontology. The previous owners had used a variety of deep drains and external inputs to try to extend Grasslands Revolution-style pasture to the maximum extent of the farm's area. They fought a costly and ultimately futile battle at the frontier between pasture and wetland, before eventually giving up during the rural downturn and selling their land to Gay and Ron Munro, who incorporated it into Manuka Mire.

The Munros tell of the day they used a digger to block up one of the main farm drains exiting the wet centre of their newly acquired swampy land. It was a revolutionary act to encourage water to hold at the centre of the farm, and in doing so they reversed the entire ontology of wetland management since colonization. Their decision to hold water rather than drain it was magnified by the material and unexpected powers of their farm – powers that began to make a different future possible, that began to flip the ontology of the farm. The blocked drain allowed the latent wetland to begin slowly refilling until it eventually became a splendid lake of dark tea-coloured water.[10] On a much grander scale than my mother's wetland, invisible worlds started to become

Figure 10 The wetland at Manuka Mire
Artist attribution: Marion Familton

visible. Lying dormant in the soil were millions of roots and seeds of a wetland floral ecosystem that progressively sprang into life. The existing mānuka began to flourish in the wet soils as the lake filled and, within a few short years, wetland tree species had fully reasserted themselves (see Figure 10). A distinct, expanding 'area' on the farm was moving out of a ragged frontier of pasture/swamp and back into a flourishing wetland ecosystem.

Thirty years on, the wetland is celebrated nationally, and when we visited it we collectively agreed it was a place of natural beauty. The Munros have placed a permanent covenant with the QEII National Trust over sixty-four hectares of it to ensure that future farmers don't succumb to the temptation of opening up the farm drain again.

The wetland at Manuka Mire has become a focal point for several important discussions. First is the question of how best to modify farms so that landscapes hold water to act as a buffer against flooding, and to enhance their function as landscape filters to improve the quality of water flowing downstream to places like Waituna Lagoon. Manuka Mire has become a site of significant restoration of indigenous biodiversity. Endangered native fish species are protected behind weirs and ladders that Ron has designed, which allow small fish to pass across the boundary of Manuka Mire while guarding against possible incursion by larger trout. As well, it is providing a habitat for wetland bird species, thus expanding the capacity of the entire Waituna Lagoon catchment to support permanent and migratory birds. Under its new management, Manuka Mire participates strongly in wider ecological networks and provides numerous ecosystem services.

At a second level, Manuka Mire has become a site of learning for those interested in how to change the future trajectory of wetlands in farming systems. In its transition from a modernist to an ecological ontology, the farm has also demonstrated an interesting economic principle. Trying to force and maintain Grasslands Revolution pastures deep into wetland systems or up de-forested hilly slopes ends up costing more in pasture management than it returns in farm income. The shifting ecological frontier at Manuka Mire may have reduced the potential productivity of the farm, but it has actually increased its profitability.

In sum, Manuka Mire has shifted the wetland frontier and brought connectedness back into a Southland pastoral farm. The Munros were key movers in this transformation, but they also credit the non-human powers on their farm. The reflorescence of the wetland with its vitality, fecundity and beauty took everyone by surprise. The human and non-human actors on Manuka Mire are collaboratively enacting a new ontology of wetland farming.

This is not an isolated story. While the Munros are restoring wetlands in a 'wet' part of Aotearoa New Zealand, other exemplar farms have emerged that are demonstrating the value of reserving wetlands for the management of water in dryland areas like Hawke's Bay and the East Coast, where small wetlands can potentially act to hold moisture in dry hill systems, filtering water and buffering the impact of major weather events.[11] These farms are sites where wider social networks are forming through landcare groups and community restoration projects. They have become key nodes in a wider network of farms and are acting to shift the wetland frontier back into pastoral lands.

The new future of trees: Waihapua and Tutira

During a prolonged discussion within the Agricultural Research Group on Sustainability (the ARGOS project), which considered farm and orchard sustainability on a group of properties over a nine-year period, trees loomed into the centre of our analysis.[12] One of our research colleagues, Chris Perley, gazed across the assembled piles of paper, post-it notes and mind-maps and declared: 'There seem to be two types of farmers in New Zealand: the ones who cut down trees, and the ones who plant trees!' If we translate that evaluation of farmer motivations into the more ontological framing of this book: 'There seem to be two kinds of farms: the ones where trees disappear and the ones where trees reappear.'

Cyclone Bola created three days of wild weather in 1988 that overturned more than half a century of expansion of the pastoral frontier into previously forested hill-country on the East Coast of Aotearoa New Zealand. The entire assemblage of pastoral farming discourse, government policy, agricultural science, the accumulated capital value of privately owned pastoral farming land, and the separated, parcel-by-parcel management of a highly destabilized landscape, collapsed during seventy-two hours of calamitous torrential rain.

Into that gaping rent in the frontier of grasslands farming, the trees returned. Given the hegemonic stranglehold of pastoral farming over land-use science, policy and planning, as recounted in Chapter 3, there was little to turn to in the way of established forestry science for help. Commercial forestry itself had also been the site of elaboration of highly modernist ontologies of land-use. In those parts of Aotearoa New Zealand where commercial forestry had been undertaken throughout the twentieth century, the outcomes were not inspiring. Commercial forestry had replaced one of the most diverse forest ecosystems on the planet with exotic plantations composed almost entirely of a single, genetically un-diverse, soft-wood tree, *Pinus radiata*.[13] The modernist configuration of commercial forestry in Aotearoa New Zealand was a less than inspirational site for generating new experiments in land-use on the devastated East Coast.

But other experiments happened anyway. One farm spent twenty years slowly failing as part of the remnant of pastoral farming in the area after Cyclone Bola. As a local farmer described it, 'Every single storm, that block got more damage from erosion. Coming from Napier it was the first thing you saw … a farm that looked absolutely bereft of trees and had huge erosion issues.'[14] The land was taken out of private ownership and purchased by the regional council in 2009 as a site for experimentation in how to farm highly erodible hill country. Now called Waihapua, it has a variable topography with multiple microclimates and soil types. As a result of collaboration between the council, local iwi (tribes) and scientists from the major forestry research institute, SCION, along with local consultants who had already been experimenting with tree species in the search for ones that might grow well and be commercially useful for that part of Aotearoa New Zealand, Waihapua is now a diverse landscape operating in much closer collaboration with its human participants.

Three material dynamics influence the outcomes of these experiments. The first is the fact that many of the most prized timber-producing native trees in Aotearoa New Zealand are slow growing (hence the commercial mania for fast-maturing *Pinus radiata*). The Waihapua experiment has involved around forty species of tree. Exotic species that will produce high-value timber relatively quickly are planted in such a way as to allow interstitial regrowth of native mānuka and kānuka 'scrub'. The scrub in turn provides an excellent long-term nursery for nurturing the growth of valuable native timber trees for later harvest.

This strategy has potential because it interacts with the second material dynamic running through Waihapua – the making of new economic values. Waihapua assembles capital in interesting new ways. First, methods of generating economic value through the planting of trees have changed with the creation of carbon markets. By participating in carbon trading, the previously challenging long-term returns of planting commercial trees can potentially be balanced with the short-term returns of sequestering carbon.[15]

The second way to generate value relates to a highly consequential new material that has re-ordered the honey industry in Aotearoa New Zealand: 'Unique Manuka Factor' or UMF. The isolation of UMF as a 'super-compound' with a range of claimed health benefits has demarcated honey that is derived from the nectar of mānuka flowers from the rest of the honey harvested in Aotearoa New Zealand.[16] Mānuka honey is now worth vastly more than other honeys in the global market. But UMF forms just one actant in an assemblage of participants that has dramatically changed the ontology of mānuka: where previously it was pejoratively characterized as 'scrub' and cursed for its speedy regrowth and tendency to reappear on cleared hill country pastures, it is now recognized as a key way that land like Waihapua is able to generate value and be understood as capital.[17]

The third material way that Waihapua creates economic value is the traditional way – by planting, managing and anticipating future harvests of trees for timber. On Waihapua, this is happening in a more heterogeneous economic enterprise and produces a more diverse landscape, while at the same time providing the potential for resilience in the face of increasing incidences of severe weather events in a changing climate.

Waihapua pushes the experimental envelope in a couple of important directions – towards diverse land-use and income streams, a more integrated ecology, and an unusual ownership and public investment structure. But there is one final element to the Waihapua story that is instructive. The turn towards transition happened late at Waihapua. The owners persisted in trying to make their modernist grasslands system work even as the ecological basis for their farm was disintegrating. When the change did come, they didn't have to invent new approaches from scratch. There were existing reservoirs of knowledge and practice in the region to turn to and adopt. Some of this knowledge came from consultants who had been experimenting in these dry and fragile eastern regions for two decades after Cyclone Bola, but other aspects of knowledge came from a special piece of land – Tutira.

Venerated as a result of Herbert Guthrie-Smith's book, Tutira became a family trust after Guthrie-Smith's death in 1940 and those 800 hectares became a site of experimentation in growing trees in hill country, eventually developing into a mature arboretum of demonstration trees and planting strategies.[18] When Cyclone Bola struck nearly fifty years later, many of the Tutira trees and landscape restoration patterns were entering their mature phase. Ecological restoration can take such a long time in a place like Aotearoa New Zealand – some of the key native trees take a long time to reach maturity – that it took half a century from Guthrie-Smith's intense reflection on the failings of modernist pastoral farming approaches before there was a full suite of demonstrable templates for landscape restoration that Waihapua could draw on. As one consultant who worked on Waihapua reflected, plans for the restoration of Bola-devastated farms were partly based on the success of Tutira's experiments over the previous fifty years.[19]

Returning trees to the landscape is happening across these and many other cases in a variety of assemblages. Each one is enacting a new ontology of land-use that involves a novel connectivity of ecology, society and economy. And those that stabilize then shift the ecological frontier of trees forward into previously colonized grassland spaces. This sits at the heart of the one of the main responses to climate change: we need more farms where trees reappear.

Keeping the drylands dry: Bonaveree Farm

The most recent frontier breach undertaken by modernist farming in Aotearoa New Zealand has been the quest to turn drylands wet through irrigation. Drylands occupy a specific place in the history of farming in Aotearoa New Zealand. Formed in the rain shadow of the Southern Alps, dry farming regions run the length of the eastern coastline of much of both main islands. They are areas of highly eroded soft rock, fast drainage, low rainfall, and are highly susceptible to hot, dry westerly winds. They are precarious farming regions requiring extensive grazing strategies, and only succeeded during the golden age due to the remarkably high price for sheepmeat and wool, along with subsidization of fertilizers to maintain ryegrass and clover pastures on fragile hillsides. Ever since the rural downturn, these dryland farms have been eyeing up exit pathways. Two possible futures arose: converting sheep farms to vineyards, where dry, hot conditions could be managed to produce high-quality grapes; or introducing a subsidy of water through irrigation in order to turn low-value extensive sheep pasture into more productive intensive cropping/grazing or dairy pasture.

Unlike its neighbouring province Canterbury, the arid Marlborough region of Aotearoa New Zealand has largely eschewed the choice of irrigation to facilitate dairying. Instead, it has tended to opt for the 'sheep to vines' transition – a story that revolves around the specific qualities of the sauvignon blanc grape, particularly when grown in the unique terroir of Marlborough.[20] But vineyards are an expensive venture and out of the reach of most exiting farmers, and for the remaining extensive sheep and cattle farmers of this extremely dry province, some other kind of possible future was needed. That potential future started with one farm (and thence a widening network of farms linked through the Landcare movement), which found a way forward following a catastrophic change in climate.[21]

Bonaveree Farm has become the centre of discussion and experimentation about sustainable futures for drylands sheep and cattle farming. While much of the narrative in this book is directed towards telling the story of the non-human powers on farms, Bonaveree is a farm with notable human powers – mainly in the form of nationally respected apostle of drylands farming, Doug Avery. Avery preaches two messages that speak to new vitalities in farm systems. His approach is based around taking a stressed, marginal, economically failing, dryland farming world and returning it to profitability through harnessing complex interactions between the natural vitalities of plants and water.[22] His first message is about how to make inert, mechanistic farm systems, which attempt to impose Grasslands Revolution pasture strategies on marginal environments, into vital, complex systems that work with landscapes and available resources.

His second message about farm vitality regards how to energize farm families who feel trapped and hopeless inside failing mechanistic systems. An influential advocate for farmers' mental wellness, Avery tells the story of his own life and farm: how learning to 'work with nature' and 'turn his system upside down' in search of more resilient systems not only released the vital powers of previously underrated elements of his farming world, but also gave him a sense of purpose and direction. Put simply, developing a new relationship with his farm saved his life.[23]

Bonaveree Farm is a complex assemblage of key actors. Avery himself is a strong contributor to enacting relationships and experimenting with new practices. He has a longstanding intellectual relationship with scientist Derrick Moot;[24] he participates in networks linking individuals interested in things like biological agriculture and, more recently, regenerative agriculture; and he talks to farmer groups around the country. But the most vital relationship on Bonaveree farm is between three actors: Avery, lucerne (alfalfa) and water – along with the wider connections they make in farming systems.[25] In the complex interplay of these three elements, Bonavaree went from being a bad farm to a good farm.

Avery's account of Bonavaree's initial pathologies involved the expansion of the small home farm to incorporate the neighbouring farm. The new farm area was 'bad' according to all the orthodox modernist evaluations: its pastures weren't good enough to maintain sufficient stocking density to earn income. Its income was insufficient to maintain buildings, fences and equipment. The lack of cash to hire labour meant that pastures were being overrun with dryland weeds like thistle. It was also completely lacking any internal resilience for the droughts that were becoming increasingly frequent. After a successful conversion to a well-maintained version of the Grasslands Revolution model – ryegrass and clover – the farm had worked well for a while until a major drought tipped it into chaos. The core of the modernist system – a tight relationship between ryegrass, clover, artificial fertilizers and adequate rainfall – failed to be resilient in the face of severe droughts. Put simply, the Grasslands Revolution model, with all its clear logic, huge scientific and policy legitimacy and cultural familiarity, was the wrong way to farm a dry landscape.

Lucerne (alfalfa) is a well-known farm crop around the world. It has great qualities as animal fodder, and its huge root systems hold water. But it also has wild vitalities and, when used in drylands systems as a forage crop for animals in Aotearoa New Zealand, had unexpected results. Bonaveree Farm became the place where human participants experimented and learned how to build new systems using lucerne to hold water in dry conditions.[26] The end result, now discussed up and down the eastern regions of both islands, is a profitable drylands system that doesn't need expensive subsidies of water through irrigation and fertilizers. It also doesn't have nearly the same level of impact downstream in freshwater systems.

The story of Bonaveree Farm is partly about moving from a mechanistic modernist farming ontology to a more complex system where the different materialities of the system have been experimentally brought into dynamic relationship in situ. The use of lucerne resonates with the re-establishment of mānuka in Waihapua. A plant that was present and either classed as a pest or utilized in a simple and well-known way became a dynamic new participant in the farm assemblage – with vital materialities that emerged once the relations around it changed.[27]

Avery tells of how wider affective relations began to align and new connections were forged. The ontological boundary of his farm was, in effect, a cage that trapped him psychologically. Part of his personal journey to escape depression involved breaking open the social boundaries of his farm to connect with wider worlds. Bonaveree subsequently became the hub of a widening network of properties connected through the Landcare movement, in which different farms experimented with a variety of drylands farming styles, transferred knowledge, built shared confidence in new approaches and expanded their vision. The result was a new way of understanding the landscape of Marlborough and the desirability of bringing native trees back into farming landscapes.[28] What commenced as a change inside Avery's farming system progressively disrupted and flipped both his farm and his wider social, ecological and economic networks, re-aligning the affective composition of his world.[29]

The Bonaveree story points in two important directions. In one crucial sense, dryland Bonaveree and its wetland counterparts around the country demonstrate the multiplier effect – of creating social networks around alternative farms that connect farms and farmers attempting similar kinds of experimentation. This has semi-formalized into what was initially known in Aotearoa New Zealand as 'biological agriculture', but is now increasingly characterized as 'regenerative agriculture'.

The second story is about a changing relationship with plants. In the ARGOS project, farm families characterized this change in different ways (and without necessarily being formal adherents to Biological or Regenerative Agriculture networks). This was what Chris Perley could see in our interview material. In one example, a pastoral farmer near Dunedin described how his father had spent his entire farming life cutting down trees on their farm. Since taking over, the son had spent his entire time *replanting* them. His rationale for change stemmed from his realization that their current management of gully systems on the farm – poisoning mānuka and trying to grow grass in its place – was an exercise in futility.[30] When discussing the pointlessness of this work, one of his neighbours quipped: 'We could have filled up these gullies with empty Tordon drums by now. They're forest areas.'[31]

At the centre of these transitions and new potentials are a changing relationship with plants and a changing set of relations that open up new plant-based potentials. In a country previously characterized by pastoral hegemony, plants are a key vector of increasing multiplicity in land-use.[32] Like other new objects and materials in these kinds of transitions, they are also sites of new affect. The adherents of these experimental approaches, like Doug Avery, the self-named 'lucerne lunatic', seem to fall in love with new objects and relations in their farming worlds.

De-colonizing landscapes: Tuaropaki, Maketu and Pamu

Pāmu is the Māori verb 'to farm'. For the last ten years or so, it has also been the brand name of New Zealand's largest commercial farmer – Landcorp.[33] Māori names have been appropriated for Pākehā farms for 150 years, but this change in name signifies something new: a profound reversal of modernity's grip on farming in Aotearoa New Zealand. Before getting to the Pamu story, however, it is important to see how numerous small and situated experiments in new styles of Māori farming laid the groundwork for the major change in direction that has emerged at Landcorp.

Simon Lambert's historical assessment of Māori farming situates modernist farming at the centre of a series of land-use dilemmas for Māori.[34] In the 1920s, as recounted in Chapter 3, Sir Āpirana Ngata saw no option but to try to encourage Māori to move towards wholesale adoption of the full suite of modernist characteristics that were then becoming the norm on Pākehā family farms. The modernization drive intensified through the mid-twentieth century, during which an assault on any remaining outposts of specifically Māori land-use practice was reinforced by the large-scale outmigration of rural Māori into urban Aotearoa New Zealand in the 1950s and 1960s. Combined with the downturn in the rural economy after 1973, Māori farmers found themselves in a desperate situation. Even Ngata's beloved Ahuwhenua Trophy ceased to be regularly awarded: after 1990, it sat in a museum for thirteen years. When their cultural and political revival began in the 1970s, many Māori had been effectively alienated from their previously familiar rural worlds for many decades, and Māori farming knowledge had almost disappeared. Lambert's account highlights the dilemmas that were to come. With the concluding of several Treaty of Waitangi settlements in the 1990s, many iwi (tribes) regained control over large landholdings, or for the first time found themselves with the capital to develop existing holdings. Multiple futures beckoned.

One option was to complete Ngata's mission to entirely modernize farming and capture maximum economic value from land, and then to use that wealth to build other areas of capacity for iwi.[35] The opposite pathway involved an ongoing search for ways to build up social and environmental capital, as well as economic returns, from iwi land.[36]

There are some inspiring examples of taking the latter path. They demonstrate the enacting of disruptive, boundary-breaking ontologies of land-use. In their evaluation of the emerging economic networks arising from Treaty settlements, dubbed the 'Taniwha Economy',[37] Le Heron and Roche cite the Tuaropaki Trust in Mokai and the Wakatu Incorporation in Nelson as inspiring examples of new forms of Māori enterprise that involve a revisioning of land, resources and their connectivity.[38]

Wakatu was incorporated in the 1970s based around 1,400 hectares of land, but a dramatic repositioning of the potential of the incorporation came with an explicit move away from traditional modernist-style pastoral farming towards an expansion into horticulture, wine, hops and seafood. For the guardians of the incorporation, this was a chance to think about the productivity of Aotearoa New Zealand in ways that broke down the modernist divisions between agriculture, horticulture, viticulture and aquaculture. Instead of forcing geographic places into a form suitable for growing particular products, they chose to grow products that were suited to the available variety of places.[39] The strategy echoed what had been the norm prior to the twentieth century, when Māori were polycultural users of resources and made good use of land and sea. Wakatu now has around 4,000 Māori co-owners and is managing assets valued at NZ$260 million.[40]

Tuaropaki Trust breaks even more boundaries, enacting a highly elaborated set of connections across a diverse range of activities.[41] Based around a mixed farm of 340 hectares, the trust has been granted access to parts of the Mokai geothermal field and has commissioned its own power station, which generates 113 MW of power. It uses heat from the geothermal field to run greenhouses for high-value vegetable crops, and uses vegetable waste to generate worm manure for its pastures and vineyard. It is also planting mānuka to bring areas of hillside into honey production. As a diverse enterprise, Tuaropaki faced an all-too-familiar challenge. The trust could not find any finance institution in Aotearoa New Zealand which would lend them money to develop their diverse vision. Instead, they had to raise capital offshore.[42]

Both Tuaropaki and Wakatu are excellent examples of diverse enterprises, and they also demonstrate high levels of social connectivity. As organizations with a large number of Māori co-owners, they place strong importance on delivering social benefits, through employment in enterprises, building capacity, or through supporting community. They prioritize their communities' access to land, jobs and opportunities for hunting and fishing.

Both these cases have innovative governance arrangements, unusual configurations of 'bounded property', unorthodox commercial visions, and a commitment to developing both social capital and community resilience. When viewed as an assemblage of human and non-human actors, however, there is more going on than just the dedication and tenacity shown by the humans. All of these assemblages include particular materials and objects that have the potential to change outcomes, introduce new vitalities and make certain futures possible. This is most obvious in the way Tuaropaki has assembled the multiple ways that geothermal power makes other activities possible.

All these experiments in land-use and enterprise have originated from within Māori communities, or from specific relationships and practices between Māori, land and other resources. At their roots are older relationships that survived on the margins of the modernist farming world throughout the twentieth century. The final example – Pamu – describes something else: how a thoroughly mainstream institution drew inspiration from these Māori exemplars. Its leaders noticed that an important new template for land-use was being developed in the Taniwha Economy. Given the direction of influence between Pākehā and Māori for most of the country's farming history, this is a startling reversal.

Arising out of the chaos of neoliberalization in the 1980s and 1990s, the state-owned enterprise Landcorp was formed out of the land development holdings of the deregulated Department of Lands and Survey. It also began to act as a 'buyer of last resort' for farmland, with the hope that the freefall in farm-land prices at the time could be halted. The result, once the crisis had stabilized, was a landholding quasi-government entity with nearly 400,000 hectares of farm-land spread across New Zealand. Landcorp carries normative, political and outright economic heft due to its size and its status as the last great state-owned farm in New Zealand. In 2012, it changed its name to Pamu.[43]

Pamu has filled an important niche in the great world of experimentation happening in twenty-first-century land-use in Aotearoa New Zealand. It takes good ideas happening on individual farms – such as fencing off wetlands on Manuka Mire, reforesting hillsides and planting mānuka at Waihapua, or new pasture strategies and matching of animals and plants to landscapes like at Bonaveree, Wakatu and Tuaropaki – and incorporates them into its management of over 125 farms. The results are impressive.[44] Pamu has already fenced 7,500 hectares of wetlands and native bush into permanent covenants and is rapidly expanding outwards from these covenants to establish permanent native vegetation on the banks of all its waterways. It is de-stocking some areas, retiring extensive amounts of hill country into forestry and converting more intensive farms to organic systems. The central vision of diversification, value-adding and sustainability is described as being guided by kaitiakitanga (guardianship) over land.[45] It is a strikingly different way of solving the 'volumes to values' conundrum that has been a core challenge for improving economic returns from farming.[46]

Pamu has taken some of the 'bad' farms that failed to survive the rural downturn and turned them into a highly valuable and highly connected landscape – by taking their inspiration from new experiments in Māori land-use, along with a host of other approaches that were being attempted on a diverse range of farms outside the margins of modernist farming. Pamu recognized newly visible farming worlds elsewhere in Aotearoa New Zealand and took the first steps towards making them normative.

Postmodern farming and de-colonization

Understanding the power of farms as something that is expressed by their ontology changes the way we understand both the past and future of farming worlds. The farms described in this chapter demonstrate a particular way of understanding the politics of being alternative in contemporary food and farming worlds. Some of the 'postmodern' farms described in this chapter are overtly political projects, but that doesn't capture the full extent of their powers and effects. They have important *ontological* powers. They assemble species, knowledge and connections/relations; they disrupt boundaries and challenge the assembling of economic value in multiple and diverse ways. They act differently in the world and make multiple possibilities real, just as their modernist predecessors acted to parcel up, contain, pacify and homogenize worlds of land-use.

While each of these farms tells its own unique story, collectively they speak to something broader: the ways in which alternative farming in all its multiplicity can be understood through its work contesting elements of the great assemblage of modernist agriculture. In the previous chapter, I described on a broader scale how various elements of modernist farming were being disrupted. These farms can be understood as acting to enact and amplify these breaches and fractures:

- Connection to wider ecologies. Modernist farms (and wider modernist worlds) tended to operate inside an ontological boundary that rendered wider ecological harms and influences invisible. New farms are reconnecting with wider ecologies and working to repair frontier breaches in older ecologies. This is a common thread across all these farms and forms a key part of how their potential futures are multiplying.
- Social connectivity. New farming ontologies are also reconnecting across the social boundary around farms in multiple ways: through the enacting of new audit

mechanisms and information flows that connect production and consumption worlds, through re-engaging with social networks and communities (often organized around new approaches to farming), or through the enacting of more connected indigenous ontologies of land-use in which social uses of land are prioritized alongside economic uses. Bonaveree Farm is a particularly poignant site of escape from the hard boundaries of the social ontology of modernist farming and demonstrates the liberation that can be found in building new networks. The need to prioritize such networks has been fundamental to all the indigenous experiments in land-use recounted here. It was fundamental to older Māori ontologies, and helps re-bind broken worlds.

- Hard boundaries and private ownership. The state acted decisively in the 1980s and 1990s to defend the 'hard' status of private property boundaries and private ownership. None of the activities reviewed in Chapter 4 have fundamentally disrupted this, although, as this chapter has shown, there are some tiny seeds of hopeful new approaches and disruptions apparent in both Māori land-ownership and experimentation, which have emerged from the settlement of Treaty of Waitangi claims and the return of land assets (among other things) into multiple ownership by iwi. Outside the Treaty settlement process, the most important innovation has been the increased use of reserves and covenanting of bush and wetland areas on private land.[47] These are only small challenges to an ongoing landscape ontology of private, separated ownership; nevertheless, they are demonstrating that different ways forward are possible, even if such alternatives are only happening in a tiny minority of cases.

- Contesting technical scientific knowledge. New Social Movements have contested the previously unchallenged status of technical, scientific expertise as the sole arbiter of what is 'good' in farming practice. For many of the farms in this chapter, new knowledge networks have taken shape around alternative approaches like organic or regenerative agriculture, which assemble expertise outside formal educational and scientific institutions. This new knowledge was intrinsic to the formation of wider social networks around alternative approaches.

- Contesting productivist rationalities of farming. Many of these farms are directly confronting the simplified rationalities of productivism. They all bring into existence values and rationalities for the existence of farms and/or the qualities of foods that differ from the usual narrow and bounded ontology inside the simplified logic of productivist rationalities. They make other ways of being a 'good farmer' thinkable. Part of this has been an increase in curiosity and innovation about new ways to create value beyond the farm (or forest, or orchard, or vineyard) gate. Pamu has sought this as part of its mission for kaitiakitanga: that good guardianship of the land is enhanced by producing high-value products, not commodities. Waihapua, Wakatu and Tuaropaki also deliberately seek ways to move away from commodities and towards higher-quality food and fibre products.[48]

- Stabilization of farms as a particular kind of capital. The modernist farm is economically composed in a very particular way, and understood as comprising a particular kind of stable and knowable economic capital. The way that new farms and arrangements are assembling new values is a key theme of recent research in Aotearoa New Zealand.[49] In some of the farms in this chapter, these dynamics of re-assembling values to create new economic possibilities is evident. From mānuka honey/UMF to the transformation of the relations around lucerne and the enacting of 'provenancing' by Māori incorporations, these farms point towards other ways to generate value.

• Enacting transitions from homogeneity and sameness to difference and multiplicity in food systems. Taken together, all these forces of disruption and experimentation reveal a new ontological pattern on farms in which the modernist impetus to simplify and homogenize is increasingly failing to hold, and greater multiplicity and complexity are emerging and making many other futures possible.

Worlds of farming that were pacified begin to heat up and change. Frontiers begin to shift. The wetland and forest frontiers expand back into land lost during colonization, and the ideas, practices and relationalities of land-use, the reality of existing and working with land, and the connectedness of landscapes that were intrinsic to Māori ontologies have increasingly emerged into view. They are the previously invisible participants in the exterior worlds lying outside the ontological boundaries of modernist farming. Collectively, their reappearance is beginning to de-colonize some modernist farming worlds.[50]

These farms demonstrate a simple truth: that the forward-looking gaze of modernist farming worlds (and their never-ending quest for progress) failed to see what could be learned from the past. Farms without deep histories have constrained futures. As Dame Anne Salmond has argued in reflecting on the potential commensurability of different colonial worlds of knowledge and learning: 'Most Europeans … saw themselves as having everything to offer, and Māori as having nothing to teach them.'[51] The inspiring example of new Māori land incorporations speaks to the resilience of a culture that has learned not once, but twice, how to live inside disrupted frontier ecologies. Around four to five centuries after having arrived from wider Polynesia, Māori faced an ecological and social crisis in the aftermath of their rapid exploitation of Aotearoa as a frontier space. It took at least until the fourteenth and fifteenth centuries for Māori land-use to transition from exploitative colonization to more stable and sustainable ways of surviving and thriving in Aotearoa. This new learning and body of land-use practices involved many things, including a shift to gardening and careful management of the harvesting of animal species.

For all researchers of land-use and farming in Aotearoa New Zealand, these wider reservoirs of knowledge and the deeper histories of our landscapes should be the first places we begin our enquiries. This is doubly true during a period in our farm history which is increasingly socially, ecologically and economically crisis-prone. For Pakeha modernist farming, the inevitable crises of farming a colonized, disrupted landscape were manageable for much of the twentieth century, until they eventually weren't. We are facing a second crisis of colonial land-use, this time even more quickly than that faced by Māori during Aotearoa's first colonization. That prior history is a vital resource: an existing pool of knowledge that enacts cultures of respect towards other species, relationality to wider ecologies and a sense of kinship with a living land, to guide new ways to farm – as is being explored by many farms in this chapter. Salmond exhorts these kinds of collaborations as the pathway to de-colonization, invoking the concept of hau (the wind of life) as the animator of shared knowledge:

> According to this philosophy [hau], one form of life studying all others is hau whitia, fundamentally out of kilter. Human understanding (as opposed to human control) requires reciprocal exchange, for all its hazards – your wisdom for mine (waananga atu, waananga mai), as we cross our thoughts together (whakawhitiwhiti whakaaro). In New Zealand, at least, a collaboration between Māori and Western knowledges seems possible.[52]

Seen in this way, it is no surprise that out of the disrupted hegemony of modernist farming worlds, Māori land-use is providing some compelling examples of the kind of future twenty-first-century farming in Aotearoa New Zealand might achieve. I like to think that the wind of life that blew through Heather's Homestead/Marotahei in the 1850s and 1860s can find even more enduring sites of farm-based collaboration in the twenty-first century.

The future of modernity's farms

Stepping outside the specific context of colonized worlds – particularly those where farms were some of the primary agents of colonization – how do these farms speak to wider transitions in modernist farming and its many alternatives? Two insights can be drawn out that can inform wider discussions about the ultimate trajectory of modernist worlds. First, what farming futures await us; and second, how do we influence which farming futures we arrive at?

The pessimistic social theorists of modernity feared that a dystopian future awaited us all. This modernist future would inevitably take on an instrumental, technologically trapped, de-humanized shape. Max Weber predicted the future dis-enchantment of a world increasingly organized by formal rationalities and logics, facilitated by bureaucratization, where humankind ends up in an 'iron cage of rationality' in which human relations, sentiments and feelings are squeezed to the margins of the world and monstrous logics dominate our lives. Jacques Ellul, alarmed at the increasing pace of the elaboration of new technologies, provided a variation on this. He feared that these modernist trajectories would eventually end up in a world dominated by technologies where human's lives would be shaped by techno-logics. Deborah Fitzgerald applied this fear to the future of farming, envisaging a world of industrial farming where industrial logics eventually marginalized the human participation in the systems until farmers simply became managers supervising human workers and animal machines in soul-less factory systems.[53] Alongside such social pathologies, many other theorists, such as Miguel Altieri, James Scott or Jules Pretty, characterized modernist farming as socially and ecologically pathological. According to them, modernist farming systems were fundamentally unresilient. They were brittle and prone to collapse. This does feel familiar – a sense of the drive to elaborate farm logics that obey internal drivers and goals, while other worlds, and a wider set of pathological outcomes, remain invisible and unable to be acted upon. But therein lies the fracture point between what we fear and what we actually experience in the elaboration of modernity. Is the dystopian future of modernity inevitable, or are we able to change course?

The farms described in this chapter speak to a different and less inevitable set of dynamics. Social theorists like Latour, Callon and Gibson-Graham are sceptical of the unchallengeable and uniform quality attributed by many scholars to the elaboration of modernist society, and point towards the constant disruption of modernist systems, the inevitability of 'overflows' and the unruly nature of ecologies and economies. Scott's modernist agricultural dreams of the twentieth-century state crashed into ruin on the rocks of social and ecological complexity. Even in the United States, the country where the modernist dystopia of farming futures has come closest to realization, Melanie DuPuis's study of the 'perfect' world of dairying and milk reveals the eternal tensions between forces of modernization/perfectibility coming up against the constant pull and rub of multiple other situated forces – both human and non-human.[54]

Farms in Aotearoa New Zealand clearly have agencies that act in ways which can disrupt the dystopian futures that pessimistic theorists of modernity imagined or feared. While the great 'unravelling' of modernist farming detailed in these last two chapters has not entirely broken the hegemonies of modernist farming in many key areas, new farms exist that are capable of challenging and disrupting modernist farming futures. Ecologies still have effects, long-term breaches accumulate consequences, political hegemonies hold – until they don't and challenges emerge. And farms act as one important site where these effects assemble and make alternatives real.[55]

One important caveat remains. Even in such an optimistic rendering of the transformative potential of farms, these farms also frame a question that Weber or Ellul would recognize as fulfilling their worst fears. Is there a 'point of no return' in damaged ecologies, a point at which things collapse and the only way back is through massive crisis and reconfiguration?

This is an important question for how we understand the ontology of farms as assembling both human and non-human powers. Are there material qualities to farm ecologies that have the capacity to close down future options? The farms in this chapter seem to be drawing on a large range of resources, some dynamic human actors, wider social networks of alternative practitioners, and critically important reservoirs of ecological capacity along with pockets of preserved knowledge and practice. These disparate resources, knowledges and ecologies *exist*, and many of them seem to be ready and waiting for their dormant powers to be awakened from the invisible exterior of bounded modernist farming worlds. There is, in all these hopeful cases, something waiting off the edge of the ontological map that can be discovered and made real, just as Aotearoa awaited Pacific voyagers who set out in search of land to the south.

In order for farms to return to more culturally and ecologically diverse worlds of land-use, however, the great modernist project of homogenization must be challenged and disrupted before it has completed its erasure of all other possibilities. Reservoirs need to survive, older knowledges must be preserved, small connections and relations nurtured and maintained. This isn't an abstract fear. During discussions about which farm cases to include in this chapter, with colleagues, friends and various situated experts, two different narratives emerged. While they happily volunteered examples of inspiring new alternative farms, much of the discussion also concerned the continuities of modernist farming and situations like the freshwater crisis in Canterbury, or the ongoing challenges for Māori whānau (families) in holding on to their land. In some cases, modernist simplification had eradicated the basis for a 'return' to more diverse, multiple forms. Many had no alternatives available to turn to in desperate situations, and precious family land was surrendered onto the market.

The farms that I selected for this chapter were chosen because they represent real and existing alternative potential futures – things that are actually being experimented with, materialized and rendered visible in Aotearoa New Zealand. But they exist in a world in which many other potential futures have already been lost. The creation of alternatives, in other words, can only be achieved if modernist farming hasn't completed its journey of erasure and annihilation of other worlds. What if we sail towards other futures and find that the farming equivalent of Terra Australis Incognita simply doesn't exist, or, Atlantis-like, was once there but has now sunk beneath the waves?

On the Munro's farm, at Pamu, or Tutira and Waihapua, and in the new hope of Bonaveree, species, practices and ideas survived and new futures emerged, but they almost didn't. All these ecological reservoirs, alternatives sources of knowledge and ideas ran the serious risk of not surviving into the twenty-first century, of not being available to be assembled into alternatives. This is the crisis of Lake Ellesmere/Te Waihora in the heart of the frontier conflict in Canterbury. It is eutrophied, possibly beyond restoration. Newly irrigated intensive dairy farms, like #370 Five-Mile Rd and its hundreds of peers, may have already taken the region past the tipping point from which the freshwater systems of Canterbury can quickly recover. The lake has tipped into a state of ecological collapse and may only recover through some as yet unknowable pathway that is beyond the ability of farms to enact. In Julie Guthman's terms, the modernist farming systems of Canterbury may have gone beyond the 'limits of repair'[56] and the only way back is through chaos, collapse and total reconfiguration.[57] It is the question that Mike Bell pondered in Iowa: had the monologic hog/corn/soybean landscape homogenized farming worlds to the point where there were no reservoirs left to support any dialogue to create alternatives?[58]

The longer history of farming colonization in Aotearoa New Zealand reminds us that catastrophic ecological scenarios happen. The threat of total erasure of the indigenous is very real. But I chose the farms in this chapter to make the opposite argument: that in this particular country, in most farming worlds, we haven't passed beyond the limits of repair; dialogue can and will happen, and alternative futures are possible. Embedded in the farm stories in this chapter are important hints about the multiple ways that farms change and farming people turn towards new futures and collaborate with their farms in new ways. Doug Avery has written a whole book about his journey and that of his farm. Gay and Ron Munro proudly tell researchers of the day they blocked a farm drain in Manuka Mire. Others tell their tales to gathered community members in Landcare groups. Some talk of the fantails returning in the wake of the adoption of a low-chemical pest management regime, to follow them down rows of kiwifruit vines. Some agents of change were inspiring women from non-farming backgrounds who married into farms and didn't find the need to conform with the rigidities of masculine 'farm culture'. Others were European migrants who came to pursue horticulture and didn't have the deeply ingrained reverence for sheep or cows that prevents many multi-generational farming Pākehā from contemplating grapes and kiwifruit vines. Included were great leaders and farm thinkers like Guthrie Smith, who declared without reservation that the destination was not what he had optimistically imagined through his long life as a farmer. And around and beneath them all lies a longer colonial history, a marginalized ontology of Māori land-use that was pushed to breaking point, but has started to find its voice again as the need for alternative futures arises.

The long history of alternative farming is partly this complex history in which great diversity and difference simmered below the surface. Seen now, many decades after the great disruption began, the most surprising aspect of this whole unmaking of modernist agriculture is the way that the hegemonic stranglehold of Pākehā pastoral farming had remained intact for so long.

Understanding farms through their ontologies reveals this kind of politics of future potentials. As complex assemblages of human and non-human actors, farms act as the material site where many powers, potentials and agencies align. Part of the political work of farms is to retain the possibility of other futures, and the farms described in this chapter demonstrate this quality. They make invisible worlds visible and new options possible; they retain reservoirs of older vitalities, and then experiment with these in dynamic combinations. As the great trajectory of modernist farming diminishes in scope and power – fractured, disrupted and challenged on numerous fronts – these are the farms that make new worlds possible.

Farming inside visible worlds means farming in full recognition of the historical contexts and consequences of our actions, searching for complexity and diversity rather than homogeneity, building and acting with recognition of our broad ecological networks, being fully engaged in social worlds and seeking new ways to create economic value. The farms described in this chapter are turned towards their exterior worlds, and are characterized by exciting new ways to emotionally and intellectually engage the great task of farming. They share the element of urgency and excitement. They are sites of affect in which new potentials inspire their participants through both the challenge of making new worlds possible and the hope that is generated when we render wider worlds visible again and become producers – not only of products, but also of new futures.

The Watching Place

After decades in which my only contact with farms was through visiting them as a researcher, my family and I bought 7.2 hectares of land on the banks of the Waitaki River in North Otago. One hundred and twenty-five years after the Campbells left Ashburn Estate, a descendant had returned to land ownership in Otago (see Figure 11). When I announced this news to Khyla Russell, a senior Māori advisor at our research centre, she responded immediately: 'Hugh, you don't own land, land owns you.'[59]

Figure 11 The Watching Place
Artist attribution: Marion Familton

My initial plan was to use the property simply as a fishing camp, but over the ensuing years as we got to know each other the powers of the land began to assert themselves. The piece of land was in a dire state. Having sat in ownership limbo for decades, and considered too poor for serious pasture development by its prior farming owners, it had become a public domain that seemed to accumulate ill intentions. The local populace used it as a place to dump rubbish. Neighbouring farmers would snip the wire holding the gate shut and run stock through it, allowing their animals to graze any edible matter down to the ground. By mid-summer its under-structure of river gravels and recently deposited sterile schist-based silt was completely exposed and so bare that, as my wife Marion put it, you could 'see a mouse run across it'. The only animals to be seen happily grazing in its gravelly banks were rabbits. High-tension power lines ran along the distant horizon. Unfertile, covered in gorse and thistle, abused by surrounding landowners, it was a modernist 'sump-oil tank' of accumulated farmland woes. It was, in other words, exactly the kind of place where it was possible to contemplate whether modernity eventually extinguishes all future options, or whether new vitalities can emerge. It was not for naught that Jenna Packer chose this exact piece of land, with our familiar range of hills in the background, as the setting for the painting that adorns the front cover of this book. This landscape speaks to her of destroyed pasts and compromised futures. Her painting is a challenge about the need to find our way back from modernist agriculture before the deluge takes us all.

My first years camping on the land were stressful. I sat in a deck chair on our newly built deck in front of a small shed reclaimed from the local school and gazed pensively out with my grandfather's eyes. What I saw was thistle, gorse and broom – weeds that surely would surge to overwhelm us if I didn't immediately fight for control. If not weeds, then hundreds of rabbits. I pondered how every blight on this land was caused by introduced species. As the spring gales turned into regular summer winds, dust would swirl around us. We had no prospect of ever turning this into an acceptable form of modernist farm. It felt like a failed piece of farmland, bordering what seemed an equally wild river valley of braided channels, cannabis plots, willows and gorse. I was secretly glad my grandfather had recently passed away and would never see this place.

In the terms used in this book, however, I was wrong. This piece of land has a life and expresses vitality. It is more than just an exemplar of failed modernity. I have come to understand that it actually sits, and acts, right at the collision zone of multiple frontiers. By the river are wetlands, around us are trees and grassland pastures are sketchily present. Down the road the advancing frontier of centre pivot irrigators is almost in view as new irrigation schemes bring the dairying world deep into our dry and windy valley. Another frontier is hinted at by the high-tension power lines in the distance: in the early 2000s our land was at the site of the climactic battle of the expanding frontier of big-river hydroelectric power schemes in Aotearoa New Zealand. All around us were frontiers being enacted or held open on this piece of land.

My first experience of being owned by this land was to cease looking at it with my modernist 'good farmer' eyes and to try to see the invisible worlds in which it existed. And after more than ten years of living with and interacting with our land, its many elements and intriguing histories, a different way of understanding it emerged. So, what became visible? How did this failed modernist farmland enact a new ontology?

Despite its first appearances the land actually had ecological reservoirs. Left fallow for a decade, the soil recovered. Ryegrass and clover naturally reseeded from the surrounding pastures and supressed most of the thistles, and we enjoyed celebrating my father's recollected childhood pleasures by burning gorse (but not driving a D2 Caterpillar into a swamp). These days we lend the paddocks to neighbours to lightly graze their horses or the occasional herd of calves, which stomp down the woody weeds. I no longer live in fear of being overwhelmed by pests.

Our land also has important histories. First, it only existed because of the kinds of social movement struggles that have characterized recent environmental politics. It was partly formed in its current shape out of a conflict over water extraction for hydroelectric power in the wider Waitaki Valley. In 2004 community opposition and organized environmental protest had halted the last 'great' hydroelectric scheme ever attempted in New Zealand, Project Aqua, in its final stages of planning. Our piece of land had been purchased by the state-owned energy company Meridian Energy for the development of a canal path between dams. When the scheme was abandoned, the previous owner didn't want the land back; it was so bad in modernist terms that he preferred to surrender it in return for monetary compensation. The modernist farming frontier shrank by 7.2 hectares. In effect, late twentieth-century environmental activism had created the political conditions that eventually sliced this land away from the modernist farming estate. This was the first, and perhaps most portentous invisible history of this place that I learned: Big Hydro had ceased its expansion in Aotearoa New Zealand right where we were sitting. When it retreated, modernist farming had not reclaimed the terrain, surrendering it instead to an interesting and fluid third space.

Over subsequent years other histories came into view. One summer I set out to grub thistles with an old mattock, hoping to get a sense of what my Scottish forebears had done on their crofts. After a few days of that I had developed a certain sympathy for the intentions of the Campbells, Laings and Atchisons who had left Scotland in a bid to find better land elsewhere! But in the process of my endeavours I uncovered different environmental histories. Beneath a thicket of African boxthorn (another annoying imported hedging material to add to the list of other self-inflicted pests) on the knoll that created nice shelter for our buildings, I discovered a large burned-out tree stump. Aerial photographs of the land go as far back as 1936, and none of them show a large tree on that windswept knoll. That stump was a sad reminder of the great burning, and the thought of anyone cutting down and burning a huge tree anchoring a nice knoll in a windy valley provided a moment of sad reflection into modernist land-use ontologies.

Local people provided us with other histories of our land. One recalled it being open to teenagers and their cars: they had fashioned a sled out of an old car bonnet and dragged each other around the paddock behind a car at high speed. Others remember an experiment with lucerne – which still occasionally pops up through the pasture. Maybe one day I'll go to a field day with Doug Avery and consider joining the lucerne lunatics.

It took ten years to begin to make progress on the other big invisible history. After eventually making contact with a local kaumatua (Māori elder), I heard the other story of our land. In prehistory it had been a camp known as 'the watching place', where journeying Māori moving up the south bank of the Waitaki River in search of orthoquartzite (and leaving rock art in their wake on limestone cliffs) camped and waited for the river to drop enough in order to wade across. Our camp is at the most 'braided' part of the river and Māori often occupied it for weeks, waiting and watching the river levels. The kaumatua didn't know if they had camped in that exact spot, but archaeological investigations have turned up multiple pre-historic sites on the nearby riverbank. I like to think the big tree would have served as both landmark and shade for Māori travellers. A giant rock in the nearby Otiake streambed was the mythological remains of a demon dog that had once been in the hunting pack of an ogre in a nearby gorge, who was slain by Māori warriors.

Understood as a small, potentially modernist farm of the kind most of my Pākehā forebears would have created, this was a hopeless piece of land. Understood as the latest iteration of a frontier camp, where people rested in their travels, hunted eels and wild pigs (and later trout, salmon and rabbits) and watched and learned, this piece of land began to assemble something new. We harvest firewood and plant new trees. Our neighbours use our land as an occasional grazing reservoir. We fish, hunt, learn new things about land and consider different futures. It has become the hinge of another frontier: between farmed terrain and the great recreational world of the Waitaki River bed, where people are free to fish, ride bikes and hunt for ducks, wild pigs and rabbits.

What we've learned at the Watching Place is that even a piece of land that seemed utterly ruined and lacking potential in a modernist sense still had ecological reservoirs, had remarkable and important histories worth knowing and learning from, and stands now as a site where multiple frontiers are being held open against modernist pressures to build dams and irrigate dairy pastures. It found a way back, with all its disturbing feralities and unexpected vitalities and, in doing so, made our lives richer as well.

Being owned by that land and open to its hidden histories, its variety of purposes and open boundaries, has started its own small work of de-colonization. It may have taken a dramatically new path compared to Glenn Rd, Te Rahui, Longridge and Windsor Lodge; but in an echo from distant history, a living breeze blows through the small door opened by the great collaboration at Heather's Homestead/Marotahei, and different futures become possible again. Next task: restore some wetlands.

Notes

1   http://www.retrolens.nz/ (accessed 17 April 2019).
2   There is also a lurking suspicion that the presence of trees in parkland-style planting reproduced the English landscape aesthetic that my grandparents admired – particularly the fetching view of the front quarter of the farm from the main road.
3   In our moist part of the Waikato, many native tree species like to have 'wet feet' and grow profusely straight out of wetlands.
4   Thus being what Rob Burton describes as the subject of special attention by farmers – 'roadside' or 'hedgerow' farming to make sure your farm looked good to your neighbours (Burton 2004a).
5   With intriguing exceptions. My forebear Arthur Heather, who spent some of his early life on Heather's Homestead/Marotahei with his Māori stepmother Unaiki and half-brother Stanley, went on to prosper greatly in business in Auckland and led a respectable and celebrated life, but was eventually bankrupted by the collapse of the kauri gum trade and left the colony in disgrace. Gum was the opposite kind of capital to a farm. It was speculative and economically unstable. One of Arthur's sons, who became a vicar in England, poignantly kept a piece of kauri gum – the substance that ruined his father's fortune and reputation – on his desk all his working life.
6   Rationalism became a force in New Zealand in the 1880s (much as in other parts of the British Empire) and sought to contest the influence of churches on the emerging character of modern society in New Zealand. It was boosted by the participation of Sir Robert Stout who became prime minister. This history is still celebrated by the currently active New Zealand Society of Rationalists and Humanists (see www.rationalists.nz).
7   Exploring this new world of farming has been a collaborative and collective task. To furnish this selection of cases, I have turned primarily to the body of work undertaken by the Biological Economies research group (including cases discussed in Le Heron et al. (2016) and Pawson et al. (2018)). Other key sources of insight into new farms are: the Agriculture Research Group on Sustainability (ARGOS) project; important scholarly collaborations like Merata Kawharu's edited collection *Whenua* (2002), which has become a crucial pivot in discussions of Māori land and resource management; the work of doctoral students (Tall forthcoming - 2021); and accounts of other well-known farms telling important stories for new social movements like Biological Agriculture and Regenerative Agriculture that have been related in media or other academic work. Clearly these cases are not representative of all the daily struggles and frustrations of the vast majority of farmers and farms still enacting

modernist farming worlds. Aotearoa New Zealand has not suddenly become a haven of widespread revolutionary change in farming. But these farms do tell an important story: that hegemonies have their limits, and that even in a shrine to modernist pastoral farming, eventually some alternatives will take shape and previously invisible worlds will become visible. They are the impertinent voices calling from the back of the crowd during the parade of the naked emperor.

8   The Ramsar Convention on Wetlands was established by UNESCO in 1971.

9   We visited as part of Ismael Tall's PhD field research (Tall forthcoming - 2021). Some photographs of the farm can be seen at the Southland Ecological Restoration Network website (https://www.sern.org.nz/project-directory/mānuka-mire-mokotua/) (accessed 18 July 2018), and in the publications of the Queen Elizabeth II National Trust (https://qeiinationaltrust.org.nz/wp-content/uploads/2018/03/QEII-Nov-issue-93.pdf (2017: 22–3)) (accessed 7 September 2018).

10 Because of residual wood and other humus, freshwater systems in this area have a remarkable dark, tea-coloured tint which produces vivid effects in the colouring of native species inhabiting these waters. This effect is visible in Figure 10.

11 In a drylands context, one oft-mentioned exemplar is Taharoa on the Mahia Peninsula in Hawke's Bay, which anchors a network of wetland and stream management across the peninsula through the actions of the Whangawehi Catchment Management Group (see https://whangawehi.com/about/) (accessed 21 April 2019).

12 We were collectively coding and sorting in-depth interview data from over 100 farms and orchards. For more information on the ARGOS project, see www.argos.org.nz.

13 The monocultural status of commercial forestry in Aotearoa New Zealand has been long debated, but never overcome, in the sector. For a good example of the modernist arguments in favour of monocultural forestry, see Hegan (1993).

14 Fenton Wilson quoted in the revealingly headlined 2018 news article: 'Bola damaged farm so badly it was only fit for trees.' https://www.stuff.co.nz/business/farming/102230595/bola-damaged-farm-so-badly-it-was-only-fit-for-trees (accessed 11 February 2019)

15 The operation of carbon markets, as geographer Adrian Nel has observed, has powerful and complex effects in territorializing new economic assemblages (Nel 2018).

16 There is a complex negotiated set of metrologies around measuring the floral origins of honey (see Bourn et al. 1999), which is currently under dispute. Millions of dollars of lucrative mānuka honey exports will be potentially included or excluded by the metrology of mānuka.

17 Waihapua is just one of many places on the East Coast where mānuka is now being actively encouraged to regrow, or even directly planted, to create foraging terrain for bees.

18 http://www.guthriesmith.org.nz/ (accessed 17 April 2019).

19 Pers. Com. Chris Perley, April, 2019.

20 Discussed by Lewis and Le Heron (2018) for Marlborough, and mirroring the 'merino to pinot' transition further south in Central Otago (Perkins et al. 2015).

21 The last year of 'good rain' in Marlborough was 1996, with the next few years being catastrophic years of 'drought', and below-average rainfall persisted for at least another ten years.

22 In his words: 'I thought my problem was drought; it wasn't. My problem was the way I farmed, and the way I thought about things' (Avery 2017: 20).

23 The story is told in Avery's book about his life and farm: *The Resilient Farmer: Weathering the Challenges of Life and the Land* (2017).

24 Moot is a professor of plant science at Lincoln University who advocates the greater use of legumes in dryland systems – particularly lucerne (alfalfa). Drylands farms like Bonavaree that experience regular serious droughts provide a test case of looming future 'drying' challenges to pastoral systems.

25 In Avery's words: 'the new idea that rescued me and set me off on my process of discovery and change came in the form of a plant – a plant we'd been growing for eighty years, but hadn't seen the potential of: lucerne, whose long tap root has the power to transform the way we utilise water … But, as a friend of mine said: "Doug, your story's not really about lucerne is it?" "No," I agreed. "It just happened to be our tool. This is a story about changing the way we integrate into the world"'(2017: 21). That integration revolved around an ontological flip from being a farmer of crops and land to being 'a farmer of water'.

26 Moving sheep from ryegrass/clover pasture to lucerne can trigger the intestinal trauma called bloat, and avoiding this was at the centre of Bonavaree experiments in how to transition from one to the other without killing your flock (Avery 2017: 135–40).

27 Avery's enchantment with lucerne transitioned into an enchantment with all sorts of trees, until eventually he became a passionate advocate and practitioner of native tree restoration in farmed landscapes (Avery 2017: 183–5).

28 This follows a familiar pattern of collective farming transition described in other parts of the world. In the United States, Bell's (2004) discussion of the Practical Farmers of Iowa follows a similar pattern. Another useful example is Hassanein's (1999) depiction of the power of grass deployed through rotational grazing and elaborated through networks of alternative farmers in the United States, to provide an alternative to industrial stock production raised in concentrated animal feed operations.

29 Avery (2017: 174). This strongly aligns with the kinds of transformation we saw taking shape on ARGOS farms and orchards (discussed in Chapter 4), in which some growers began to express greater 'breadth of view' that linked their orchards or farms into wider social, economic and ecological networks (see Hunt et al. 2011).

30 The return of mānuka into gully systems across the region of Otago is the subject of decades-long experimentation by farm foresters like Ken Stephens of Kakapuaka (https://www.nzffa.org.nz/branches/south-otago-branch/branch-member-videos/ken-stephens-balclutha-south-otago-branch/) (accessed 21 April 2019). He and his father started allowing mānuka back into their gullies for purely pragmatic economic reasons: removing the trees was costing more than they could earn from grazing any resulting pasture. But over time, their great reservoir of mānuka became a key resource in the establishment of a regional farm forestry association and they became a major source of mānuka seedlings for replanting across the region (https://www.odt.co.nz/business/farming/fun-ride-says-award-recipient) (accessed 29 May 2019).

31 Quoted in https://chrisperleyblog.com/2019/05/14/the-economics-of-space-in-land-use-and-our-unrealised-potential-in-new-zealand/ (accessed 15 May 2019). Tordon is the brand name for a widely used herbicide designed to control woody weeds like gorse and broom – and mānuka. Avery talks about the same transition in his life: he spent days in his youth 'scrub cutting' mānuka off his hillsides, only to find himself back there with a spade later in life replanting them (Avery 2017: 179).

32 But not the only one. Smith (2010) and Le Heron et al. (2016b) describe the emergence of Biological Agriculture in dairy systems around networks of farmers, scientists and other vitalities in their shared focus on the powers of *soils*. As a vital

material, soils have become central to numerous new farm ontologies, but they generally align around one important binary. In modernist farm ontologies, soils are treated as if they are best understood as a combination of chemical elements and compounds. In other approaches like organic, biodynamic or Biological Agriculture, soil is considered alive.

33   Le Heron and Roche (2018).

34   Lambert (2011).

35   Some of the most complex politics of this approach have played out across the South Island where the major iwi – Ngāi Tahu – faced significant internal conflict as it positioned itself as both a guardian of freshwater systems like Lake Ellesmere/ Te Waihora and the Waituna Lagoon, while simultaneously cutting down its forests on the Canterbury Plains to establish intensive dairy farms (discussed in Hansford 2014).

36   As Lambert (2011) recounts, even the Ahuwhenua Trophy became a site of this struggle, with some of the early winners after 2003 being rewarded as excellent exemplars of successful modernist 'agribusiness', whereupon pressure came to bear on the committee to expand the judging criteria to include more social and ecological qualities in the evaluation of success.

37   *Taniwha* are mythical creatures of great power: 'Taniwha Economy' is a Māori transliteration of terms like the 'tiger economy'. It has been used to characterize the emerging economic networks arising from Treaty settlements that have returned land, forests and fisheries to iwi, or the revival of existing land-holding through the injection of capital from settlements.

38   Le Heron and Roche (2018).

39   Hence their move not only into the traditional Māori area of horticulture, but also into less traditional areas like wine production under their Tohu and Kono labels. Wine is understood in global contexts as having a particularly vital set of relations between plants, land and production culture – *terroir* – which is a concept that translates well into Māori understandings of the relationship between products and land. This supports the wider argument by Le Heron and Roche (2018) about how such assemblages enact and build upon 'provenancing'.

40   Le Heron and Roche (2018: 167–8).

41   Le Heron and Roche (2018: 166–7).

42   This resonates strongly with the significant barriers to access to capital that characterized the decline of Māori farming in the late nineteenth and early twentieth centuries, and is in stark contrast with Pākehā farms, for which government credit schemes provided ready access to capital.

43   Le Heron and Roche (2018).

44   And proudly proclaimed by Carden and McKenzie (2018).

45   Where did that kaitiakitanga come from? It wasn't sitting dormant in history books, but was the precious project of generations of inspirational Māori leaders through the dark years of the twentieth century. From Te Puea to Dame Whina Cooper, political struggle and an ongoing quest to keep indigenous knowledge alive (often by women such as these), kept a reservoir of knowledge intact and available when it was later needed.

46   The economic dimensions of this, including a recognition of diverse ways to create new value, are discussed extensively in Pawson et al. (2018).

47   It is worth noting that there have also been significant political contests and dialogues on public access to farmland for recreation, which have led to the

formation of the Walking Access Commission (https://www.walkingaccess.govt.nz/) (accessed 18 July 2018). Its actions and the ongoing negotiation of access to trails and elaboration of online maps are not directly addressed in any of the farm cases in this chapter.

48   I have only gestured towards these kinds of 'quantities to qualities' transitions in economic worlds of land-use, partly because this is a major focus of a recent publication of the Biological Economies group in Aotearoa New Zealand (Pawson et al. 2018).

49   Pawson et al. (2018).

50   It is important to note that while this narrative concerns farming, there are huge worlds of action taking shape around Treaty of Waitangi settlements in other fields, including the co-governance of rivers (Muru-Lanning 2016; Ngata 2018) and the development of fisheries (Russell and Campbell 1999).

51   Salmond (1997: 509).

52   Salmond (1997: 513).

53   Something that echoes with much of the New Rural Sociology which, in its Marxist inflected approach, looked for the way that farms were being inevitably subsumed into wider, socially pathological, capitalist forms of production.

54   DuPuis (2002).

55   But not the only ones. I'll return in the Epilogue to a consideration of how farms aren't the only assemblages that disrupt modernity and enact change.

56   Guthman's (2019) study of the Californian strawberry industry provides a compelling picture of what happens when a central element of a highly tuned and simplified industrial assemblage – methyl bromide fumigation – is removed. In her terms, the industrial strawberry assemblage has been tipped beyond the 'limits of repair' within which orthodox science and technical expertise can re-assemble their systems (2019: 11).

57   The consequences of what happens next are traversed in Tsing (2015), who contemplates pathways back from collapsing socio-ecological and economic systems. While encouraging on many levels, Tsing's prognosis doesn't bode well if applied to modernist farming systems on the Canterbury Plains.

58   Bell (2004) poses this problem as one of 'monologic' industrial agriculture in a world which needs farming dialogue. For dialogue to happen, both sides need to exist.

59   This phrase echoes through almost any world of indigenous land-use and has been repeated so many times it forms something of a core rationale for how indigenous land-use ontologies stand in contrast to modernist ownership of land.

Epilogue: Theorizing the ontology of farms

In setting out to examine the power of farms as expressed through their ontology, this story has been focused on farms, their histories and their futures. My intention was to write a book that was accessible to anyone who was familiar with farms. This epilogue, however, undertakes another task: reflecting on the implications of taking a political ontologies approach for some specific theoretical discussions in agrifood studies.[1]

The recent emergence of post-structuralist approaches in agrifood studies has introduced important new ideas: the more-than-human turn, Foucauldian-inspired re-interpretations of the formation and disciplining of economic worlds, engagements with the formation of social worlds through theories of assemblage, the power of post-colonial critique, and a more reflexive awareness of the enactive power of practices of scholarship and research.[2] All of these have the potential to inform significant questions about farms and their pasts and futures in modernity.

While my intention in this book has been to try and use some of these new post-structuralist insights to create fresh ways of thinking about farms, their histories and their agencies, I also wanted to do this in ways that could bridge structuralist and post-structuralist approaches in agrifood scholarship. Put simply, I wanted to create an account of farms that would be useful both for those who seek their answers in the structural imperatives of capitalism and for those who seek to understand the current problems of the world in the elaboration of processes of modernity.

In Chapter 1 of this book, I drew up a list of potential ways in which the politics of farm and food ontologies might inform areas of critical agrifood research: (1) by opening up the 'black box' of the farm to reveal its multiple agencies, (2) by engaging with farm histories to reveal the agency of farms in creating colonial and modern worlds, (3) by revealing the ontology of farms and their relationship to science, (4) by understanding how farms act to make alternative worlds possible, and (5) by recognizing the enactive power of scholarship. Having now traversed the great history of farming, colonization and modernity (and its disruption) in Aotearoa New Zealand, the following reflection initially identifies three ways that political ontologies can operate in bridging roles in agrifood scholarship: by revealing the invisible stories of the historical agency of farms (particularly, in this case, in colonized worlds), by exploring their exterior and interior ontological character, and by examining the ways that farms are assembled as capital. These three insights inform the large political concern: how do we de-colonize agrifood scholarship in colonized worlds?[3]

Revealing farm histories: Political and ecological frontiers

The radical scholarly turn that emerged after the 1970s, which began to situate farms inside the wider history of capitalism, was transformative in providing a much-needed alternative to orthodox approaches to studying farms. Farms had a history, and it was a history characterized by the larger trajectories of capitalism. This approach, however, had the unfortunate tendency to romanticize family farms as a form of enduring land-use with great virtues – many of which were defensible – but without meaningful histories. In the context of colonized worlds where farms had acted as the agents of colonization, this was a particularly problematic lapse.

Any erasure of history is politically powerful and has many consequences. The modernist farm as described in this book became a free-floating vessel in an ahistorical sea, free to write its own history and silence older land-use cultures and ecologies, and thus doomed constantly to face the feral powers of disrupted ecologies and broken social relations. The political ontologies approach searches for the missing histories. For Aotearoa New Zealand, the existing body of historical scholarship around colonization and environments was enormously helpful for writing such an account. My account pointed towards key sites – frontiers – where farms had agency in enacting those histories.[4] At one level, farms were agents that pushed back political frontiers and drove the expansion of settlement into indigenous cultural worlds. At another level, farms were the agents that breached important ecological frontiers, turning forests, wetlands and indigenous grasslands into bounded and segmented territories of exotic pasture.

The idea of an 'ecological frontier' usefully reveals farms as socio-ecological agents. It exposes their material powers as bounded units that are enacted by erasing and silencing prior land-use. Farms silence and pacify, by setting up camp in the ecological chaos that is the product of such erasures and enacting a series of interventions to stabilize new ecological patterns and practices. In Aotearoa New Zealand, farms enacted a patch-by-patch assembling of new ecological domains that became zones of control (or semi-control) of disrupted ecosystems.

These farms and their frontiers made political futures happen. Various political institutions and initiatives constantly reinforced the Pākehā pastoral family farm as the appropriate form of land-use for Aotearoa New Zealand. Pākehā farmers seeking to buy and develop these little bounded territories were granted land, given access to credit, provided with technical knowledge and prospered politically. This was not a racially neutral venture: in the apportioning of title, credit and access to scientific knowledge and political influence, it differentiated between Pākehā single-family farms (considered desirable/modern) and Māori lands held in complex indigenous 'ownership' (considered undesirable/backward). This was not simply an effect of national-level racial preference by the state: it was also generated farm by farm.

This is the hidden political ontology of farms in colonial history: rendering invisible past land-use, breaching frontiers and erasing existing ecological systems, unleashing social and ecological chaos, and then fencing off and attempting to re-stabilize these disrupted worlds. In so doing farms helped enact modernity in colonized worlds: separating the land from the colonized peoples (and their futures); segmenting the landscape in ways that helped reinforce the wider binary division of land into nature and culture; creating divisions between that which was managed and productive and that which was wild and wasted; and creating human domains that were knowable, measurable and – as I will address shortly – exchangeable in an otherwise complex and disrupted landscape.

This is the first bridge towards a new style of agrifood theorization. Recognizing the full history of farms brings contemporary agrifood scholarship into dynamic engagement with longer histories of political and ecological colonization. As the farms discussed in the previous chapter show, these longer histories enacted some of the most problematic character of modernist farms, and also shaped much of the contemporary experimentation on farms. Without having these in full view, agrifood politics risks narrowing 'alternative' food and farm politics in ways that reduce or even totally erase the historical status and/or regenerative powers and capacities of colonized peoples and ecosystems.

The ontology of modernist farms

I have elaborated the two main characteristics of the modernist farm in this book as being a 'bounded ontology' and having a 'machine-like interior'. These emerged through the twentieth century in ways that stabilized a new land-use ontology. While the 'machine-like' ontology is very much in line with other critical characterizations of modern farming systems (particularly by ecologists critiquing the ignoring of complex internal and external ecological and social relationalities in farming), the 'bounded' quality has been less well considered.[5]

At the specific level of the farm, I've articulated how a set of processes, objects and practices created a boundary around farms and, in so doing, enacted the farm in its modern form. At the level of state politics, this boundary is legally constituted, but operates only when political processes and coercions support its existence. Legal boundaries operate alongside a social ontology of the farm boundary. Social practice defines an interior and exterior world that is socially transacted and reinforced by institutions like the kinship structure of Pākehā family farms – in which major kinship ties are contained inside a farm boundary (or operated, like my own family, between bounded units) rather than being spread across a landscape, as in the Māori world. The social boundary is also enacted through boundary-crossing practices, such as the social transaction of visitor rights and access for recreation. A final significant boundary operates at the farm gate, which historically created a 'silence of markets' and a focus on the production of food and fibre, along with an altogether diminished sense of connection to product destinations, markets and consumers.

This social boundary operated in tandem with an ecological boundary which, in a material sense, was partly fictitious, since in reality ecological processes flow across farm boundaries. Nevertheless, modernist farming constantly attempted ecological demarcation through the delineating of the foraging range of stock, the planting of productive species, the creation of hedges and shelterbelts, the attempted eradication of pests, the development of pastures, the planting and/or removal of trees, and fertilizing, spraying and managing 'farmed' ecologies in ways that created a demarcation between interior and exterior ecological worlds.

The enacting of all these ontological boundaries around the modern farm creates a division between worlds: an exterior and interior. Things in the exterior world become less relevant: less subject to the actions of farmers, they are sites of diminished responsibility. At the same time, the interior of farms becomes a site where a particular ontology can take shape. First, a world of contained and unified knowledge – the product of new ways of scientifically dividing up the world – populates the farming world with technical relations, measures and practices. As argued by other scholars, it is a world of mechanistic relations, technically defined, obeying natural laws of cause and effect. These combine to make systems dynamics less visible and, consequently, harder to act upon. Farms like this can become understood as 'machines for producing X, Y or Z'.

This bounded and mechanistic modernist farm ontology has many important political consequences. It segments and divides realities and narrows realms of expertise, reducing authority and legitimacy to only being that which can be articulated in technical and scientific knowledge, thereby undermining the legitimacy of other conversations. Furthermore, it creates a boundary around actions, disguises consequences outside this boundary and diminishes responsibility. Finally, it has the overall effect of pacifying and de-politicizing worlds. In Callon's terms, its relations are 'cold' rather than 'hot' – or, in Tania Li's description, 'anti-political' – in that they make the 'opposite of politics'; they enact undisputed, uncontested worlds in which it is difficult to consider alternatives.[6]

This is the second bridge, bringing farms back into a more dynamic role in wider agrifood analyses. Understanding modernist farms through their ontology brings some novel theoretical framings and approaches into agrifood studies, particularly by bringing farms back into central focus along with science and scientific knowledge production. Farm ontologies enact particular kinds of politics. The capacity of modernist farms to segment realities, to silence exterior worlds, to reduce responsibilities for actions and to enact racialized and gendered outcomes are all of central interest to critical agrifood scholars from both structuralist and post-structuralist traditions.

Stable ontologies create stable capital

One of the most interesting contemporary areas of interest in agrifood studies has been the examination of financialization of farmland and other elements of farming worlds.[7] Contemporary land grabs have taken shape around processes that Li describes as 'making land investible': a series of alignments that turn a piece of land into a metrologized and thus globally fungible and tradeable unit of capital or commodity.[8] This important account of the contemporary economic politics of farms and land has a deep historical echo. In the furthest recesses of colonial history, modern farms were also assembled and became viable items of capital. The story in Aotearoa New Zealand vividly portrays how land went from complex indigenous ownership in which it was embedded in collaborative economic activity, to becoming the anchor of a settler capitalist economy based around the capacity of privately owned family farms to act as capital.

How the colonial farm became stabilized and able to act as capital follows a similar theoretical path to prior accounts of stabilizing economic worlds. These include Tim Mitchell's account of the colonial state–economy relationship in Egypt, Tania Li's description of the emergence of a development economy in Indonesia (including how forests became stabilized and able to act in certain ways), and Anna Tsing's account of how, even in capitalist ruins, new economic assemblages can form out of unlikely materials.[9]

This path is one of assemblage, and my account understands the assembling of farms as capital in two parts. First, the stable-bounded ontology of the farm – secured legally, socially, ecologically and politically – was essential for demarcating a fungible 'thing'. The enacting of its boundaries created the enclosure of a particular set of relations and things, and thus rendered it able to be traded as a commodity.

The second part of the assembling of colonial farms as capital was the populating of the interior of farms with new objects, new scientific knowledge and new relations that made it knowable, predictable and thus also exploitable. Of particular interest are the metrologies of farm production and farm accounting, which combined to make grassy paddocks into economically knowable and predictable agents of production. As the great unified project of scientifically knowable farm production took shape, so the economically knowable value of potential production, land-valuation and markets in farms and their products also became stabilized.

Finally, this stable assemblage became a cultural and emotional site of positive affect. The bounded space of the farm, its productivity and valuation, its objects, its vistas, its managed landscapes and its key human relations, became sites of affect which not only helped farmers to be farmers, but also generated a love for farms and created an economy of affect. The romanticized Pākehā farm histories and autobiographies that filled the twentieth century may have elided much real colonial history, but they clearly narrated the farm as a site of affect and deep attachment and a creator of wealth and prosperity.

In order to become stable capital, farms need a stable ontology. And in colonial Aotearoa New Zealand, that stable ontology had racialized consequences. The new stable ontology of farms secured their status as capital and sites of knowledge in ways that privileged Pākehā settlers over Māori, anchored the elaboration of wider networks of investment and valuation, and provided the platform for producing the goods that enacted colonial trade circuits. In doing so, they unpicked the ties of the collaborative economy in colonial Aotearoa New Zealand and cemented the relations that would secure part of Friedmann and McMichael's Imperial Food Regime.[10]

This understanding of farms creates an important bridge between theoretical positions in agrifood scholarship. From the earliest origins of economic networks in modernist farming worlds to the globalizing, financializing dynamics of the current moment, the question of how farms and land assemble as capital is one that can unite both structuralist and post-structuralist scholars.[11]

De-colonizing agrifood scholarship

The final bridge is the most important for any scholar living and working in a colonized land. The 'enactive turn' points towards a much greater need to recognize the power of scholarship to help make (and unmake) ontological worlds of farming. This book points to the scale and consequences of these kinds of enactive powers of scholarship.

Historically, scientists and other scholars who elaborated a new modernist approach to farming played an important role in rendering many worlds invisible and closing down possible futures, as well as erasing links to multiple pasts. The social and ecological pathologies of modernist agriculture can be partly explained by the ontological politics of knowledge production by scholars participating in enacting bounded, mechanistic farm ontologies. In light of this legacy in Aotearoa New Zealand, how do we participate in enacting the de-colonization of farming and living land?

As a researcher *and* a descendent of six generations of Pākehā family farmers in Aotearoa New Zealand, the need to de-colonize landscapes and renew and regenerate indigeneity presents a fundamental political and epistemic challenge for me. At the outset of this book I argued that, in seeking to write a history of colonization grounded in the actions and consequences of my own families' farms, I was hoping to open up one pathway into a large and problematic gap in our agrifood scholarship. With the notable exception of Guthrie Smith's *Tutira* I was concerned by the relative lack of ecologically grounded and historically nuanced historical accounts of family farming in Aotearoa New Zealand – particularly of the period during the twentieth century when modernist Pākehā farming became normalized and uncontested.[12] This is partly the result of exactly the kinds of modernist dynamics I have elaborated in this book. Farming was 'rendered technical'. It became a realm defined mainly by narrow and instrumental economic measures of production and by a scientific narrative of its technical componentry. Most histories of these worlds speak only of moments of invention, of human ingenuity and achievement, written with a large dose of historical amnesia. Written cultural history, when it emerged mid-century, took the form of a solid serving of Pākehā self-mythologization.

As yet there is no solid body of literature creating a subaltern history of Māori farming in twentieth-century Aotearoa New Zealand. As Simon Lambert argued, Māori farm histories of the kind I explored in Chapter 3 must be implied, either from individual biographies or through works of scholarship focusing on national-level political and legal contests. When Māori farms do appear in archival records through the mid-twentieth century, what emerges is often a dire tale of paternalistic, racialized persecution justified by the ongoing drive for modernity and progress. Māori who lived through the last decades of the attempt to assimilate Māori farming know this as part of their lived experience. The next generation of Māori scholars will, in time, make sure more of these voices are heard.[13]

The kaupapa (rationale) of this book has been to recognize that a conversation has already commenced about the great conflicts of land in Aotearoa New Zealand; authoritative voices have already framed how that discussion will unfold.[14] The purpose of this book has been to join that emerging dialogue and to provide an account of some of the ways that other worlds were rendered invisible by Pākehā family farms. But it is also important to recognize other agencies and powers for change. Academic dialogue will, in time, become more elaborated, but while we, as researchers, are the key agents in generating that dialogue, farms themselves have already begun to change worlds. They are sites of dialogue, multiplicity, experimentation and, in some important ways, de-colonization.

The narrative in this book has shown how, farm by farm, alternative worlds are assembling and new realities are being made tangible. Even where scholarly histories haven't yet been written, farms themselves are enacting answers to questions like 'how do we de-colonize colonized worlds?' and 'what is it we are trying to be alternative to?' New farms reveal fresh potentials and novel ways of being alternative. Some of them were crisis experiments during neoliberalization; some operate as a rejection and search for alternative ways to farm in the face of quite specific individual family crises or ecological pressures; and some are a search for an older ontology of indigenous land-use that can potentially open up farm boundaries, allowing the wider influence of social, economic and ecological worlds into the interior world of farms. In all of these farms, experiments with farming inside visible worlds have provided a point of purchase for real, situated, new human/more-than-human collaborations on the land. They also point the way forward for grasping how to act as academics and researchers when trying to theorize and research in ways that make the invisible visible again and, in so doing, make new futures possible.

Notes

1   In a book characterized by some long theoretical endnotes, consider this epilogue to be the place where theoretical discussion breaks out into the main text for some extended treatment.

2   Reviewed in Le Heron et al. (2016).

3   And it is important to insert my caveats early in this summative chapter. This book has been shaped by consequential choices, but none more so than my choice to focus explicitly on the farm. I did this to reveal the world-making qualities of an otherwise mundane assemblage. I also have chosen to concentrate on the actions of farms as they are situated in very particular kinds of frontiers. This is a productive place to open up wider worlds of colonization, landscape-change, science and the arbitration of racialized futures in New Zealand. This choice, however, does enact its own boundaries and closures. Farms are only one kind of political agent and frontiers are a very specific kind of setting. Analytically privileging them above all others does risk obscuring other powers and sites of possible action and potential futures. My foregrounding of farms and frontiers should be understood as using them to indicate the kinds of ontological politics that might equally be applied to other dynamics and settings, as is discussed in Le Heron et al. (2016) and Pawson et al. (2018). I am happy to acknowledge a wide variety of other new ways of enacting food-land-people relationships, including: backyard gardening, urban gleaning, wild harvesting and hunting, community gardens, guerrilla gardening, shared land ownership of land, etc., all of which are exciting and experimental, and many of which are the subject matter of books like Mayes et al. (2007) and Goodman et al. (2011). Many of these not only enact alternatives to modernist agriculture, they enact alternatives to the idea of the farm itself. In the face of those new sites of creativity and experimentation, I must acknowledge the specificities of my framing. The world is not all about farms – even in Aotearoa New Zealand.

4   In choosing to focus on frontiers as the site where the agency of farms was decisive in colonization, I do not wish to ignore other important dynamics of farming and colonization. For example, the role of farms and 'land hunger' in creating a flow of migrants to a new colony in the first place, the importance of farm commodities

in solidifying colonial trade circuits, or the role of privately owned family farms in generating a sense of a new political allegiances to an emerging state and, later, a sense of nationalism are important and addressed by other scholars (e.g. see McMichael 1984, Belich 2009, and Fuglestad 2018).

5   The closest cognate is Andro Linklater's sweeping history of property, which includes the power of property boundaries in the creation of capitalism and modernity (Linklater 2013). There are also hints towards the consequential power of privately bounded farms (along with weeds!) in Cronon's account of the New England colonies (Cronon 1983).

6   Callon (1998), Li (2007b).

7   For example, see Lawrence and Smith (2018), Bjorkhaug et al. (2020).

8   Li (2014, 2017). My use of the term 'capital' may seem unnecessary to assemblage thinkers, but is intended to make this discussion more recognizable to critical political economists.

9   Mitchell (2002), Li (2007a), Tsing (2015).

10   Friedmann and McMichael (1989).

11   Something that we have elsewhere termed 'post structuralist political economy' (Le Heron et al. 2016).

12   It is a question that any agrifood researcher working in an colonized landscape may ask themself. While the story is different in other colonized worlds where farms played a major role as agents in what unfolded – such as Canada, Australia and the United States – some important commonalities emerge around the simple recognition of the potential centrality of farms as agents of colonization (and, hopefully, de-colonization). For the United States, Cronon's ([1983] 2003) classic *Changes in the Land* was celebrated for its clear statement of the need to place ecological histories at the heart of narratives of the political and economic enacting of frontiers in American history. His story told of the ecological power of private boundaries, farms and domesticated species (along with other pests and weeds) that were central agents in the colonization of New England. His subsequent masterwork *Nature's Metropolis* tells the story of how a city – Chicago – became the crucial node in the colonization of three ecosystems and their commoditization in the service of capitalist economies, two of which – meat and wheat – enacted consequential new farming worlds (Cronon 1991). Other US scholars point towards the power of barbed wire fences, the eradication of the bison and the military/legal sanction on nomadic harvesting of migratory animals, as central to the way in which the colonization of indigenous worlds was enacted. Recent Australian scholarship by Pascoe (2018) and Gammage (2012) has profoundly challenged the understanding of aboriginal land-use practices at the moment of colonization, and revealed a world of farming activity and unbounded land-use practices that pose important questions for what post-colonial farming (and scholarship about farming) might look like in Australia. As Mayes (2018) argues, putting this new colonial history at the centre of Australian agrifood studies demands a different approach to how we act as agrifood scholars. These colonial histories of farming and land-use in Australia and the United States form the profound starting point for sets of reflections parallel to those which I've created for Aotearoa New Zealand. The specific histories, conflicts, agencies and outcomes are often different, but they share an understanding: in order to de-colonize farming worlds we must first understand farms as agents of colonization and, in my narrative, understand how modernist farming locked in those powers and rendered invisible the possibility of alternatives.

13   Many of these new voices have been important resources for this book. The next generation of Māori scholars like Simon Lambert, John Reid, Michael Stevens, Maria Bargh, Tremane Barr, Marama Muru-Lanning and Merata Kawharu are telling new stories and revealing fresh possible futures for Māori land-use. One excellent example was published just as this book was going to press: Kawharu and Tapsell (2019).

14   Informed by the great volume of careful historical scholarship of the Waitangi Tribunal and drawing inspiration from important scholarly voices like Sir Ranginui Walker and Linda Tuhiwai Smith speaking for Māori, and Geoff Park, Dame Evelyn Stokes and Dame Anne Salmond responding for Pākehā.

References

Agrawal, A. (2005), *Environmentality: Technologies of Government and Political Subjects*, Durham: Duke University Press.

Ahmed, S. (2004), *The Cultural Politics of Emotion*, Edinburgh: Edinburgh University Press.

Alexander, R., G. Gibson and A. LaRoche (1997), *The Royal New Zealand Fencibles, 1847–1852*, Auckland: New Zealand Fencibles Society.

Almas, R. and H. Campbell eds. (2012), *Rethinking Agricultural Policy Regimes: Food Security, Climate Change and the Future Resilience of Global Agriculture*, Bingley: Emerald.

Altieri, M. A. (2002a), 'The Ecological Impact of Industrial Agriculture', in A. Kimbrell (ed), *Fatal Harvest: The Tragedy of Industrial Agriculture*, 197–202, California: Foundation for Deep Ecology.

Altieri, M. A. (2002b), 'Agroecology: The Science of Natural Resource Management for Poor Farmers in Marginal Environments', *Agriculture, Ecosystems and Environment*, 93(1–3): 1–24.

Altieri, M. A. and C. I. Nicholls (2017), 'Agroecology: A Brief Account of Its Origins and Currents of Thought in Latin America', *Agroecology and Sustainable Food Systems*, 41(3–4): 231–7.

Anderson, A. (2002), 'A Fragile Plenty: Pre-European Maori and the New Zealand Environment', in E. Pawson and T. Brooking (eds), *Environmental Histories of New Zealand*, 19–34, Melbourne: Oxford University Press.

Ansems de Vries, L. A. (2016), 'Politics of (In)visibility: Governance-resistance and the Constitution of Refugee Subjectivities in Malaysia', *Review of International Studies*, 42(5): 876–94.

Ansems de Vries, L. A., L. M. Coleman, D. Rosenow, M. Tazzioli and R. Vázquez (2017), 'Collective Discussion: Fracturing Politics (or, How to Avoid the Tacit Reproduction of Modern/Colonial Ontologies in Critical Thought)', *International Political Sociology*, 11(1): 90–108.

Ansley, B. (2012), *A Fabled Land: The Story of Canterbury's Famous Mesopotamia Station*, Auckland: Random House.

Anthony, F. (1977), *Gus Tomlins: Together with Original Stories of 'Me and Gus'*, Auckland: Auckland University Press.

Arnold, R. (1994), *New Zealand's Burning: The Settlers' World in the Mid-1880s*, Wellington: Victoria University Press.

Avery, D. (2017), *The Resilient Farmer: Weathering the Challenges of Life and the Land*, Auckland: The Penguin Press.

Ballantyne, T. (2011), 'On Place, Space and Mobility in Nineteenth-Century New Zealand', *New Zealand Journal of History*, 45(1): 50–70.

Bargh, M. ed. (2007), *Resistance: An Indigenous Response to Neoliberalism*, Wellington: Huia Publishers.

Bargh, M. (2013), 'The Post-Settlement World (So Far): Impacts for Maori', in N. Wheen and J. Hayward (eds), *Treaty of Waitangi Settlements*, 166–81, Wellington: Bridget Williams Books.

Bargh, M. (2014), 'A Blue Economy for Aotearoa New Zealand?', *Environment, Development and Sustainability*, 16(3): 459–70.

Bargh, M. and J. Otter (2009), 'Progressive Spaces of Neoliberalism in Aotearoa: A Genealogy and Critique', *Asia Pacific Viewpoint*, 50(2): 154–65.

Barr, T. L. (2000), *Maori Issues in Organic Farming in Aotearoa/New Zealand*, PhD diss., Canterbury: Lincoln University.

Barr, T. L., J. Reid, P. Catska, G. Varona and M. Rout (2018), 'Development of Indigenous Enterprise in a Contemporary Business Environment – the Ngāi Tahu Ahikā Approach', *Journal of Enterprising Communities: People and Places in the Global Economy*, 12(4): 454–71.

Beaglehole, J. C. (1974), *The Journals of Captain James Cook: The Voyage of the Endeavour, 1768-1771*, 2nd edn, London: Cambridge University Press.

Belich, J. (1986), *The New Zealand Wars and the Victorian Interpretation of Racial Conflict*, Auckland: Auckland University Press.

Belich, J. (1996), *Making Peoples: A History of the New Zealanders from Polynesian Settlement to the End of the Nineteenth Century*, Auckland: The Penguin Press.

Belich, J. (2001), *Paradise Reforged*, Auckland: The Penguin Press.

Belich, J. (2009), *Replenishing the Earth: The Settler Revolution and the Rise of the Anglo-World, 1783-1939*, New York: Oxford University Press.

Bell, C. (1996), *Inventing New Zealand: Everyday Myths of Pakeha Identity*, Auckland: Penguin.

Bell, M. M. (2004), *Farming for Us All: Practical Agriculture and the Cultivation of Sustainability*, University Park: Penn State Press.

Bell, M. M. (2009), *An Invitation to Environmental Sociology*, 3rd edn, Thousand Oaks: Pine Forge Press.

Bell, S. and S. Morse (2008), *Sustainability Indicators: Measuring the Immeasurable?* London: Earthscan.

Bennett, J. (2010), *Vibrant Matter: A Political Ecology of Things*, Durham: Duke University Press.

Berry, W. (1977), *The Unsettling of America: Culture and Agriculture*, San Francisco: Sierra Club.

Best, E. (1941), *The Maori, Vol 2*, Memoirs of the Polynesian Society, Volume 5, Wellington: The Polynesian Society.

Beus, C. and R. Dunlap (1990), 'Conventional versus Alternative Agriculture: The Paradigmatic Roots of the Debate', *Rural Sociology*, 55: 590–616.

Beus, C. and R. Dunlap (1991), 'Measuring Adherence to Alternative vs. Conventional Agricultural Paradigms: A Proposed Scale', *Rural Sociology*, 56: 432–60.

Björkhaug, H., P. McMichael and B. Muirhead eds. (2020), *Finance or Food?: The Role of Cultures, Values and Ethics in Land-Use Negotiations*, Toronto: University of Toronto Press.

Blackett, P. and R. Le Heron (2008), 'Maintaining the "Clean Green" Image: Governance of On-Farm Environmental Practices in the New Zealand Dairy Industry', in C. Stringer and R. Le Heron (eds), *Agri-Food Commodity Chains and Globalising Networks*, 75–88, Avebury: Ashgate.

Blake, N. (1983), *The Story of Howick, 1847-1864: A Village Founded by the Royal New Zealand Fencibles*. Auckland: Howick Historical Society.

Blaser, M. (2009), 'Political Ontology', *Cultural Studies*, 23(5–6): 873–96.

Blaser, M. (2013), 'Ontological Conflicts and the Stories of Peoples in spite of Europe: Toward a Conversation on Political Ontology', *Current Anthropology*, 54(5): 547–68.

Blaser, M. (2014), 'Ontology and Indigeneity: On the Political Ontology of Heterogeneous Assemblages', *Cultural Geographies*, 21(1): 49–58.

Bourn, D., B. Newton and H. Campbell (1999), *Strategies for 'Greening' the New Zealand Honey Industry: An Evaluation of the Development of Organic and Other Standards*, Studies in Rural Sustainability Research Report No. 8, Department of Anthropology, Dunedin: University of Otago.

Brewer, J. P. and P. V. Stock (2016), 'Beyond Extension: Strengthening the Federally Recognized Tribal Extension Program (FRTEP)', *Journal of Agriculture, Food Systems, and Community Development*, 6(3): 91–101.

Brewer, J. P. and M. K. Dennis (2019), 'A Land Neither Here nor There: Voices from the Margins and the Untenuring of Lakota Lands', *GeoJournal*, 84(3): 571–91.

Britton, S., R. Le Heron and E. Pawson (Eds.),(1992), *Changing Places in New Zealand: A Geography of Restructuring*, Wellington: New Zealand Geographical Society.

Brooking, T. (1996), *Lands for the People?: The Highland Clearances and the Colonisation of New Zealand: A Biography of John McKenzie*, Dunedin: University of Otago Press.

Brooking, T. and E. Pawson (2007), 'Silences of Grass: Retrieving the Role of Pasture Plants in the Development of New Zealand and the British Empire', *Journal of Imperial and Commonwealth History*, 35(3): 417–35.

Brooking, T. and E. Pawson (2011), 'The Contours of Transformation', in T. Brooking and E. Pawson (eds), *Seeds of Empire: The Environmental Transformation of New Zealand*, 13–33, London: I.B. Tauris.

Brooking, T. and E. Pawson eds. (2011), *Seeds of Empire: The Environmental Transformation of New Zealand*, London: I.B. Tauris.

Brooking, T. and P. Star (2011), 'Remaking the Grasslands: The 1920s and 1930s', in T. Brooking and E. Pawson (eds), *Seeds of Empire: The Environmental Transformation of New Zealand*, 178–99, London: I.B. Tauris.

Brooking, T., R. Hodge and V. Wood (2002), 'The Grasslands Revolution Reconsidered', in E. Pawson and T. Brooking (eds), *Environmental Histories of New Zealand*, 169–82, Melbourne: Oxford University Press.

Buller, H., and C. Morris (2003), 'Farm Animal Welfare: A New Repertoire of Nature–Society Relations or Modernism Re-Embedded?' *Sociologia Ruralis*, 43(3): 216–37.

Burch, K. A, K. A. Legun and H. Campbell (2018), 'Not Defined by the Numbers: Distinction, Dissent and Democratic Possibilities in Debating the Data', in J. Forney, C. Rosin and H. Campbell (eds), *Agri-Environmental Governance as an Assemblage: Multiplicity, Power and Transformation*, 127–44, London: Routledge.

Burton R. (1998), 'The Role of Farmer Self-Identity in Agricultural Decision-Making in the Marston Vale Community Forest', PhD Diss., Leicester: DeMontfort University.

Burton, R. (2004a), 'Seeing Through the "Good Farmer's Eyes": Towards Developing an Understanding of the Social Symbolic Value of "Productivist" Behaviour', *Sociologia Ruralis*, 44(2): 195–214.

Burton, R. (2004b), 'Reconceptualising the "Behavioural Approach" in Agricultural Studies: The Socio-Psychological Perspective', *Journal of Rural Studies*, 20(3): 359–71.

Burton, R. and G. A. Wilson (2006), 'Injecting Social Psychology Theory into Conceptualisations of Agricultural Agency: Towards a Post-Productivist Farmer Self-Identity?' *Journal of Rural Studies*, 22(1): 95–115.

Burton, R. and G. A. Wilson (2012), 'The Rejuvenation of Productivist Agriculture: The Case for "Cooperative Neo-Productivism"', in R. Almas and H. Campbell (eds), *Rethinking Agricultural Policy Regimes: Food Security, Climate Change and the Future Resilience of Global Agriculture*, 51–72, Bingley: Emerald.

Burton, R., S. Peoples and M. Cooper (2012), 'Building "Cowshed Cultures": A Cultural Perspective on the Promotion of Stockmanship and Animal Welfare on Dairy Farms', *Journal of Rural Studies*, 28(2): 174–87.

Busch, L., V. Gunter, T. Mentele, M. Tachikawa and K. Tanaka (1994), 'Socializing Nature: Technoscience and the Transformation of Rapeseed into Canola', *Crop Science*, 34(3): 607–14.

Buttel, F. H. (1993), 'The Production of Agricultural Sustainability: Observations from the Sociology of Science and Technology', in P. Allen (ed), *Food for the Future: Conditions and Contradictions of Sustainability*, 19–45, New York: Wiley.

Buttel, F. (1999), 'Agricultural Biotechnology: Its Recent Evolution and Implications for Agrofood Political Economy', *Sociological Research Online*, 4(3): 1–13.

Buttel, F. H. and H. Newby eds. (1980), *The Rural Sociology of the Advanced Societies: Critical Perspectives*, Montclair: Allanheld, Osmun.

Buttel, F. H., O. F. Larson and G. W. Gillespie (1990), *The Sociology of Agriculture*, New York: Greenwood Press.

Butterworth, G. V. (1974), *The Maori People in the New Zealand Economy*, Dept of Social Anthropology and Maori Studies, Massey University: Palmerston North.

Calder, A. (2011), *The Settler's Plot: How Stories Take Place in New Zealand*, Auckland: Auckland University Press.

Callon, M. (1998), 'An Essay on Framing and Overflowing: Economic Externalities Revisited by Sociology', *The Sociological Review*, 46(1): 244–69.

Çalışkan, K. and M. Callon (2010), 'Economization, Part 2: A Research Programme for the Study of Markets', *Economy and Society*, 39(1): 1–32.

Campbell, H. (1995), *Regulation and Crisis in New Zealand Agriculture: The Case of Ashburton County, 1984–1992*, PhD Diss., Australia: Charles Sturt University.

Campbell, H. (1996), *Recent Developments in Organic Food Production in New Zealand: Part 1, Organic Food Exporting in Canterbury*, Studies in Rural Sustainability No. 1, Department of Anthropology, Dunedin: University of Otago.

Campbell, H. (2004), 'Organics Ascendant? The Curious Politics of Resistance to GM', in R. Hindmarsh and G. Lawrence (eds), *Recoding Nature: Critical Perspectives on GM*, 41–52, Sydney: University of New South Wales Press.

Campbell, H. (2005), 'The Rise and Rise of EurepGAP: The European (Re)Invention of Colonial Food Relations?', *International Journal of Sociology of Agriculture and Food*, 13(2): 6–19.

Campbell, H. (2009), 'Breaking New Ground in Food Regimes Theory; Corporate Environmentalism, Ecological Feedbacks and the "Food from Somewhere" Regime', *Agriculture and Human Values*, 26(4): 309–19.

Campbell, H. (2011), 'Neoliberalism, Science Institutions and New Experiments in Knowledge Production', *Dialogues in Human Geography*, 1(3): 350–4.

Campbell, H. (2013), 'Food and the Audit Society', in A. Murcott, W. Belasco and P. Jackson (eds), *The Handbook of Food Research*, 177–91, London: Bloomsbury.

Campbell, H. (2016), 'In the Long Run, Will We Be Fed?' *Agriculture and Human Values*, 33(1): 215–23.

Campbell, H. (2018), 'The Two Lives of the Kiwifruit Industry', in E. Pawson and the Biological Economies Team (eds), *The New Biological Economy: How New Zealanders Are Creating Value from the Land*, 79–97, Auckland: University of Auckland Press.

Campbell, H. and D. Moore (1991), 'Crisis Time for Rural Crisis Meetings: Ruralia Contra Mundum', *Rural Society*, 1(2): 15–16.

Campbell, H. and S. Wards (1992), 'Farm Politics in New Zealand: Pushing on to "Drier" Ground?' *Rural Society*, 2(2): 12–15.

Campbell, H. and R. Liepins (2001), 'Naming Organics: Understanding Organic Standards in New Zealand as a Discursive Field', *Sociologia Ruralis*, 41(1): 21–39.

Campbell, H. and G. Lawrence (2003), 'Assessing the Neo-liberal Experiment in Antipodean Agriculture', in R. Almas and G. Lawrence (eds), *Globalization, Localization and Sustainable Livelihoods*, 89–102, Aldershot: Ashgate.

Campbell, H. and J. Dixon (2009), 'Introduction to the Special Symposium: Reflecting on Twenty Years of the Food Regimes Approach in Agri-Food Studies', *Agriculture and Human Values*, 26(4): 261–5.

Campbell, H. and C. Rosin (2011), 'After the "Organic Industrial Complex": An Ontological Expedition through Commercial Organic Agriculture in New Zealand', *Journal of Rural Studies*, 27(4): 350–61.

Campbell, H. and D. Reynolds (2020), 'Last in, First Out?: The Uncertain Future of Agricultural Trade Liberalisation', in H. Björkhaug, P. McMichael and B. Muirhead (eds), *Finance or Food?: The Role of Cultures, Values and Ethics in Land-Use Negotiations*, 42–58, Toronto: University of Toronto Press.

Campbell, H., M. M. Bell and M. Finney eds. (2006), *Country Boys: Masculinity and Rural Life*, University Park: Penn State Press.

Campbell, H., R. Burton, M. Cooper, M. Henry, E. Le Heron, R. Le Heron, N. Lewis, E. Pawson, H. Perkins, M. Roche, C. Rosin and T. White (2009a), 'From Agricultural Science to "Biological Economies"?' *New Zealand Journal of Agricultural Research*, 52: 91–7.

Campbell, H., C. Rosin, S. Norton, P. Carey, J. Benge and H. Moller (2009b), 'Examining the Mythologies of Organics: Moving beyond the Organic/Conventional Binary?' in G. Lawrence, K. Lyons and T. Wallington (eds), *Food Security, Nutrition and Sustainability*, 238–51, London: Earthscan.

Campbell, H., C. Rosin, L. Hunt and J. Fairweather (2012), 'The Social Practice of Sustainable Agriculture under Audit Discipline: Initial Insights from the ARGOS Project in New Zealand', *Journal of Rural Studies*, 28(1): 129–41.

Carden, S. and P. McKenzie (2018), 'Pamu – A New Future of Food', in M. Joy (ed), *Mountains to Sea: Solving New Zealand's Freshwater Crisis*, 61–5, Wellington: Bridget Williams Books.

Carnegie, G. D., P. Foreman and B. P. West (2006), 'F. E. Vigars' Station Book-Keeping: A Specialist Australian Text Enabling the Adaptation and Transfer of Accounting Technology', *Accounting Historians Journal*, 33(2): 103–30.

Carolan, M. (2004), 'Ontological Politics: Mapping a Complex Environmental Problem', *Environmental Values*, 13(4): 497–522.

Carolan, M. (2011), *Embodied Food Politics*, Farnham: Ashgate Publishing.

Carolan, M. (2013), 'Final Word: Putting the "Alter" in Alternative Food Futures', *New Zealand Sociology*, 28(4): 145–50.

Carolan, M. (2015), 'Affective Sustainable Landscapes and Care Ecologies: Getting a Real Feel for Alternative Food Communities', *Sustainability Science*, 10(2): 317–29.

Carolan, M. (2016), 'Adventurous Food Futures: Knowing about Alternatives Is Not Enough, We Need to Feel Them', *Agriculture and Human Values*, 33(1): 141–52.

Carson, R. ([1962] 2002), *Silent Spring*, Boston: Houghton Mifflin Harcourt.

Carter, I. and N. Perry (1987), 'Rembrandt in Gumboots: Rural Imagery in New Zealand Television Advertisements', in Phillips, J. (ed), *Te Whenua, Te Iwi – The Land and the People*, 61–72, Wellington: Port Nicholson Press.

Clark, A. H. (1949), *The Invasion of New Zealand by People, Plants and Animals*, New Brunswick: Rutgers University Press.

Clark, N. (1999), 'Wild Life: Ferality and the Frontier with Chaos', in K. Neumann, N. Thomas and H. Erickson (eds), *Quicksands: Foundational Histories in Australia and Aotearoa New Zealand*, 133–52, Sydney: University of New South Wales Press.

Cocklin, C. and M. Wall (1997), 'Contested Rural Futures: New Zealand's East Coast Forestry Project', *Journal of Rural Studies*, 13(2): 149–62.

Coombes, B. and H. Campbell (1996), 'Pluriactivity in (and beyond?) a Regulationist Crisis', *New Zealand Geographer*, 52(2): 11–17.

Coombes, B. and H. Campbell (1998), 'Dependent Reproduction of Alternative Modes of Agriculture: Organic Farming in New Zealand', *Sociologia Ruralis*, 38(2): 127–45.

Cooper, A., L. Paterson and A. Wanhalla (2015), *The Lives of Colonial Objects*, Dunedin: University of Otago Press.

Craig, D. (2005), 'Taranaki Gothic and the Political Economy of New Zealand Narrative and Sensibility', *New Zealand Sociology*, 20(2): 18–40.

Cram, F., L. Pihama and G. Philip-Barbara (2000), *Māori and Genetic Engineering*, Auckland: International Research Institute for Māori and Indigenous Education.

Cronon, W. (1987), 'Revisiting the Vanishing Frontier: The Legacy of Frederick Jackson Turner', *The Western Historical Quarterly*, 18(2): 157–76.

Cronon, W. (1991), *Nature's Metropolis: Chicago and the Great West*, New York: W. W. Norton.

Cronon, W. ([1983] 2003), *Changes in the Land: Indians, Colonists, and the Ecology of New England*, New York: Hill and Wang.

Crosby, A. W. (1986), *Ecological Imperialism: The Biological Expansion of Europe, 900–1900*, New York: Cambridge University Press.

Curtis, B. (2002), 'Actor Network Theory Let Loose: Ferality, Colonialism and Other Material Relations', *New Zealand Sociology*, 17(1): 91–109.

Dalziel, P. and R. Lattimore (1991), *A Briefing on the New Zealand Macroeconomy: 1960–1990*, Auckland: Oxford University Press.

Dalziel, P. and C. Saunders (2014), *Wellbeing Economics: Future Directions for New Zealand*, Wellington: Bridget Williams Books.

Dalziel, P., C. Saunders and J. Saunders (2018), *Wellbeing Economics: A Capabilities Approach to Prosperity*, Switzerland: Palgrave McMillan.

Dann, C. (2002), 'Losing Ground? Environmental Problems and Prospects at the Beginning of the Twenty-first Century', in E. Pawson and T. Brooking (eds), *Environmental Histories of New Zealand*, 275–87, Melbourne: Oxford University Press.

Davis, M. (2002), *Late Victorian Holocausts: El Niño Famines and the Making of the Third World*, London: Verso Books.

Deans, N. and K. Hackwell (2008), *Dairying and Declining Water Quality: Why Has the Dairying and Clean Streams Accord Not Delivered Cleaner Streams?* Wellington: Joint publication of Fish and Game New Zealand and the Forest and Bird Protection Society.

Demeulenaere, E. (2014), 'A Political Ontology of Seeds: The Transformative Frictions of a Farmers' Movement in Europe', *Focaal*, 69: 45–61.

Dominy, M. D. (2001), *Calling the Station Home: Place and Identity in New Zealand's High Country*, Lanham: Rowman and Littlefield.

DuPuis, E. M. (2002), *Nature's Perfect Food: How Milk Became America's Drink*, New York: New York University Press.

Dwiartama, A. and C. Piatti (2016), 'Assembling Local, Assembling Food Security', *Agriculture and Human Values*, 33(1): 153–64.

Edwards, P. and S. Trafford (2016), 'Social Licence in New Zealand – What Is It?', *Journal of the Royal Society of New Zealand*, 46(3–4): 165–80.

Egoz, S., J. Bowring and H. Perkins (2001), 'Tastes in Tension: Form, Function, and Meaning in New Zealand's Farmed Landscapes', *Landscape and Urban Planning*, 57(3–4): 177–96.

Eketone, A. (2020), 'Wiremu Patene and the Early Peace Movement at Karakariki', in R.Jackson, J. Llewellyn, G. Leonard, A. Gnoth and T. Karena (eds), *Revolutionary Nonviolence: Concepts, Cases and Controversies*, 181–99, London: Zed Books.

Ellul, J. (1963), *The Technological Society*, New York: Vintage Books.

Escobar, A. (2007), 'The "Ontological Turn" in Social Theory. A Commentary on "Human Geography without Scale", by Sallie Marston, John Paul Jones II and Keith Woodward' *Transactions of the Institute of British Geographers*, 32: 106–11.

Fairburn, M. (1989), *The Ideal Society and Its Enemies: Foundations of Modern New Zealand Society, 1850–1900*, Auckland: Auckland University Press.

Fairweather, J. (1985), 'White-Settler Colonial Development: Early New Zealand Pastoralism and the Formation of Estates', *Journal of Sociology*, 21(2): 237–57.

Fairweather, J. (1989), *Some Recent Changes in New Zealand Society*, AERU Discussion Paper No. 124, Agribusiness and Economics Research Unit, Canterbury: Lincoln University.

Fairweather, J. (1992), *Agrarian Restructuring in New Zealand*, Research Report No. 213, Agribusiness and Economics Research Unit, Canterbury: Lincoln University.

Fairweather, J., C. Maslin, P. Gossman and H. Campbell (2003), *Farmer Views on the Use of Genetic Engineering in Agriculture*, AERU Research Report No 258, Agribusiness and Economics Research Unit, Canterbury: Lincoln University.

Fairweather, J., C. Rosin, L. Hunt and H. Campbell (2009), 'Are Conventional Farmers Conventional? Analysis of the Environmental Orientation of Conventional New Zealand Farmers', *Rural Sociology*, 74(3): 430–54.

Fish and Game New Zealand (2002), *Dairy Farming and the Environment*. Position statement by Fish and Game New Zealand. Available online: https://fishandgame.org.nz/about/f-and-g-position-statements/dairy-farming-and-the-environment/ (accessed 25 October 2019).

Fitzgerald, D. K. (2003), *Every Farm a Factory: The Industrial Ideal in American Agriculture*, New Haven: Yale University Press.

Fitzgerald, R., H. Campbell and L. Sivak (2002), 'Content Analysis of Bias in International Print Media Coverage of GM Food', *Rural Society*, 11(3): 181–96.

Flinders, M. and M. Wood (2014), 'Depoliticisation, Governance and the State', *Policy and Politics*, 42(2): 135–49.

Flora, C. B. (1992), 'Reconstructing Agriculture: The Case for Local Knowledge', *Rural Sociology*, 57(1): 92–97.

Forney, J. (2016), 'Enacting Swiss Cheese: About the Multiple Ontologies of Local Food', in R. Le Heron, H. Campbell, N. Lewis and M. Carolan (eds), *Biological Economies: Experimentation and the Politics of Agrifood Frontiers*, 67–81, London: Routledge (Earthscan).

Forney, J. and P. Stock (2014), 'Conversion of Family Farms and Resilience in Southland, New Zealand', *International Journal of Sociology of Agriculture and Food*, 21(1): 7–29.

Forney, J., C. Rosin and H. Campbell eds. (2018), *Agri-Environmental Governance as an Assemblage*, London: Routledge (Earthscan).

Fox, W. (1851), *The Six Colonies of New Zealand*, London: John W Parker and Son.

Friedland, W. H. (1984), 'Commodity Systems Analysis: An Approach to the Sociology of Agriculture', in H. K. Schwarzweller (ed), *Research in Rural Sociology and Development: A Research Annual*, 221–35, Greenwich: JAI Press.

Friedland, W. H., Barton, A. and Thomas, R. (1981), *Manufacturing Green Gold: Capital Labour and Technology in the Lettuce Industry*. Cambridge: Cambridge University Press.

Friedmann, H. (1978), 'World Market, State, and Family Farm: Social Bases of Household Production in the Era of Wage Labor', *Comparative Studies in Society and History*, 20(4): 545–86.

Friedmann, H. and P. McMichael (1989), 'Agriculture and the State System: The Rise and Decline of National Agricultures, 1870 to the Present', *Sociologia Ruralis*, 29(2): 93–117.

Fuglestad, E. M. (2018), *Private Property and the Origins of Nationalism in the United States and Norway: The Making of Propertied Communities*, London: Palgrave Macmillan.

Gammage, B. (2012), *The Biggest Estate on Earth: How Aborigines Made Australia*, Sydney: Allen and Unwin.

Gasson, R. (1980), 'Roles of Farm Women in England', *Sociologia Ruralis*, 20(3): 165–80.

Gibb, J. A. and J. M. Williams (1994), 'The Rabbit in New Zealand', in H. V. Thompson and C. M. King (eds), *The European Rabbit: The History and Biology of a Successful Colonizer*, 158–204, Oxford: Oxford University Press.

Gibson-Graham J. K. (2006), *A Postcapitalist Politics*, Minneapolis: University of Minnesota Press.

Giddens, A. (1980), *The Consequences of Modernity*, Cambridge: Polity Press.

Gieryn, T. F. (1983), 'Boundary-work and the Demarcation of Science from Non-science: Strains and Interests in Professional Ideologies of Scientists', *American Sociological Review*, 48: 781–95.

Gill, T., P. Koopman-Boyden, A. Parr and W. E. Willmott (1975), *The Rural Women of New Zealand: A National Survey*. Wellington: Women's Division, Federated Farmers of New Zealand.

Goodman, D. and M. Watts (1997), *Globalizing Food: Agrarian Questions and Global Restructuring*, London: Routledge.

Goodman, D. (1999), 'Agro Food Studies in the "Age of Ecology": Nature, Corporeality, Bio Politics', *Sociologia Ruralis*, 39(1): 17–38.

Goodman, D. (2001), 'Ontology Matters: The Relational Materiality of Nature and Agro Food Studies', *Sociologia Ruralis*, 41(2): 182–200.

Goodman, D. and M. DuPuis (2002), 'Knowing Food and Growing Food: Beyond the Production–Consumption Debate in the Sociology of Agriculture', *Sociologia Ruralis*, 42(1): 5–22.

Goodman, D., M. DuPuis and M. Goodman (2011), *Alternative Food Networks*, London: Routledge.

Goodman, J. (2005), *Tobacco in History: The Cultures of Dependence*, London: Routledge.

Goven, J. (2006), 'Processes of Inclusion, Cultures of Calculation, Structures of Power: Scientific Citizenship and the Royal Commission on Genetic Modification', *Science, Technology and Human Values*, 31(5): 565–98.

Goven, J. and J. Wuthnow (2004), 'Challenging Scientific Legitimacy: Citizen Participation in Technoscience', in K. Dew and R. Fitzgerald (eds), *Challenging Science: Issues for New Zealand Society in the 21st Century*, 51–67, Palmerston North: Dunmore Press.

Gray, I. (1996), 'The Detraditionalization of Farming', in D. Burch, R. Rickson and G. Lawrence (eds), *Globalization and Agri-food Restructuring: Perspectives from the Australasia Region*, 91–103, Aldershot: Avebury.

Gray, I. and G. Lawrence (2001), *A Future for Regional Australia: Escaping Global Misfortune*, Melbourne: Cambridge University Press.

Gray, S. and R. Le Heron (2010), 'Globalising New Zealand: Fonterra Co-operative Group, and Shaping the Future', *New Zealand Geographer*, 66(1): 1–13.

Gray, S., R. Le Heron, C. Stringer and C. Tamásy (2007), 'Competing from the Edge of the Global Economy: The Globalising World Dairy Industry and the Emergence of Fonterra's Strategic Networks', *Die Erde*, 138(2): 127–47.

Griffiths, T. (2002), 'The Outside Country', in T. Bonyhady and T. Griffiths (eds), *Words for Country: Landscape and Language in Australia*, 222–44, Sydney: University of New South Wales Press.

Gurney, P. J. (2009), '"Rejoicing in Potatoes": The Politics of Consumption in England During the "Hungry Forties"', *Past and Present*, 203(1): 99–136.

Guthman, J. (2008), 'Neoliberalism and the Making of Food Politics in California', *Geoforum*, 39(3): 1171–83.

Guthman, J. (2011), *Weighing In: Obesity, Food Justice, and the Limits of Capitalism*, Berkeley: University of California Press.

Guthman, J. (2019), *Wilted: Pathogens, Chemicals, and the Fragile Future of the Strawberry Industry*, Berkeley: University of California Press.

Guthman, J., A. W. Morris and P. Allen (2006), 'Squaring Farm Security and Food Security in Two Types of Alternative Food Institutions', *Rural Sociology*, 71(4): 662–84.

Guthrie Smith, H. ([1921] 1999), *Tutira: The Story of a New Zealand Sheep Station*, Cambridge: Cambridge University Press.

Haggerty, J. H. (2007), '"I'm Not a Greenie but …": Environmentality, Eco-Populism and Governance in New Zealand Experiences from the Southland Whitebait Fishery', *Journal of Rural Studies*, 23(2): 222–37.

Hale, J., K. A. Legun, H. Campbell and M. Carolan (2019), 'Social Sustainability Indicators as Performance', *Geoforum*, 103: 47–55.

Hansford, D. (2014), 'Liquidation', *New Zealand Geographic*, Issue 125 (January to February). Available online: https://www.nzgeo.com/stories/liquidation/ (accessed 4 November 2018).

Haraway, D. (2015), 'Anthropocene, Capitalocene, Plantationocene, Chthulucene: Making Kin', *Environmental Humanities*, 6(1): 159–65.

Harrison, R. (1964, reissued 2013), *Animal Machines: The New Factory Farming*, Wallingford and Boston: CABI International.

Hassanein, N. (1999), *Changing the Way America Farms: Knowledge and Community in the Sustainable Agriculture Movement*, Lincoln: University of Nebraska Press.

Hassanein, N. and J. R. Kloppenburg (1995), 'Where the Grass Grows Again: Knowledge Exchange in the Sustainable Agriculture Movement', *Rural Sociology*, 60(4): 721–40.

Hatch, E. (1992), *Respectable Lives: Social Standing in Rural New Zealand*, Berkeley: University of California Press.

Hay, C. (2014), 'Neither Real nor Fictitious but "as if Real"? A Political Ontology of the State', *The British Journal of Sociology*, 65(3): 459–80.

Hegan, C. (1993), 'Radiata – Prince of Pines', *New Zealand Geographer*, Issue 20 (October/December 1993). Available online: https://www.nzgeo.com/stories/radiata-prince-of-pines/ (accessed 9 March 2019).

Henry, M. (2019), 'Making Agricultural Science: Ontological Projects and the Conditions of Possibility in Agricultural Knowledge Production in New Zealand, Post-World War Two', paper presented to *Agrifood XVI*, University of Canterbury, 3 December 2019.

Henry, M. and M. M. Roche (2016), 'Materialising Taste: Fatty Lambs to Eating Quality-Taste Projects in New Zealand's Red Meat Industry', in R. Le Heron, H. Campbell, N. Lewis and M. Carolan (eds), *Biological Economies: Experimentation and the Politics of Agrifood Frontiers*, 95–108, London: Routledge (Earthscan).

Henry, M. and M. M. Roche (2018), 'Making Lamb Futures', in E. Pawson and the Biological Economies Team (eds), *The New Biological Economy: How New Zealanders Are Creating Value from the Land*, 41–60, Auckland: Auckland University Press.

Hicks, D. (1991), 'Erosion under Pasture, Pine Plantations, Scrub and Indigenous Forest: A Comparison from Cyclone Bola', *New Zealand Journal of Forestry*, 36(3): 21–22.

Hindmarsh, R. and G. Lawrence eds. (2004), *Recoding Nature: Critical Perspectives on Genetic Engineering*, Sydney: University of New South Wales Press.

Hindmarsh, R., G. Lawrence and J. Norton (1998), *Altered Genes, Reconstructing Nature: The Debate*, Sydney: Allen and Unwin.

Hiroa, Te Rangi. (1938), *Vikings of the Sunrise*, New Zealand and New York: Frederick A. Stokes Company.

Holbraad, M., M. Pedersen and E. Viveiros de Castro (2014), 'The Politics of Ontology: Anthropological Positions', *Cultural Anthropology* – online. Available online: https://culanth.org/fieldsights/the-politics-of-ontology-anthropological-positions (accessed 10 November 2018).

Holland, Peter (P. G.) (2013), *Home in the Howling Wilderness: Settlers and the Environment in Southern New Zealand*, Auckland: Auckland University Press.

Holland, P. G., K. O'Connor and A. Wearing (2002), 'Remaking the Grasslands of the Open Country', in E. Pawson and T. Brooking (eds), *Environmental Histories of New Zealand*, 69–83, Melbourne: Oxford University Press.

Holland, P. G., J. Williams and V. Wood (2011a), 'Learning about the Environment in Early Colonial New Zealand', in T. Brooking and E. Pawson (eds), *Seeds of Empire: The Environmental Transformation of New Zealand*, 34–50, London: I.B. Tauris.

Holland, P. G., P. Star and V. Wood (2011b), 'Pioneer Grassland Farming: Pragmatism, Innovation and Experimentation', in T. Brooking and E. Pawson (eds), *Seeds of Empire: The Environmental Transformation of New Zealand*, 51–72, London: I.B. Tauris.

Holland, Philip (2015), 'The Dirty Dairying Campaign and the Clean Streams Accord', *Lincoln Planning Review*, 6(1–2): 63–69.

Holloway, L. (2007), 'Subjecting Cows to Robots: Farming Technologies and the Making of Animal Subjects', *Environment and Planning D*, 25(6): 1041–60.

Holmes, D. (1989), *Cultural Disenchantments: Worker Peasantries in Northern Italy*, Princeton: Princeton University Press.

Hunn, J. K. (1961), *Report on Department of Maori Affairs*, Wellington: Government Printers.

Hunt, L. (2004), 'The Rise and Fall of DDT in New Zealand', *New Zealand Sociology*, 19(2): 240–59.

Hunt, L., C. Rosin, H. Campbell and J. Fairweather (2013), 'The Impact of Neoliberalism on New Zealand Farmers: Changing What It Means to Be a "Good Farmer"', *Extension Farming Systems Journal*, 9(1): 34–42.

Hunt, L., J. Fairweather, C. Rosin, H. Campbell, D. Lucock and G. Greer (2011), 'Doing the Unthinkable: Linking Farmers' Breadth of View and Adaptive Propensity to the Achievement of Social, Environment and Economic Outcomes', Paper presented to *18th International Farm Management Congress*, Methven, New Zealand.

Hutchings, J., P. Tipene, G. Carney, A. Greensill, P. Skelton and M. Baker (2012), 'Hua Parakore: An Indigenous Food Sovereignty Initiative and Hallmark of Excellence for Food and Product Production', *MAI Journal: A New Zealand Journal of Indigenous Scholarship*, 1(2): 131–45.

Isern, T. (2002), 'Companions, Stowaways, Imperialists, Invaders: Pests and Weeds in New Zealand', in E. Pawson and T. Brooking (eds), *Environmental Histories of New Zealand*, 233–45, Melbourne: Oxford University Press.

Jack, L. (2005), 'Stocks of Knowledge, Simplification and Unintended Consequences: The Persistence of Post-war Accounting Practices in UK Agriculture', *Management Accounting Research*, 16(1): 59–79.

Jay, M. (2007), 'The Political Economy of Productivist Agriculture: New Zealand Dairy Discourses', *Food Policy*, 32(2): 266–79.

Joy, M. (2015), *Polluted Inheritance: New Zealand's Freshwater Crisis*, Wellington: Bridget Williams Books.

Joy, M. ed. (2018), *Mountains to Sea: Solving New Zealand's Freshwater Crisis*, Wellington: Bridget Williams Books.

Juska, A. and L. Busch (1994), 'The Production of Knowledge and the Production of Commodities: The Case of Rapeseed Technoscience', *Rural Sociology*, 59(4): 581–97.

Kawharu, H. (1977), *Maori Land Tenure*, Oxford: Clarendon Press.

Kawharu, M. ed. (2002), *Whenua: Managing Our Resources*, Auckland: Raupo Press (Penguin Group).

Kawharu, M. and P. Tapsell (2019), *Whāriki: The Growth of Māori Community Entrepreneurship*, Auckland: Oratia Media.

Keating, N. and H. Little (1991), *Generations in Farm Families: Transfer of the Family Farm in New Zealand*. Research Report No. 208. Agribusiness and Economics Research Unit, Lincoln University, Canterbury.

Keating, N. and H. Little (1994), 'Getting into It: Farm Roles and Careers of New Zealand Women', *Rural Sociology*, 59(4): 720–36.

Keenan, D. (2002), 'Bound to the Land: Maori Retention and Assertion of Land and Identity', in E. Pawson and T. Brooking (eds), *Environmental Histories of New Zealand*, 246–60, Melbourne: Oxford University Press.

Keenan, D. (2013), *Ahuwhenua: Celebrating 80 Years of Maori Farming*, Wellington: Huia Publishers.

King, M. (2003), *The Penguin History of New Zealand*, Auckland: Penguin Books.

Kirwan, J. (2004), 'Alternative Strategies in the UK Agro Food System: Interrogating the Alterity of Farmers' Markets', *Sociologia Ruralis*, 44(4): 395–415.

Kloppenburg, J. (1991), 'Social Theory and the De/Reconstruction of Agricultural Science: Local Knowledge for an Alternative Agriculture', *Rural Sociology*, 56(4): 519–48.

Knorr-Cetina, K. (1999), *Epistemic Cultures: How the Sciences Make Knowledge*, Cambridge: Harvard University Press.

Lambert, S. (2008), *The Expansion of Sustainability through New Economic Space: Māori Potatoes and Cultural Resilience*, PhD Diss., Lincoln University: Canterbury.

Lambert, S. (2011), 'Te Ahuwhenua and the "Sons of the Soil": A History of the Māori-Farmer-of-the-Year Award', *MAI Journal: A New Zealand Journal of Indigenous Scholarship*, 2011(1): 1–13.

Latour, B. (1993), *We Have Never Been Modern*, Cambridge: Harvard University Press.

Law, J. and Urry, J. (2004), 'Enacting the Social', *Economy and Society*, 33(3): 390–410.

Law, R., H. Campbell and J. Dolan eds. (1999), *Masculinities in Aotearoa/New Zealand*, Palmerston North: Dunmore Press.

Lawrence, G. (1987), *Capitalism and the Countryside: The Rural Crisis in Australia*, Sydney: Pluto Press.

Lawrence, G. and H. Campbell (2013), 'Neoliberalism in the Antipodes: Understanding the Influence and Limits of the Neoliberal Political Project', in S. Wolf and A. Bonanno (eds), *The Neoliberal Regime in the Agri-Food Sector: Crisis, Resilience, and Restructuring*, 263–83, London: Routledge.

Lawrence, G. and K. Smith (2018), 'The Concept of Financialization: Criticisms and Insights', in H. Bjorkhaug, A. Magnan and G. Lawrence (eds), *The Financialization of Agri-Food Systems: Contested Transformations*, 23–41, London: Routledge (Earthscan).

Le Heron, R. (1988), 'State, Economy and Crisis in New Zealand in the 1980s: Implications for Land-Based Production of a New Mode of Regulation', *Applied Geography*, 8(4): 273–90.

Le Heron, R. (1989a), 'A Political Economy Perspective on the Expansion of New Zealand Livestock Farming, 1960–1984 – Part I: Agricultural Policy', *Journal of Rural Studies*, 5(1): 17–32.

Le Heron, R. (1989b), 'A Political Economy Perspective on the Expansion of New Zealand Livestock Farming, 1960–1984 – Part II: Aggregate Farmer Responses – Evidence and Policy Implications', *Journal of Rural Studies*, 5(1): 33–43.

Le Heron, R. (1993), *Globalized Agriculture: Political Choice*, Oxford: Pergamon Press.

Le Heron, R. (2018), 'Dairying in Question', E. Pawson and the Biological Economies Team (eds), *The New Biological Economy: How New Zealanders Are Creating Value from the Land*, 20–40, Auckland: Auckland University Press.

Le Heron, R. and E. Pawson (1996), *Changing Places: New Zealand in the Nineties*, Auckland: Longman Paul.

Le Heron, R. and M. Roche (2018), 'The Taniwha Economy', in E. Pawson and the Biological Economies Team (eds), *The New Biological Economy: How New Zealanders Are Creating Value from the Land*, 157–76, Auckland: Auckland University Press.

Le Heron, E., N. Lewis and R. Le Heron (2016), 'Geographers at Work in Disruptive Human-Biophysical Projects', in R. Le Heron, H. Campbell, N. Lewis and M. Carolan (eds), *Biological Economies: Experimentation and the Politics of Agrifood Frontiers*, 196–211, London: Routledge (Earthscan).

Le Heron, R., H. Campbell, N. Lewis and M. Carolan eds. (2016a), *Biological Economies: Experimentation and the Politics of Agrifood Frontiers*, London: Routledge (Earthscan).

Le Heron, R., G. Smith, E. Le Heron and M. Roche (2016b), 'Enacting BA dairying as a System of Farm Practices in New Zealand: Towards an Emergent Politics of New Soil Resourcefulness?', in R. Le Heron, H. Campbell, N. Lewis and M. Carolan (eds), *Biological Economies: Experimentation and the Politics of Agrifood Frontiers*, 170–86, London: Routledge (Earthscan).

Leach, H. M. (1984), *1000 Years of Gardening in New Zealand*, Wellington: A H and A W Reed.

Legun, K. A. (2015), 'Club Apples: A Biology of Markets Built on the Social Life of Variety', *Economy and Society*, 44(2): 293–315.

Legun, K. A. (2016), 'Ever-Redder Apples: How Aesthetics Shape the Biology of Markets', in R. Le Heron, H. Campbell, N. Lewis and M. Carolan (eds), *Biological Economies: Experimentation and the Politics of Agrifood Frontiers*, 39–52, London: Routledge (Earthscan).

Legun, K. A. (2018), 'Securing the Future of Apple Production', in E. Pawson and the Biological Economies Team (eds), *The New Biological Economy: How New Zealanders Are Creating Value from the Land*, 98–115, Auckland: Auckland University Press.

Legun, K. A. and M. Henry (2017), 'Introduction to the Special Issue on the Post-Human Turn in Agri-Food Studies: Thinking about Things from the Office to the Page', *Journal of Rural Studies*, 100(52): 77–80.

Levy, B. (1955), *Grasslands of New Zealand*, Technical Correspondence School, Wellington: Dept of Education, Government Printer.

Lewis, N. and E. Le Heron (2018), 'New Zealand Wine: Seeking Success beyond Growth', in E. Pawson and the Biological Economies Team (eds), *The New Biological Economy:*

How New Zealanders Are Creating Value from the Land, 116–36, Auckland: Auckland University Press.

Lewis, N., R. Le Heron and H. Campbell (2017), 'The Mouse That Died: Stabilizing Economic Practices in Free Trade Space', in V. Higgins and W. Larner (eds), *Assembling Neoliberalism: Expertise, Practises, Subjects*, 151–70, New York: Palgrave Macmillan.

Lewis, N., R. Le Heron, M. Carolan, H. Campbell and T. Marsden (2016), 'Introduction: Assembling Generative Approaches in Agrifood Research', in R. Le Heron, H. Campbell, N. Lewis and M. Carolan (eds), *Biological Economies: Experimentation and the Politics of Agrifood Frontiers*, 1–20, London: Routledge (Earthscan).

Lewis, N., R. Le Heron, H. Campbell, M. Henry, E. Le Heron, E. Pawson, H. Perkins, M. Roche and C. Rosin (2013), 'Assembling Biological Economies: Region Shaping Initiatives in Making and Retaining Value', *New Zealand Geographer*, 69(3): 180–96.

Li, T. M. (2007a), *The Will to Improve: Governmentality, Development, and the Practice of Politics*, Durham: Duke University Press.

Li, T. M. (2007b), 'Practices of Assemblage and Community Forest Management', *Economy and Society*, 36(2): 263–93.

Li, T. M. (2010), 'Indigeneity, Capitalism, and the Management of Dispossession', *Current Anthropology*, 51(3): 385–414.

Li, T. M. (2014), 'What Is Land? Assembling a Resource for Global Investment', *Transactions of the Institute of British Geographers*, 39(4): 589–602.

Li, T. M. (2017), 'Rendering Land Investible: Five Notes on Time', *Geoforum*, 82: 276–78.

Liepins, R. (1998), 'The Gendering of Farming and Agricultural Politics: A Matter of Discourse and Power', *The Australian Geographer*, 29(3): 371–88.

Liepins, R. (2000), 'Making Men: The Construction and Representation of Agriculture-Based Masculinities in Australia and New Zealand', *Rural Sociology*, 65(4): 605–20.

Liepins, R. and B. Bradshaw (1999), 'Neoliberal Agricultural Discourse in New Zealand: Economy, Culture and Politics Linked', *Sociologia Ruralis*, 39(4): 563–82.

Limerick, P. (2000), *Something in the Soil: Legacies and Reckonings in the New West*, New York: W. W. Norton.

Linklater, A. (2013), *Owning the Earth: The Transforming History of Land Ownership*, London: Bloomsbury.

Little, J. (2003), '"Riding the Rural Love Train": Heterosexuality and the Rural Community', *Sociologia Ruralis*, 43(4): 401–17.

Loveridge, A. (2004), 'Crisis and Identity: Autobiographies and Farm Life in the 1930s and 1980s', *New Zealand Sociology*, 19(2): 260–80.

Loveridge, A. (2009), 'Farm Children's Understanding of Animals in Changing Times: Autobiographies and Farming Culture', *Australian Zoologist*, 35(1): 28–38.

Loveridge, A. (2016), 'Rural Sociology in New Zealand: Companion Planting?' *New Zealand Sociology*, 31(3): 207–29.

Lowe, P. (2010), 'Enacting Rural Sociology: Or What Are the Creativity Claims of the Engaged Sciences?' *Sociologia Ruralis*, 50(4): 311–30.

Mayes, C. (2018), *Unsettling Food Politics: Agriculture, Dispossession and Sovereignty in Australia*, London: Rowman and Littlefield.

McAloon, J. (2002), 'Resource Frontiers, Environment, and Settler Capitalism: 1769–1860', in E. Pawson and T. Brooking (eds), *Environmental Histories of New Zealand*, 52–66, Melbourne: Oxford University Press.

McConnell, D. J. and J. L. Dillon (1997), *Farm Management for Asia: A Systems Approach*, FAO Farm Systems Management Series, No. 13, Rome: Food and Agriculture Organization of the UN.

McCullum, H. and F. McCullum (1965), *The Wire That Fenced the West*, Norman: University of Oklahoma Press.

McKerchar, C., S. Bowers, C. Heta, L. Signal and L. Matoe (2015), 'Enhancing Māori Food Security Using Traditional Kai', *Global Health Promotion*, 22(3): 15–24.

MacLeod, C. and H. Moller (2006), 'Intensification and Diversification of New Zealand Agriculture since 1960: An Evaluation of Current Indicators of Sustainable Land Use', *Agriculture, Ecosystems and Environment*, 115(1–4): 201–18.

McLaughlan, G. ([1981] 2006), *The Farming of New Zealand: The People and the Land*. Auckland: Viking (Penguin Group).

McMichael, P. (1984), *Settlers and the Agrarian Question: Foundations of Capitalism in Colonial Australia*, New York: Cambridge University Press.

McMichael, P. (2012), 'Food Regime Crisis and Revaluing the Agrarian Question', in R. Almas and H. Campbell (eds), *Rethinking Agricultural Policy Regimes: Food Security, Climate Change and the Future Resilience of Global Agriculture*, 99–122, Bingley: Emerald.

McMichael, P. (2013), *Food Regimes and Agrarian Questions*, Nova Scotia: Fernwood Publishing.

McNeill, J. (2000), *Something New under the Sun: An Environmental History of the Twentieth Century*, London: The Penguin Press.

McTavish, C. (2015), *Making Milking Bodies in the Manawatu. Assembling 'Good Cow'– 'Good Farmer' Relationships in Productionist Dairy Farming*. MA Diss., Palmerston North: Massey University.

Mann, S. A., and J. M. Dickinson (1978), 'Obstacles to the Development of a Capitalist Agriculture', *The Journal of Peasant Studies*, 5(4): 466–81.

Mark, A. (1994), 'Effects of Burning and Grazing on Sustainable Utilization of Upland Snow Tussock (*Chionochloa spp*) Rangelands for Pastoralism in South Island, New Zealand', *Australian Journal of Botany*, 42(2): 149–61.

Mark, A. F. and B. McLennan (2005), 'The Conservation Status of New Zealand's Indigenous Grasslands', *New Zealand Journal of Botany*, 43(1): 245–70.

Mark, A., K. Dickinson and B. Patrick (2003), 'Indigenous Grassland Protection in New Zealand', *Frontiers in Ecology and the Environment*, 1(6): 290–1.

Massy, C. (2017), *Call of the Reed Warbler: A New Agriculture for a New Earth*, White River Junction, Vermont: Chelsea Green Publishing.

Mayes, D., L. Holloway and M. Kneafsey (2007), *Alternative Food Geographies: Representation and Practice*, Oxford: Elsevier.

Mintz, S. (1985), *Sweetness and Power*, New York: Elisabeth Sifton Books.

Mitchell, T. (2002), *Rule of Experts: Egypt, Techno-politics, Modernity*, Berkeley: University of California Press.

Mol, A. (1999), 'Ontological Politics. A Word and Some Questions', *The Sociological Review*, 47(1): 74–89.

Mol, A. (2002), *The Body Multiple: Ontology in Medical Practice*, Durham: Duke University Press.

Mol, A. (2008), 'I Eat an Apple. On Theorizing Subjectivities', *Subjectivity*, 22(1): 28–37.

Moller, H., F. Berkes, P. Lyver and M. Kislalioglu (2004), 'Combining Science and Traditional Ecological Knowledge: Monitoring Populations for Co-Management', *Ecology and Society*, 9(3), Article 2. Available online: https://www.ecologyandsociety.org/vol9/iss3/art2/ (accessed 26 September 2016).

Moore, J. (2000), 'Sugar and the Expansion of the Early Modern World-Economy: Commodity Frontiers, Ecological Transformation, and Industrialization', *Review* (Fernand Braudel Center), 23(3): 409–33.

Moore, J. (2015), *Capitalism in the Web of Life*, London: Verso.

Moran, W., G. Blunden and J. Greenwood (1993), 'The Role of Family Farming in Agrarian Change', *Progress in Human Geography*, 17(1): 22–42.

Morris, C. M. (2002), *Station Wives in New Zealand: Narrating Continuity in the High Country*, PhD Diss., University of Auckland: Auckland.

Morris, C. M. (2007), 'A Dog of One's Own: Canines, Ovines and the Gendering of High Country Farming', Paper presented at *Animals and Society II: Considering Animals*, Hobart, July 2007, Tasmania: Australia.

Morris, C. M. (2010), 'The Politics of Palatability: On the Absence of Māori Restaurants', *Food, Culture and Society*, 13(1): 5–28.

Morris, C. M. (2014), 'Art, Action and Tenure Review: Landscape and Politics in the High Country of Aotearoa New Zealand', *Journal of Rural Studies*, 34(April 2014): 184–92.

Murcott, A. (2019), *Introducing the Sociology of Food and Eating*, London: Bloomsbury.

Muru-Lanning, M. (2016), *Tupuna Awa: People and Politics of the Waikato River*, Auckland: University of Auckland Press.

Nel, A. (2018), 'Assembling Value in Carbon Forestry: Practices of Assemblage, Overflows and Counter-Performativities in Ugandan Carbon Forestry', in J. Forney, C. Rosin and H. Campbell (eds), *Agri-Environmental Governance as an Assemblage*, 107–26, London: Routledge (Earthscan).

Ngata, T. (2018), 'Wai Maori', in M. Joy (ed), *Mountains to Sea: Solving New Zealand's Freshwater Crisis*, 6–11, Wellington: Bridget Williams Books.

Ó'Gráda, C. (1993), *Ireland before and after the Famine: Explorations in Economic History, 1800–1925*, 2nd edn, Manchester: Manchester University Press.

O'Malley, V., B. Stirling and W. Penitito (2010), *The Treaty of Waitangi Companion: Maori and Pakeha from Tasman to Today*, Auckland: Auckland University Press.

Park, G. (1995), *Nga Uruora (The Groves of Life): Ecology and History in a New Zealand Landscape*, Wellington: Victoria University Press.

Park, G. (1999), 'Going between Goddesses', in K. Neumann, N. Thomas and H. Erickson (eds), *Quicksands: Foundational Histories in Australia and Aotearoa New Zealand*, 176–97, Sydney: University of New South Wales Press.

Park, G. (2002), '"Swamps Which Might Doubtless Easily Be Drained": Swamp Drainage and Its Impact on the Indigenous', E. Pawson and T. Brooking (eds), *Environmental Histories of New Zealand*, 151–65, Melbourne: Oxford University Press.

Park, J., K. Scott, C. Cocklin and P. Davis (2002), 'The Moral Life of Trees: Farming and Production Forestry in Northern New Zealand', *Journal of Anthropological Research*, 58(4): 521–44.

Parliamentary Commissioner for the Environment (2004), *Growing for Good: Intensive Farming, Sustainability and New Zealand's Environment*, Wellington: Office of the Parliamentary Commissioner for the Environment.

Pascoe, B. (2018), *Dark Emu: Aboriginal Australia and the Birth of Farming*, Melbourne: Scribe.

Pawson, E. (2011), 'Creating Public Spaces for Geography in New Zealand: Towards an Assessment of the Contributions of Kenneth Cumberland', *New Zealand Geographer*, 67(2): 102–15.

Pawson, E. and T. Brooking eds. (2002), *Environmental Histories of New Zealand*, Melbourne: Oxford University Press.

Pawson, E. and T. Brooking (2011), 'Introduction', in T. Brooking and E. Pawson (eds), *Seeds of Empire: The Environmental Transformation of New Zealand*, 1–12, London: I.B. Tauris.

Pawson, E. and V. Wood (2011), 'The Grass Seed Trade', in T. Brooking and E. Pawson (eds), *Seeds of Empire: The Environmental Transformation of New Zealand*, 117–38, London: I. B. Tauris.

Pawson, E., R. Le Heron, H. Campbell, M. Henry, E. Le Heron, K. A. Legun, N. Lewis, H. C. Perkins, M. Roche and C. Rosin (2018), *The New Biological Economy: How New Zealanders Are Creating Value from the Land*, Auckland: Auckland University Press.

Perkins, H. C., M. Mackay and S. Espiner (2015), 'Putting Pinot alongside Merino in Cromwell District, Central Otago, New Zealand: Rural Amenity and the Making of the Global Countryside', *Journal of Rural Studies*, 39(June 2015): 85–98.

Phillips, J. (1987), *A Man's Country?: The Image of the Pakeha Male, A History*, Auckland: Penguin Group.

Phillips, C. and M. Marden (2005), 'Reforestation Schemes to Manage Regional Landslide Risk', in Glade, T., Anderson, M. and Crozier, M. (eds), *Landslide Hazard and Risk*, 517–48, Oxford: Wiley.

Piatti, C. (2015), *Enacting the Alter-Native: A Theoretical Reframing of Local Food Initiatives in Aotearoa/New Zealand*, PhD Diss., Dunedin: University of Otago.

Pihama, L., F. Cram and S. Walker (2002), 'Creating Methodological Space: A Literature Review of Kaupapa Māori Research', *Canadian Journal of Native Education*, 26(1): 30–42.

Pini, B. (2005), 'The Third Sex: Women Leaders in Australian Agriculture', *Gender, Work and Organization*, 12(1): 73–88.

Piper, L. and J. Sandlos (2007), 'A Broken Frontier: Ecological Imperialism in the Canadian North', *Environmental History*, 12(4): 759–95.

Polanyi, K. (1944), *The Great Transformation*, New York: Farrar and Rinehart.

Pollan, M. (2006), *The Omnivore's Dilemma: A Natural History of Four Meals*, New York: Penguin.

Pomeroy, A. (1995), 'Matching New Zealand Rural Development Policy to a Changing Clientele: The Emerging Contribution of MAF', *New Zealand Geographer*, 51(1): 49–56.

Pretty, J. (2012), 'Agriculture and Food Systems: Our Current Challenge', in C. Rosin, P. Stock and H. Campbell (eds), *Food Systems Failure: The Global Food Crisis and the Future of Agriculture*, 17–29, London: Earthscan.

Pretty, J. (2013), *Agri-Culture: Reconnecting People, Land and Nature*, London: Routledge.

Reid, J. (2011), *Maori Land: A Strategy for Overcoming Constraints on Development*, PhD Diss., New Zealand: Lincoln University.

Reid, J. and M. Rout (2016), 'Getting to Know Your Food: The Insights of Indigenous Thinking in Food Provenance', *Agriculture and Human Values*, 33(2): 427–38.

Reid, J., T. Barr and S. Lambert (2013), *The New Zealand Sustainability Dashboard: Indigenous Sustainability Indicators for Maori Farming and Fishing Enterprises – A Theoretical Framework*, Research Report No. 13/16, Agriculture Research Group on Sustainability: Christchurch.

Reynolds, D. (2016), *The Depoliticisation of Deprivation: Food Insecurity in Aotearoa New Zealand*. MA Diss., Dunedin: University of Otago.

Rivers, M. J., A. Pomeroy, D. Buchan, B. Pomeroy and R. Fogarty (1997), *Change and Diversity: Opportunities for and Constraints on Rural Women in New Zealand*. MAF Policy Technical Paper 97/11, Wellington: Ministry of Agriculture and Fisheries.

Roche, M. M. (1990), 'The New Zealand Timber Economy, 1840–1935', *Journal of Historical Geography*, 16(3): 295–313.

Roche, M. M., T. Johnston and R. Le Heron (1992), 'Farmers' Interest Groups and Agricultural Policy in New Zealand during the 1980s', *Environment and Planning A*, 24(12): 1749–67.

Rogers-Hayden, T. and R. Hindmarsh (2002), 'Modernity Contextualises New Zealand's Royal Commission on Genetic Modification: A Discourse Analysis', *Journal of New Zealand Studies*, 1(October 2002): 41–61.

Rose, D. B. (2004), *Reports From A Wild Country: Ethics for Decolonisation*, Sydney: University of New South Wales Press.

Rosenberg, G. (1966), 'Maori Land Tenure and Land Use: A Planner's Point of View', *Journal of the Polynesian Society*, 75(2): 210–22.

Rosin, C. (2008), 'The Conventions of Agri-Environmental Practice in New Zealand: Farmers, Retail Driven Audit Schemes and a New Spirit of Farming', *GeoJournal*, 73(1): 45–54.

Rosin, C. (2013), 'Food Security and the Justification of Productivism in New Zealand', *Journal of Rural Studies*, 29 (January 2013): 50–8.

Rosin, C. (2014), 'Engaging the Productivist Ideology through Utopian Politics', *Dialogues in Human Geography*, 4(2): 221–24.

Rosin, C., P. Stock and H. Campbell eds. (2012), *Food Systems Failure: The Global Food Crisis and the Future of Agriculture*, London: Earthscan.

Rosin, C., H. Campbell and J. Reid (2016), 'Metrology and Sustainability: Using Sustainability Audits in New Zealand to Elaborate the Complex Politics of Measuring', *Journal of Rural Studies*, 52(May 2017): 90–9.

Rosin, C. J., K. A. Legun, H. Campbell and M. Sautier (2017), 'From Compliance to Co-Production: Emergent Forms of Agency in Sustainable Wine Production in New Zealand', *Environment and Planning A*, 49(12): 2780–99.

Roskruge, N. (2007), *Hokia Ki Te Whenua*. PhD Diss., Palmerston North: Massey University.

Russell, K. and H. Campbell (1999), 'Capitalism, the State, and Kai Moana: Māori, the New Zealand Fishing Industry and Restructuring', in D. Burch, J. Goss, and G. Lawrence (eds), *Restructuring Global and Regional Agricultures: Transformations in Australasian Agri-Food Economies and Spaces*, 113–30, Aldershot: Ashgate.

Sachs, C. (1983), *The Invisible Farmers: Women in Agricultural Production*, New Jersey: Rowman and Allenheld.

Salaman, R. (1949), The *History and Social Influence of the Potato*, Cambridge: Cambridge University Press.

Salmond, A. (1997), *Between Worlds: Early Exchanges between Maori and Europeans, 1773-1815*, Auckland: Viking (Penguin Books).

Salmond, A. (2017), *Tears of Rangi: Experiments across Worlds*, Auckland: Auckland University Press.

Sandrey, R. and R. Reynolds (1990), *Farming without Subsidies: New Zealand's Recent Experience*, Wellington: Ministry of Agriculture and Fisheries.

Saunders, C. M., A. Barber and G. J. Taylor (2006), *Food Miles – Comparative Energy/ Emissions Performance of New Zealand's Agriculture Industry*. AERU Research Report No. 285, Agribusiness and Economics Research Unit, Canterbury: Lincoln University.

Sautier, M., K. A. Legun, C. Rosin and H. Campbell (2018), 'Sustainability: A Tool for Governing Wine Production in New Zealand?', *Journal of Cleaner Production*, 179 (April 2018): 347–56.

Schama, S. (1995), *Landscape and Memory*, New York: Vintage Books.

Scott, J. C. (1998), *Seeing Like a State: How Certain Schemes to Improve the Human Condition Have Failed*, New Haven: Yale University Press.

Shiva, V. (2016), *The Violence of the Green Revolution: Third World Agriculture, Ecology and Politics*, Lexington: University of Kentucky Press.

Smith, G. (2010), *A Convention Theory Analysis of Justifications for Biological Agricultural Practices in New Zealand Dairy Farming*, MSc Diss., Auckland: University of Auckland.

Smith, L. T. (2012), *Decolonizing Methodologies*, 2nd edn, Dunedin: University of Otago Press.

Spiers, R. and N. Lewis (2016), 'Enactive Encounters with the Langstroth Hive: Post-human Framing of the Work of Bees in the Bay of Plenty', in R. Le Heron, H. Campbell, N. Lewis and M. Carolan (eds), *Biological Economies: Experimentation and the Politics of Agrifood Frontiers*, 109–26, London: Routledge (Earthscan).

Star, P. and L. Lochhead (2002), 'Children of the Burnt Bush: New Zealanders and the Indigenous Remnant, 1880–1930', in E. Pawson and T. Brooking (eds), *Environmental Histories of New Zealand*, 119–35, Melbourne: Oxford University Press.

Star, P. and T. Brooking (2011), 'The Farmer, Science and the State in New Zealand', in T. Brooking and E. Pawson (eds), *Seeds of Empire: The Environmental Transformation of New Zealand*, 159–77, London: I.B. Tauris.

Stevens, M. (2009), *Muttonbirds and Modernity in Murihiku : Continuity and Change in Kāi Tahu Knowledge*, PhD Diss., Dunedin: University of Otago.

Stock, P. and S. Peoples (2012), 'Commodity Competition: Divergent Trajectories in New Zealand Pastoral Farming', in R. Almas and H. Campbell (eds), *Rethinking Agricultural Policy Regimes: Food Security, Climate Change and the Future Resilience of Global Agriculture*, 263–84, Bingley: Emerald.

Stock, P. and C. Brickell (2013), 'Nature's Good for You: Sir Truby King, Seacliff Asylum, and the Greening of Health Care in New Zealand, 1889–1922', *Health and Place*, 22: 107–14.

Stock, P. and J. Forney (2014), 'Farmer Autonomy and the Farming Self', *Journal of Rural Studies*, 36(October 2014): 160–71.

Stock, P., M. Carolan and C. Rosin eds. (2015), *Food Utopias: Reimagining Citizenship, Ethics and Community*, London: Routledge.

Stokes, E. (1987), 'Maori Geography or Geography of Maoris', *New Zealand Geographer*, 43(3),118–23.

Stokes, E. (1992), 'The Treaty of Waitangi and the Waitangi Tribunal: Maori claims in New Zealand', *Applied Geography*, 12(2): 176–91.

Stokes, E. (2002), 'Contesting Resources: Maori, Pakeha, and a Tenurial Revolution', in E. Pawson and T. Brooking (eds), *Environmental Histories of New Zealand*, 35–51, Melbourne: Oxford University Press.

Tall, I. (forthcoming – 2021), *Wading through Uncertain Waters: The Unfolding of Government-led Agri-Environmental Policies and Their Appropriation by Farmers. The Case of Southland, New Zealand*, PhD Diss., Switzerland: University of Neuchatel.

Tall, I. and H. Campbell (2018), 'The "Dirty Dairying" Campaign in New Zealand: Constructing Problems and Assembling Responses', in J. Forney, C. Rosin and H. Campbell (eds), *Agri-Environmental Governance as an Assemblage: Multiplicity, Power and Transformation*, 161–76, London: Routledge.

Tannahill, R. (1973), *Food in History*, London: Penguin.

Taylor, C. N. and H. McCrostie Little (1995), *Means of Survival?: A Study of Off- Farm Employment*, Christchurch: Taylor Baines Associates.

Trotter, C. (1988), 'Cyclone Bola: The Inevitable Disaster', *New Zealand Engineering*, 43(6): 13–16.

Tsing, A. L. (2015), *The Mushroom at the End of the World: On the Possibility of Life in Capitalist Ruins*, Princeton: Princeton University Press.

Turner, S. (1999), 'Settlement as Forgetting', in K. Neumann, N. Thomas and H. Erickson (eds), *Quicksands: Foundational Histories in Australia and Aotearoa New Zealand*, 20–38, Sydney: University of New South Wales Press.

Van der Ploeg, J. D. (2008), *The New Peasantries: Struggles for Autonomy and Sustainability in an Era of Empire and Globalization*, London: Earthscan.

Vivieros de Castro, E. (1998), 'Cosmological Deixis and Amerindian Perspectivism', *Journal of the Royal Anthropological Institute*, 4(3): 469–88.

Walker, R. (2004), *Ka Whawhai Tonu Matou – Struggle without End*, Auckland: Penguin Books.

Warne, K. (2017), 'Troubled Waters', *New Zealand Geographic*, Issue 146 (July–August 2017). Available online: https://www.nzgeo.com/stories/troubled-waters/ (accessed 1 September 2017).

Wharfe, L. and J. Manhire (2004), *The SAMsn Initiative: Advancing Sustainable Management Systems in Agriculture and Horticulture: An Analysis of International and New Zealand Programmes and Their Contribution to Sustainability*, Christchurch: The Agribusiness Group.

Williams, J. and P. Martin eds. (2011), *Defending the Social Licence of Farming: Issues, Challenges and New Directions for Agriculture*, Canberra: CSIRO Publishing.

Wilson, P. (1991), *The Domestication of the Human Species*, New Haven: Yale University Press.

Wolf, E. (1982), *Europe and the People without History*, Berkeley: University of California Press.

Wood, V. and E. Pawson (2011), 'Flows of Agricultural Information', in T. Brooking and E. Pawson (eds), *Seeds of Empire: The Environmental Transformation of New Zealand*, 139–58, London: I.B. Tauris.

Wood, V., T. Brooking and P. Perry (2008), 'Pastoralism and Politics: Reinterpreting Contests for Territory in Auckland Province, New Zealand, 1853–1864', *Journal of Historical Geography*, 34(2): 220–41.

Woolgar, S. and J. Lezaun (2013), 'The Wrong Bin Bag: A Turn to Ontology in Science and Technology Studies?' *Social Studies of Science*, 43(3): 321–40.

Worster, D. (1990), 'Transformations of the Earth: Toward an Agroecological Perspective in History', *The Journal of American History*, 76(4): 1087–106.

Wynne, G. (2002), 'Destruction under the Guise of Improvement?: The Forest, 1840–1920', in E. Pawson and T. Brooking (eds), *Environmental Histories of New Zealand*, 100–16, Melbourne: Oxford University Press.

Index